The Painful News
I Have to Write

Letters and Diaries
of Four Hite Brothers of Page County
in the Service of the Confederacy

The Painful News
I Have to Write

Letters and Diaries
of Four Hite Brothers of Page County
in the Service of the Confederacy

compiled and edited

by

Harlan R. Jessup

First Edition
Butternut & Blue
1998

Copyright 1998 by Harlan R. Jessup.

No part of this book may be reproduced in any form or by any means without the written consent of the publisher.

ISBN 0-935523-72-3

Printed in the United States of America on acid-free paper.

Published in 1998

by

Butternut & Blue
3411 Northwind Road
Baltimore, MD 21234
410-256-9220

This first edition is limited to 1,000 copies

Dedicated to
Eva Mae Jessup & Gladys Mary Fahrney,
granddaughters of Isaac Hite,
whose cheerful fortitude
throughout their long lives
has reflected the strength and patience
of their Hite ancestors.

CONTENTS

Editor's Preface i

List of Maps and Photographs v

Introduction - The People and the Times 1

Chapter 1 - Hopeful Beginnings and First Blood 7

Chapter 2 - John: Quiet Interlude 24

Chapter 3 - William: Recuperation and Relapse 45

Chapter 4 - The First Year Ends 64

Chapter 5 - Winter, 1862 73

Chapter 6 - The Valley Campaign 93

Chapter 7 - Distant Battles and Yankees in the Valley 104

Chapter 8 - Winter and Spring, 1863 121

Chapter 9 - Gettysburg 142

Chapter 10 - Homefront and Headquarters, 1863 and 1864 155

Chapter 11 - David: Declining Fortunes & a Third Fatal Blow 165

Chapter 12 - War's End and Epilogue 176

Appendices 183

Index 189

EDITOR'S PREFACE

One day, in the downstairs bedroom improvised after her stroke, my grandmother, Ella (Hite) Murray, was found crying "for all those boys dying in the war." "Over in Korea?" asked my mother, for this was 1952. "No," she sniffed, "in the War Between the States." At age eighty she was weeping for those uncles she had never met and who had died a decade before she was born.

Soon after that my aunt read me one or two letters from these uncles. I was intrigued by what I thought to be ancient, curious, and rare examples of living history. It was nearly forty years later that I came to a greater awareness. Aunt Gladys had quite a few such letters. A second cousin in Luray had even more. And the diary of John Hite, one of the brothers, was reportedly to be found in some obscure repository.

As I read these old papers and similar ones from other families, I began to realize that Civil War letters and diaries were not particularly rare (nor indeed so ancient). But there were few such sizeable collections which told such a complete family story. And there were not many families whose lives had been so touched, indeed pierced, by this, the most bloody American war.

A 1942 article in The Page News and Courier calls the Hites "A Family of Heroes," but these letters and diaries say nothing of fearless gallantry. Rather, they describe a very ordinary family coping as best they can with most extraordinary circumstances.

Objectives

In putting the story together I tried to satisfy two audiences with differing interests.

First, I wanted to preserve and disseminate the original materials for researchers of this period. For them, nothing has been left out. Included are all of the wartime letters and diaries of this family with their original spelling and (for the most part) their punctuation, reflecting, for example,

Preface

the partiality of Ella Buswell for semicolons and the disdain of Daniel Hite for any punctuation whatsoever.

Secondly, I wanted the story to flow for the general reader. And especially I wanted the descendants of the Hites and their Page County neighbors to grow in their affinity to ancestors separated by just a few generations. For them, I have added the brief explanatory notes I thought necessary, trying not to burden the story, but rather to identify the participants and to position the events in the context of the more familiar schoolbook history.

Portions of the unpublished diaries of George Daniel Buswell, Michael Shuler, and Oliver Hazard Perry Kite, all members of Co. H, the "Page Greys," in which David, William, and John Hite served, have been included to fill out the narrative where Hite family materials are sparse. For researchers and other readers an index is provided to the (mostly) Page County soldiers, neighbors and relatives named here.

Source materials

There are three primary sources for this book, two collections of family letters and a transcription of John Hite's diary.

The largest group of letters, almost fifty of them, passed to James E. Gander of Page County, Virginia, from his deceased first cousin, Walter Gander. James and Walter are grandsons of Martin and Bettie (Hite) Gander. The original transcription of this collection by the Genealogical Society of Page County has been edited after careful comparisons with the original letters.

My aunt, Gladys Fahrney of Frederick, Maryland, a granddaughter of Isaac Hite and Mary Ann Gander, has another group of some thirty letters. With due care, I have transcribed these myself.

Except for one small notebook for April 21 to May 25, 1862, the original diaries of John Hite have not been found, and our source is a typescript authorized by Walter Gander, probably before 1960. Here,

PREFACE

without comment, I have corrected what appear to be simple typographical errors.

The original letters, on paper of various sizes, are written both in pen and, frequently, in pencil. Surprisingly, almost all are quite legible. The transcriptions repeat the spelling and punctuation of the originals, except that omitted periods (but not initial capitals) have been added where sentences run together, and a few omitted words and letters have been added [in brackets]. Such omissions are somehow less noticeable in manuscript but stand out in print. The originals fill most of every page, rarely indenting, and forcing the paragraphing here to be somewhat arbitrary.

Addresses on envelopes and on the covers of folded letters are often very simple, for example, to "Daniel Hite, Luray." Many envelopes can no longer be matched with specific letters. Many are not postmarked, having been carried by friends and private couriers. And just one has a Confederate States postage stamp. Cover addresses are not described unless they provide information of interest such as the name of the courier.

Acknowledgements

First to be thanked, among the many who helped bring this project to a conclusion, are the holders of the original letters. My aunt, Gladys M. Fahrney, has not only let me copy and transcribe the letters in her possession, but she has offered continuous encouragement in getting this work into print. My double-second-cousin-once-removed, James E. Gander of Luray, has graciously allowed me to borrow his letters on several occasions and has helped to search his family photo collection looking for pictures of the Hite soldiers.

Next, I must thank those who first transcribed the letters and diaries, both known and unknown. Robert Sims of Middle Ground Institute first transcribed the Gander letters under the direction of Debby J. Owens of the Genealogical Society of Page County. They provided me a copy on disc, saving hours of keyboarding. Without the transcription of John Hite's diary arranged by Walter Gander, now deceased, we might be deprived of this family information, for the original has since been lost. I must similarly thank the unknown transcribers of the diaries of O.H.P. Kite and John H. Grabill. And Jean Buswell Sutton of Mulberry, Indiana,

Preface

has not only permitted quoting her transcription of George Buswell's diary, but she has also offered valuable clues to the identities of several people named in the letters.

First among the library staffs deserving special mention is, of course, Vicky Cyphert and others of the Page County Library. Next is the Handley Library of Winchester, the source of many of these materials, where archivist Rebecca Ebert has offered assistance and encouragement. The staff of the Thomas Balch Library in Leesburg were helpful with their excellent military collection. Other materials have come from the Library of Virginia and the Library of Congress.

I greatly appreciate the work of the Genealogical Society of Page County under the leadership of Debby Owens and Vicky Cyphert. Besides their transcription of these letters, the *Page County Federal Census, 1860,* transcribed and given an every name index by Debby, has been especially helpful.

Special thanks are offered to Robert L. Smith of Alexandria, Virginia, for his research and nicely presented genealogies of the Hite and Gander families and for permission to include several of his photographs.

And finally, the encouragement, counsel and moral support of friends and family cannot be overlooked. The home of my mother and aunt in Frederick has often provided bed and breakfast service enroute to research trips. And my wife, Shirley, has put up with my long hours in front of the computer and the sometimes lengthy conversations exclusively about *my* family.

LIST OF MAPS AND PHOTOGRAPHS

Daniel Hite Farmhouse 2

Map: Shenandoah Valley and Surroundings 9

Isaac Maggart Farm 39

William Francis Hite Grave 63

Mill Creek Church 90

Map: Neighbors of Daniel Hite (Page County, Virginia) 111

Mary Ann (Gander) Hite 125

Map: Army of Northern Virginia's Theater of Operations 144

John Hite's Memorial Notice 154

Isaac Martin Hite 160

David Christian Hite and Dianah (Cline) Hite 166

David Hite's Memorial Notice 175

INTRODUCTION

The People and the Times

No war has come closer to Americans than the War Between the States. Then, more young men suffer death and mutilating wounds than in any war before or since. And the battlegrounds and campgrounds of the opposing armies are in the fields of American family farmers.

No place is closer to that war than the Valley of the Shenandoah. Depredations, both from foragers and from deliberate destruction, are perhaps more keenly felt than the ravages of the local battles themselves. The young men go to serve in front-line regiments. Their companies, recruited county by county, are visited regularly by the fathers and uncles (and sometimes by the mothers and sisters and aunts) of the soldiers, for they are seldom more than a day or two from home. And the soldiers often visit home, both when furlough is granted and when it is not.

Few families have been as close to war as Daniel and Rebecca Hite's family of Page County, Virginia. Four sons fight in Confederate armies. Three die of wounds inflicted in battles not so far away—Manassas, Gettysburg, and Winchester. This is the story of that family as told in their own diaries and letters—not as memoirs from later years, but while it is happening—and before they die.

The Family

In June of 1861, as Virginia confirms its secession from the Union, the Hites are living at the farm on Mill Creek, some two miles southwest of the Page County courthouse at Luray. The household includes parents Daniel and Rebecca, in their fifties, and children John, 20, Sarah Elizabeth (Bettie), nearly 18, Eliza Ellen (Ella), 15, Daniel, nearly 12, and Nebraska (Braskie), 7. The older sons, Isaac, 25, and William, 23, are away from home. William is a merchant clerk living at the Luray residence of his "Uncle Stage," Augustus Staige Modesitt. Isaac, not found in the 1860 census, may have a similar position in a neighboring county. David,

INTRODUCTION

Daniel Hite Farmhouse

Built circa 1850
[Photo circa 1960, Jennie Ann Kerkhoff]

INTRODUCTION

28, the oldest and only married brother, lives with his wife Dianah in a separate dwelling on the family farm. David's twin sister, Mary, lives with her husband John A. Burner and four small children at their farm a few miles away just across the Shenandoah River.

Daniel Hite married Rebecca Grove in 1829. Their first child, Susannah, died as an infant just before the twins were born. Daniel's grandfather, also named Daniel, had first appeared in the Valley in 1771 with his brothers Abraham, Andrew, and (possibly) John. The first Daniel and his wife, Appolonia Keller, had eight children. Their youngest, David, married Susannah Spitler, and they had six children, including Daniel, the father of the four Confederate soldiers. Both of Daniel's grandfathers, Daniel Hite and Abraham Spitler, saw Revolutionary War service in Michael Reader's Shenandoah County company.

Rebecca's grandfather, Christian Grove (or Groff), also served in Michael Reader's company, having purchased a farm on the Hawksbill Creek in 1756. His son, Christian, Jr., married Mary Gochenour and had ten children including Rebecca.

The Military Units

The young men of Page County are recruited together and serve together in just a handful of military units. In 1861 Isaac Hite and his future brother-in-law Martin Gander are in the 97th Virginia Militia. In 1862 they serve in the Dixie Artillery and its successor, Cayce's Artillery Company. In January, 1863, they join Robert E. Lee's Bodyguard, Company C of Richardson's Battalion of Scouts, Guides, and Couriers, where they serve until war's end.

The three who are to die, David, William, and John Hite, are all in Company H, 33rd Regiment, Stonewall Brigade. Like other Virginia companies this unit has a nickname, the Page Greys, but the contemporary letters and diaries mostly call it just Co. H. The history of that military unit is intertwined with the story of this family.

INTRODUCTION

Appearing here also are many soldiers from the other units recruited in Page County: Co. K of the 10th Virginia Infantry, Co. E of the 35th Battalion Virginia Cavalry, and Co. D of the 7th Virginia Cavalry.

The Correspondents

Through fourteen aunts and uncles, the Hite soldiers have no less than 70 first cousins, most of them living in Page County at the time of the War. Besides Hite and Grove, they are surnamed Huffman, Modesitt, Yowell, and Coffman. Many appear in the letters and diaries here transcribed, together with friends, acquaintances, and comrades in arms. Many live within four or five miles south and west of Luray in places called Mill Creek, Leaksville, Riverdale, and Massanutten. These are the families appearing most frequently, with children's ages as of June, 1861:

Augustus Staige Modesitt (Uncle Stage) is married to Daniel Hite's sister, Mary. A merchant in Luray, his household includes oldest daughter Mary Ellen, 15, plus Lucy, Elizabeth, Martha, Rebecca, Andrew, and a year-old infant. Living with them (at 1860 census time) are three young male clerks including William Hite and a free black servant, Catharine Blanham.

Henry and Mary (Coffman) Gander live at the family farm on the Shenandoah River with children Martin, 22, Mary Ann (Mollie), 19, Frances (Fannie), 17, Sarah Jane (Sally), 14, Martha Ellen (Mat), 12, and David Henry, almost 10. Martin's military service parallels that of Isaac Hite, and he is later to marry Isaac's sister Bettie. Mollie and Fannie are frequent correspondents with John Hite, but Mollie is eventually to marry Isaac. Older Gander sons, Isaac Franklin and Joseph Thomas, have married and moved to Cooper Co., Missouri, about 1858. There is an unconfirmed family story that both once wore Union blue.

Thomas and Rebecca (Spitler) Buswell live in Leaksville, about two miles from the Hite farm. Rebecca is a first cousin to Daniel Hite. Their children include Sarah Ellen (Ella), 19, George Daniel, 18, Mary (Molly), 17, Wesley, 13, Abram, 11, and Willie, 10. Thomas has been a Major General in the Virginia Militia and has served several terms in the Virginia House of Delegates and State Senate. At the beginning of the War he is called to active duty with a regular rank of Lt. Col. in the 97th Va. Militia. George D. Buswell, who first serves as 2nd Lt. in Co. E of that regiment, enlists in the Page Greys in March, 1862, becomes lieutenant of that company in September 1862, and serves there until put out of further action by a leg wound at Spotsylvania in May 1864. In 1863 Thomas Buswell is to move his family to Salem, Virginia, where he is in Confederate government service, perhaps in a procurement role.

The family of Gideon W. Jones of Warren County become close friends and frequent correspondents after nursing William Hite in his recuperation and final illness. Jones is a successful merchant whose house adjoins the store at 11 Chester Street in the center of Front Royal, the county seat on the Manassas Gap Rail Road some 25 miles north of Luray. Gideon's household includes wife Elizabeth A.; children Henrietta, 12, Gideon E., 11, and Earnest A., 6; his mother Miriam; his sisters Evaline and Jane C. Jones; and three young male clerks. He also employs a mulatto slave girl, age 14, and has separate slave quarters on the premises.

Other important correspondents include the three successive captains of Co. H. The first, William D. Rippetoe, is a Methodist minister, age 25, living with his wife in James Modesitt's Luray hotel at 1860 census time. When ill health forces Rippetoe's resignation, Ambrose Booten Shenk, a salesman and Hite cousin, age 31, is promoted to captain. He is killed at Kernstown on March 23, 1862. Michael Shuler, only 18 as the War begins, becomes the third captain, to be killed, in turn, at the Wilderness in May, 1864, leaving the diary quoted here.

The Personalities

There are few photographs here, but those who read—and reread—these letters and diaries will form ever sharper mental images of the writers and their personalities.

Father Daniel is the farmer, ever concerned with the product of the land. His letters are forthright and remarkably articulate, and his handwriting is perhaps the best of any. But his spelling, though phonetic, is unique, and he utterly disdains punctuation. There are no letters from mother Rebecca and none addressed solely to her. She remains in the shadows, quietly performing the duties of the farm wife. Any letters from oldest son David, the intended heir of the family farm, were probably kept only by his widow, Dianah, and are now lost to the family.

Surprisingly, all of the Hite brothers write with better grammar and spelling than that seen in two letters of their first cousin and near neighbor, Ambrose Hite. William, and probably Isaac, have apprenticed for merchant careers and their letters are mature and grammatically correct. As the family tragedy deepens and the Confederacy's prospects fade in 1864, Isaac becomes ever more philosphical and devout. John, the youngest (and shortest) of the soldiers, seems the most lively. He is especially devoted to keeping his options open with, it would seem, *all* of the single girls within courting distance.

Among these young ladies, including Fannie and Mollie Gander, Ella Buswell, and Mary Ellen Modesitt, there are enough letters that we may also gain a sense of their individual personalities.

But the reader will best form his own mental images as we begin in the late spring of 1861.

CHAPTER 1

Hopeful Beginnings and First Blood

*"Merciful God look down with
an eye of compassion"*

On April 12, 1861, Confederate batteries in Charleston Harbor fire on Fort Sumter. On April 17 Virginia adopts an Ordinance of Secession. On April 18 Virginia militia companies occupy the arsenal at Harpers Ferry and extinguish the fires set by the retreating Federal garrison.

For the next six weeks military action is mostly confined to recruiting, positioning of forces, and reorganization of poorly prepared militias. Federals begin to blockade Confederate ports. Robert E. Lee takes command of all Virginia forces. VMI professor Thomas J. Jackson is commissioned as colonel. Soon he is put in command of the newly formed First Brigade and begins his regimen of military drill and regular religious services.

Recruiting proceeds steadily. It is probably stimulated in Virginia as Capt. John Q. Marr becomes one of the first Confederate fatalities in a skirmish at Arlington Mills on June 1. At Bethel Church on June 10, another small battle results in 18 Federal troops killed and just one more Southern death.

In the Shenandoah Valley recruiting has become earnest by mid-June. "As of June first" John and William Hite enlist in Company H, the Page Greys, John as private and William as 1st Lt. Isaac delays—because he is needed to work the farm or because of the illness reported below. David is soon called into militia service.

Regular entries in John's diary do not begin until July 11, but they commence with this preface:

June 1861. I left Luray June 19th 1861 in a volunteer company under the Command of Capt W. B. Rippetoe. Wm T. Hite, A. B. Shenk, M. Shuler, 1st, 2nd, and 3rd Lieuts respectively. Arrived at

Winchester June 29th. Cheered on the rout by the waving of handerchiefs and reciept of bouquets from the ladies. We take quarters in a warehouse, where we were mustered into service 21st June, numbering 101 men, and four officers. Have considerable discention in the company on account of the rigidness of the Captain.

On June 27 John begins his first letter to sister Bettie. His description of camp life takes several days to complete. His regimental commander, Arthur Campbell Cummings, V.M.I. class of 1844, has practiced law after serving in the Mexican War. The Irish of Co. E, the Emerald Guard, are to become famous for drinking and brawling. Militia colonel Mann Spitler heads the 97th Regiment from Page County, and George W. Murphy commands the 13th Regiment from Shenandoah County. Begun on June 27, this letter takes several days to complete.

Winchester Frederick Va. June 27th 61.
Dear Sister:
  I embrace this opportunity of writing to you, for I expect you have been looking for a letter ere this; but as many of our company has been writing back I thought I would hold on a little longer. I have been quite unwell for the last several days, but am about right again.
  The rest of our company are well I believe, and all in good spirits. We have a very good house for barracks since we cleaned it for there was great objections to it when we arrived; and we sleept out of doors the first night. The next day we taken out all the straw that was put in by other troops, who formerly occupied it; and then we white-washed it and put lime around on the outside. From the best information I can get there is about 15 or 18,000 troops here now, of whom about 1,000 are sick though not a great many dangerously; for its mumps and measles principally. Last sunday there were several buried in the cemetery here and a few since then; one Georgian who shot himself accidentally yesterday morning with his pistol.
  We have plenty of the very best of bread as good as Mother ever baked, and bacon or beef, also sweetened coffee twice a day, (of course that suits me) besides many of the company buy molasses; which can be had for 8 cts per quart, very best of sirup too. We mustered into service last Saturday for twelve months from the 1st of June. Since I wrote the above I taken my dinner on bread and fat meat, and no one can have more than is allotted him. For the last several nights we have been sleeping with all of our clothes on, so as to be prepared to march at a moments warning if necessary in an emergency; and I

HOPEFUL BEGINNINGS AND FIRST BLOOD

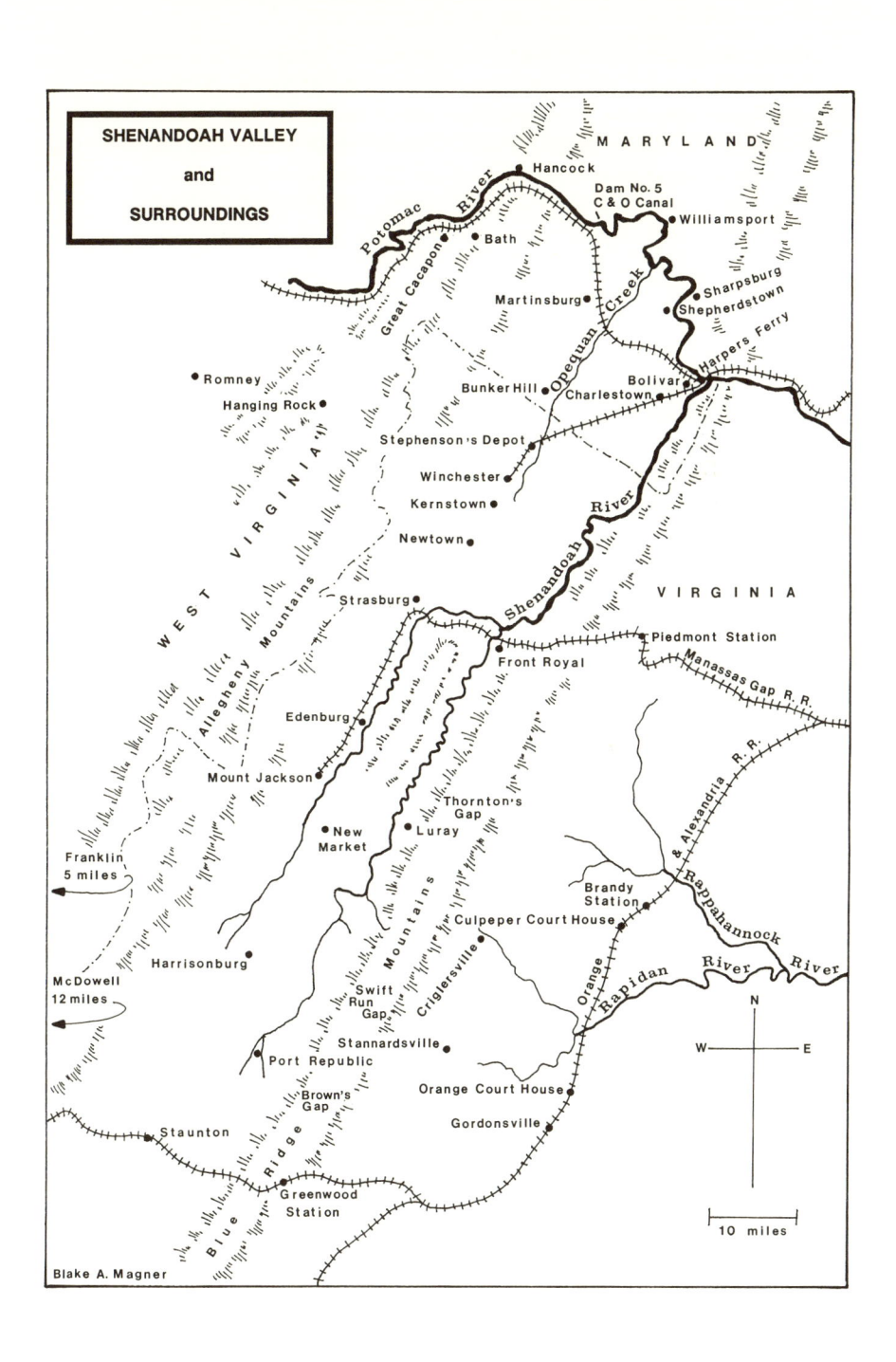

expect we will move about two miles from town this evening.

    I believe we are the most civil company here, for I have not saw a man with liquor of our company since I been here; and but little swearing. We have the praise of the whole town above all others, and we are the largest company here that I know of; though they are many very good companies here. The revele beats every morning at 5 O'clock and then every man must get up that can; and then we go on drill till breakfast, (7 o'clock) at 8 drill again until towards dinner. We also go on a few other drills till evening at 6 O'clock when we go on dress parade, which is the best drill we have; for we march all through town, some of the regiments attended with the best of bands which is enough to make the hair stand upon our heads when they all keep the step. I must stop rite off and prepare to leave, and can't tell when I will finish it.

    [Letter resumes, now in pencil.] Well I'll try and write a little as we have arrived at our journey's end; and the soldiers are busily gathering leaves to sleep on; we have also joined Col. Cummings regiment. There are only two other companies here besides ours, both from Shenandoah one of which is all Irishman; stout fellows too. Cols. Spitler & Murphy visited us a few days ago; who informed us that you were busy harvesting, also that Isaac is sick, and has the Typhoid fever and indeed I was sorry to hear that, for I don't know how you will get along with your work, but hope you will get through it; that is if you can hire. The people down here have not harvested but very little yet, for the grain is not ripe yet; though the crops are good. The soldiers have turned their horses into some of the wheatfields.

    Last Sunday nine soldiers of our company and I taken up seven soldiers and put them in the prison for trying to break into a private house. At first some of them did not like very much to go but soon saw we were determined to take them, and if they had opposed us we would have made daylight shine through every one of them. For I certainly did feel like fighting; neither can I say I was afraid. We marched them through the streets untill we came to the prison house where we delivered them.

    Flour is worth about $4 per barrel. I have not time to write more but hope some of you will write immediately and give me all the news. Some of us have our knapsacks; I have mine, and got all in it but blanket and pants. I feel first rate sitting cool shade here this evening. You need not show this letter to critics to criticise it for any one will make mistakes where there is as much going on around them as there is around me.

HOPEFUL BEGINNINGS AND FIRST BLOOD

Yours affectionately
Address   John P. Hite
Winchester
Frederick Cty
Virginia
Care of Capt. Rippetoe.
N.B. I have not time to look over to correct; hoping you will excuse mistakes.

William's first letter, also about camp routine, is to his parents, Daniel and Rebecca Hite. He has received word from Benjamin F. Grayson, Sheriff of Page County, who will soon enlist as private in Co. F, 97th Va. Militia.

Camp E. K. Smith near Winchester
July 2nd 1861

Dear Father and Mother

I have a little time now of which I will avail myself of writing to you.

I heared yesterday by B. F. Grayson that Isaac is quite sick with fever. We have not heared from home by letter since we left. I am quite anxious to hear especially from Isaac. We are all well at this time. There are but few days however that there is not some one two or three reported on the sick list. There is a report of the company made out by the Orderly sergeant every morning Stating the number sick, on guard duty, the number capable for service &c. to the adjutant. There are 4 Com. here under the command of Col. Cummings, Who figured in the Mexican War. He was there wounded by a ball passing through his side. There was a silk Handkerchief drawn through the wound. I think he is an excellent officer. He is here now waiting for more Companies to come in to fill up the Regiment. 10 Companies constitute a Regiment.

Some of the men of all companies are dissatisfied. It seems that they started from home without first counting the cost of a soldiers life, and believed that it would be as it was for the first few days after they volunteered. They had read but little about wars and thought less; hence when first fun has worn away and the realities are coming upon them they are disappointed. I hear the drum beating for parade. The Revellie or getting up time 5 oclock. The companies then rise and drill till 7 (Breakfast) Then from 9 till 11. Then officers drill 11 to $^1/_2$ Past 12. Dinner at 1. drilling commences again at 2 and con-

tinues till 4. Officers drill 4 to $5^{1}/2$, Dress parade at $6^{1}/2$, tattoo (retiring) 9, taps $9^{1}/2$ extinguishing lights. There are 48 men detailed each day for guard duty, 14 of which are from the Page Grays. They go to the guard tent at 8 oclock A.M. Each day, $^{1}/3$ stand guard at a time 2 Hours so that they will be 2 Hours on and 4 off guard. The Camp is $1^{1}/4$ miles South [of] town on the old road to F. Royal. It is in a delightful grove a few hundred yards from water. I have not been sick a day since I left home, have found the hardship not as severe as I anticipated, But I tell the boys we are now only _playing_ the soldier and _not_ experiencing it. I can put up without a murmur if it comes no harder.

There are 6 or 8 Regiments North and West of Winchester. Some from the South. I have been in them. There is a great difference in the appearance of the men. The 10th Georgia Reg. was the cleanest and the Tennessee Regiments were the dirtyest and most Ragged that I Saw. Write to me soon. tell Bettie, Ella and them all to write and give me the news we don't anticipate a fight soon.

from your Son   William

Danel and Rebecca Hite

One of the first letters to William and John comes from "Uncle Stage," Augustus Staige Modesitt, who is married to their father's sister Mary. He reports the calling up of Page County's 97th Regiment of Virginia Militia by Gen. Gilbert S. Meem, responding to a call from Gen. Joseph E. Johnston. The regimental commander is Col. Mann Spitler, a cousin of Daniel Hite. Officers include for Co. E, Capt. David M. Dovel and 2nd Lt. George Daniel Buswell (of whom more later); for Co. F, Capt. Henry F. Bradley and 1st Lt. Daniel Judd; and for Co. I, 1st Lt. Thomas M. Offenbacker. A July 13 proclamation by Virginia Governor Letcher mobilizing all northern Virginia militia units will soon ratify Meem's possibly precipitate action. The news of the unwelcome call-up is brought by Francis H. Jordan, a teacher, age 39, who is himself soon to be embroiled in the controversy.

Recd your & Jno. letter

Luray July 3rd 61

Lieut. Wm F. Hite & Bro..

I was at your Fathers last late yesterday evening. All well but Isaac. he is no better or worse stands at about the same. They do not have to set up with him he says dont suffer any thing much keeps his

Hopeful Beginnings and First Blood

bed. You[r] mother sent by me 2 loaves bread one Cheese to send you & John. Mary Ellen sends one can peaches some leakes some dried beef which I hope you may be able to enjoy when recd by A[br?]. Stover. would send some butter but have none. your mother hasent either. Col Spitler Capt D. M. Doval Capt H.F. Bradly was Detailed to go with the Militia on Friday next. Lieut. Thomas Ofenbacker Lieut. Danl. Judd Do. [ditto] George Buswell Also the Bal. of the officers. I havent yet heard of who they were. this news was brought by F. H. Jordan from Gen. <u>Meem</u>. this morning it is thought the Militia will not be out long.. Seems to be altogether the doings of General Meem from what I can hear. Meem had better be careful with him self if he is the only man causing this march of Militia for I do assure the People here as well as other Places look uppon him with Bitterness I think and may want to reward him for it

in haste Yours Truly A.S.M.

Along margin: *If mistakes mark them out. havent time to look over this*

Besides writing regularly to his family, John Hite keeps up a lively correspondence with the young ladies at home. Among the first to respond is second cousin Sarah Ellen (Ella) Buswell, about 20 years old, a sister of George Buswell who is later to become John's comrade in the Page Greys. In a newsy letter from Leaksville, a crossroads not far from the Hite's farm, she reports details of the desultory militia muster and something of the controversy involving Francis H. Jordan, who will later become a captain on the staff of the adjutant general. Martin VanBuren Gander (M.V.G.), James R. Modesitt, Andrew Jackson (Jack) Kite, Frank Yowell, Alexander (Elic) Rothgeb, and Isaac Hite are enlisted in Co. I of this regiment as of July 22, where Modesitt is soon to be promoted to 1st Lt. John's first cousin Ambrose M. Hite is in Co. E. Henry J. Smoot is a young Luray physician. Joseph E. Johnston, now a brigadier, is soon promoted to command the Confederate Army of Northern Virginia. Randall L. Gibson, a Confederate brigadier from Maryland, is later to fight in many western battles. Joseph Johnston (not to be confused with the general) and Gideon Long have enlisted in the Page Greys. Mary Jane is the 19-year-old daughter of Sarah Davis, a neighbor of "Uncle" Mann Spitler in Luray, and Barbara Ann, 15, is the daughter of Isaac Rothgeb, a neighbor of the Hite family. Reuben S. Booten, James H. Dorraugh (or Derrough), and Francis W. Yowell are in Co. D of the 7th Va. Cavalry.

The Painful News I Have to Write

Ella Yowell is soon to be married to her "Elic" Rothgeb. Susan Rebecca (Becca) and Frances (Fannie) are sisters, ages 17 and 13, of Ambrose Hite. Mary is Ella Buswell's sister, now 18, and Wesley and Abram are her two brothers, about 15 and 12.

Leaksville Page Co. Virginia
July 6th 1861

Cousin John
 I received your very kind letter Wednesday; and should have answered it sooner, but was very busy in getting George ready to march. I suppose you have heared of the draft. <u>it seems as if the Militia will get in battle as soon as your company</u>. I was at the <u>Whitehouse</u> Friday evening to see the company pass   there were a good many of my acquaintances in the company. I spoke to nearly all of them. They seemed in very good humor. I gave none of them goodbye as I did you. I will save the next one for M.V.G. I suppose you will see our men if they get to Winchester. Dr. <u>Smoot</u> brought the news up here yesterday evening the Northern troops were in Martinsburg and Gen Johnson & <u>Gibson</u> had marched there; did not say where you were. I hope there yet; so I think your boys will be needed; and not get home as soon as some expected: We had a very small crowd here yesterday to muster; Modesitte acted as Lieut. & D.S. both; & Martin G. took George's place; Capt. said I was very much needed in the field that day so I think I uniform untill next Saturday and take a <u>squad</u>.
 I was glad to hear you was doing so well; I think of you all when it rains you ought to have your tents & coats; I would like to see you cook & wash though I heard you did not bake your own bread; Joe Johnston was in the shop here Thursday but did not come over I would liked to have seen him. I think you had better get someone to run a way so you could come for them; though I should not like to be the one to run away;
 I suppose you thought it rather strange I did not come to Town when you started; [then?] I thought you would not start before seven Oclock untill <u>Tuesday evening</u> about dark and then I thought I could not get to speak to you all that morning and if so I did not care to see you; had I have known it Tuesday I would have gone down then; I hope you will come back and then I will get to see you; though it will be a long time yet if you stay 12 mo.
 I have been no where since you left but at the Seminary to hear Mr. Grant preach; and at Town last Monday so I have not seen many of the <u>youngsters</u> since you have. I saw Mary Jane Monday. She asked me how Barbara Ann took your departure   I told her I did not [think] she thought as much of your leaving as Jack Kite's. Mary

HOPEFUL BEGINNINGS AND FIRST BLOOD

Jane and I liked to had a quarrel about Capt. Jordon's company coming back & his not going up the Country that Sunday; she says he nor none of his company are cowards and Jordon had more sense than to go up there without knowing it was so; & unless a Magistrate had sent for him & then he would have gone I said a Magistrate did not send for the rest of them and he was no better than they were; don't say anything about it so they will hear it; though I expect she will write to him about it. R.L. Booton passed here while ago he & Jim <u>Dorough</u> came home last Wednesday, they say for more Volunteers; I expect glad to get home; I heared Booton was shot at; by the <u>Enemy</u> (though missed as you see). Frank Yowell passed last Thursday evening after sundown I guess going to tell his lady goodbye. I should not wonder if she cried then; I heared Ella Yowel was very much out of heart when the whole Regiment was called out about <u>Elic's</u> going; I do not expect he was far behind; though Ambrose wants to go very much; says he volunteered as soon as he left school to go & then they would not take him: Rebecca & Fannie Hite were here to day, I told <u>Becca</u> I was writing to a Volunteer but did not tell who, and she sends her love to you; Mary also; they do not seem to mind Ambrose going much; they are like the rest of us koun [knowing] it has to be and they can not help it; I am afraid George will get the measels; he never had them.

John, to day was preaching at the Hawksbill did you go up; I did not go. Wesley and Abram went; I presume you hardly know when Sunday comes; think all rainey days are Sunday, that has been very the case here, for a great many harvested on Sunday; I believe the people are nearly all through, now. Did you see the Comet they say that is a Sign of War but as it is war time now; perhaps it is for peace; or a long war; I hope the former; I have not seen any of your folks since you left; I saw Gideon Long's picture Friday, it is a very good one. I wish I could see some more of them;

I believe I have told you all the news I know to write if you were here I could find more to tell you; and as they are all in bed but me; and I have to keep snuffing the candle, I will stop; Give my love to all my friends; your-self not excepted; be a good boy & take good care of yourself.

We are all well at present. Excuse all errors and bad writing for I am like you writing on my lap. Hoping you will favour us with another letter soon,

I remain as ever your friend & cousin
Ella Buswell
<u>*Sunday night 9 Oclock*</u>

The Painful News I Have to Write

William writes again to the family at home. Like many such alarms, this one proves false. William Hite and Michael Shuler are 1st and 3rd Lts., and William D. Rippetoe, a young Methodist minister, the inexperienced captain of Company H.

Camp E. K. Smith near
Winchester Va July 10th 1861

Dear Father Mother Sisters & Bros,

We received an order 1/2 an hour ago from the Col. to prepare to leave at a minutes warning We went to the drilling field this morning as usual at 9 Oclock. At 11 we received the order, We are now at the Camp preparing dinner and something to put in our haversacks to march toward the enemy. Lieut Shuler was at town this morning and said that the Regiments around town had received marching orders. We have since learn[ed] that the enemy were within 8 miles of the place, We expect to fight. The Soldiers here are making every preparation. We are all composed and will Soon be ready to march. All I regret is the inefficiency of our Captain. The mail boy is waiting Jno got 2 Letter but not opened Yet

Good to you all until I see you again

W. F. Hite

P.S.
I have not time to look over this letter
WFH

Regular entries in John's diary begin with a note on the same false alarm. He continues derogatory comments about Capt. Rippetoe whose temporary disappearance and eventual resignation are caused by personal health problems.

July 11th. Recieve orders from the Col. to cook three days rations and be ready at a moments warning to march as it is said the Federals are advancing from Martinsburg, but proved to be false. Rained very hard in the evening.

July 12th. Captain leaves but don't let his Company know where he is going to. Rains after night, lightens and thunders a great deal.

Hopeful Beginnings and First Blood

By July 15, the requisite ten companies, including Co. H, have been assembled and designated as the 33rd Infantry Regiment of Virginia Volunteers. They join the First Brigade under T. J. Jackson and begin the movement toward the critical Manassas Junction, where the Manassas Gap R.R. from the Shenandoah Valley meets the Orange and Alexandria R.R. connecting Richmond to Washington.

15th. We move from Camp E. K. Smith below Winchester and join General Jackson's Brigade. Marched behind the breastwork after night for a fight; but disappointed. and soon marched back to our tents. Ordered to sleep on our arms ready at a moments warning.

July 16th. Have no alarm during the night. The enemy supposed to be within six miles distance.

17th. Still dissatisfied with the Captain. We are ordered out to pull down fencing in double quick time to prepare for a fight; but the enemy won't come.

18th. We receive orders at 11 o'clock PM to strike tents, and begin our march for the junction 7 o'clock, A.M. on the receipt of a dispatch from Beauregard to Johnston that the Federals are advancing with an overwhelming force. We march on in quick time all night, wading the Shenandoah River at midnight, and a great many broke down.

The rather flamboyant Confederate general, P. G. T. Beauregard, who holds Manassas Junction with some 20,000 troops, knows that Gen. McDowell has advanced from Washington on the 16th of July with about 35,000 men. Gen. Joseph E. Johnston, who outranks Beauregard, has about 9,000 troops in the Shenandoah Valley. His feints toward Harpers Ferry have frightened the Federals there into defensive positions, and this permits him to slip away and send most of his force to support Beauregard on the "cars," the first ever large military movement by rail.

19th. Arrive at pedemont station at 8 o'clock A.M. almost broke down. Took the cars at 7 P.M., arrive at the Junction 2 o'clock at night and remain the cars until morning. I don't sleep any or very little for 48 hours. Almost entirely worn out.

18   THE PAINFUL NEWS I HAVE TO WRITE

20th. We get our breakfast and start to meet the enemy; but don't come in contact with them. We have very sorry water to drink. We lay within two miles of the enemy on our arms expecting an alarm in the night; but disappointed.

July 21st. We take a cold bite this morning, then to march in quick time; and continue marching around until about 10 o'clock when we march in front of the enemy. The thickett behind a small hill. Form a line a battle, then lay down for about 20 minutes, when we make a charge on Sherman's battery with loaded guns, fire as soon as we get out of the pines, and the yankees fall, like the leaves of autumn, many fleeing that don't get killed; also many of our company fall, six killed and 18 wounded; but thank God that I escaped with a wound. I helped to carry a northcaralinean off the field.

In these few words, John has described the successful attack on the Federal battery on Henry House Hill, a critical turning point in this first Manassas battle. The diary of John H. Grabill of Co. C, the "Shenandoah Riflemen" of the 33rd Virginia gives a more comprehensive report of the regiment's involvement.

July 21st. This morning we were awakened by the firing of our pickets. After eating a hearty breakfast and filling our haversacks with provisions, we were again on the march. The artillery of the enemy could be distinctly heard on our right. After marching and counter marching for sometime, we were stationed within a-half mile of the battle ground. The regular roaring of the cannon, enlivened by volleys of musketry and the shouts of our boys, whenever they charged, produced a combination of sounds as rare as grand.

We were then marched to a position on the left of Capt. Pendleton's battery and almost in front of a battery of the enemy at a distance of 150 yards, where we were ordered to lie down. We remained for more than an hour, exposed to heavy fire. At length the enemy appeared in sight of the left wing of our regiment. After a partial fire we charged them and drove them from their battery of rifled cannon. We had but 375 men and lost in killed and wounded 160. ... [Names of Co. C. casualties] ...After holding the field for sometime, our number becoming less every moment, we left the battery expecting to rally our men for another charge. So many were killed, wounded and scattered that an attempt to rally proved ineffectual. The rest of the afternoon I spent in having the wounds of the wounded dressed

HOPEFUL BEGINNINGS AND FIRST BLOOD

and in sending them to the Junction. When night came the same sad duty was to be performed. At length having seen that all our wounded had their wounds dressed or were on the way to the junction, I lay down surrounded by the wounded and dying. I was so wearied that in a few moments, I was asleep and slept as pleasantly as if nothing had happened.

This battle of First Manassas or Bull Run is where the Yankees learn this war is real, where T. J. Jackson receives his nickname "Stonewall", and where the 33rd Virginia suffers 146 casualties, including 1st Lt. William Hite. A small square of paper with a list of Co. H men wounded on July 21 was found in an envelope with a later letter:

Wounded
Lieut. W F Hite
Corp. G. B. Long
privates Paul Miller
*   Peter Sours [Sowers]*
*   Silas A. Summers [Somers]*
*   Danl. Smith*

John Hite's diary resumes:

22nd. I go in search of brother Wm who had been badly wounded; find near the battlefield, and take him with other[s] to the Junction. I then go in search of some other wounded, and find a few. Start to F. Royal at midnight with them. I am very wet from being in the rain all day.

23rd. Arrive at F. Royal at 7 o'clock AM and put the wounded at [a] private house where every attention is given them.

A diarist from Front Royal reports:

July 23. By an extra train, Capt. Rippetoe brought 3 of his Page Grays, seriously wounded in the battle. One of them, Mr. Coontz [Pvt. Martin V. B. Koontz], died in the evening.

The Painful News I Have to Write

The war becomes a sad reality to the Hites as Isaac reports William's wound to sisters Bettie and Ella who are away from home, perhaps visiting their older sister Mary Burner. As of July 22, Isaac has enlisted in Capt. John D. Aleshire's Militia Co. I, soon to be posted to Winchester. His illness, reported earlier, may have been keeping him at home to receive the news of William's wound. Nancy Corbin, aged 51 in 1860 census, is one of three spinster sisters heading a household which includes a sister-in-law and her children. Catherine Rothgeb, 79, is a widow living with the Reuben Dadisman family, near neighbors of the Hites.

Home July 24th 1861

Dear Sisters:

We received late yestarday evening the melancholy news that William was shot through the body & and also th[r]ough the leg. Oh! awful to contemplate. The cars brough[t] him To Frontryal yestarday, but there he got so weak that it was impossible to bring him any farther. Father & Mother left last night about half past ten o,clock for to see him in Frontroyal, and to bring him home if possible alive. It is thought he can't possible get well. He was shot Sunday last. As for John we have not heard from and perhaps never will. Merciful God look down with an eye of compassion

It was father's and Mother's request that you should know this our troubles as soon as possible, and to bear it as light as possible. They also thought it would be much better for you both to stay there, and try to attend to things until they brought him home. We will let you know as soon as they get back. Father said he would bring him as soon as possible dead or alive.

Your affectionate brother
Isaac

P.S. one of Corbins will bear this who perhaps will tell you more about it. be as much composed as possible. We had a long night last night. Nancy Corbin & Catherine Rothgeb stayed with us.

John, of course, is very much alive. His diary continues with hopes for William's recovery.

24th. Father and Mother arrive here at 7 o'clock A.M. to see Wm. find him very low. I go to Winchester in the evening after the officer's baggage.

HOPEFUL BEGINNINGS AND FIRST BLOOD

July 25th. I am kept very busy giving the malitia a slight description of the battle, I go back to F. Royal in the evening with the baggage, also brother David. Wm begins to improve a little.

26th. I start for the Junction at 4 o'clock AM arrive there at 7. Go to the battlefield find a good many dead yankees; then go to the company find it small and lowspirited.

27th. We move to Magot Camp about two miles northwest from the Junction.

Though sources say the camp is officially unnamed, John calls this Camp Jackson in his letter of July 30. The only water source is a stream draining from the battlefield still strewn with shallow graves and corpses of men and horses, and Camp Maggot soon becomes the common nickname. A few days later an outbreak of typhoid fever forces a relocation.

28th. I go to preaching at Jackson's Head-Quarters the congregation very solemn. The [water] very sorry here.

29th, Monday. Have only a small squad to drill on account of a good deal of sickness. The Capt leaves for home on account of being sick.

Father Daniel writes to his son David. Daniel's brother, Uncle Martin, is now in Co. I, 97th Va. Militia, and John Burner, the husband of David's twin sister Mary Ann, may also be there with the militia. Postmarked and addressed:

"FRONT ROYAL JUL 29 – PAID 5"

In the cear of
    Captn
D. M. Dovel

David C. Hite
Winchester Po.
       Va.

Frontroyal Va July 29th 1861
    Dear son David thinking, perhaps you have not heard from Willam since you left here I thought I would write a few lines and let you hear from him, he is still improving but very Slowly, I am in good hopes of his recovering, unless something unexpected Should thake

place, which soon mite in his critical condition, the doctors visit him twise every day and say, he is doing very well, but not out of dange[r], Mr.. Jones and his family do every thing for him in their power, he could not gotten to any better place, I dont know when I Shall go home, Mother went on Saturday, we had avery fine rain here yesterday, I have not heard wether your Uncle Martin and the rest of the militia have gone to that place or wether they are still at Strawsburge yet, if he is I wish you would send word to him and John Bunner [Burner] how William is, if I knew they ware still there I would write to them, but thinking they have come townther [down there], if the[y] have you can tell them allabout it   nothing more but remain your affectionate Father

Daniel Hite

As William recuperates at the home of Gideon W. Jones in Front Royal, John, back with his regiment, writes one more letter home.

Prince William Va. July 30th 61
Camp Jackson near Manassa.

Dear Father:

as I have not heard from you all since I left, I thought I would drop you a few lines; though I told Mr. Jones where to direct your letter. I hope that Wm. is getting better by this time, but I have not heard from him since I left. It is reported that dispatches has come here from Washington asking for an armistice for a month so as to determine whether the majority of the North are in favor of peace but from the best information I can get, it will not be granted; because it is thought they only want time to recruit. Most of the men have been in very low spirits since the battle, and many went home without a furlough; and some are sick, which is caused mostly from the water we have to use which is very sorry, no better than pond water or very little.

I could have got a furlough, had not so many left without a permit so that those who ought to have them cannot get any now. We had a fine rain day before yesterday, and the lightning struck a walnut not more than twenty steps from me, some others were closer than I, and knocked them down, it did not knocked me down for I was lying down but jarred me very much. We also had a fine rain yesterday. I must close for the present; hoping it will find you in better spirits than when I left. We are now about 4 miles below the junction.

HOPEFUL BEGINNINGS AND FIRST BLOOD

From your affection[ate] Son   John;

Very warm here now.   Address   John P. Hite
Manassa Junction
Virginia.
Care of Capt. Rippetoe Col. Cumming's Regt.

CHAPTER 2

John – Quiet Interlude

*"I thought you could be a good Soldier, if <u>you were little</u>.
It is not the largest people that are the best men."*

Were it not for various widespread illnesses, the few months after the fight at Manassas are to prove about as pleasant as a soldier's life can be. Morale is high with good water in the camps and sufficient if not abundant food rations. Jackson keeps the troops busy drilling and attending worship services, and there is perhaps too much rain and early cold. But there is plenty of time for letter-writing, for visits from family, and for visits home to the valley by feigned illness or "French furlough." Little fighting, but rumors of victory, reviews by the general staff and dignitaries, both foreign and domestic, and the promotion of their "Stonewall" Jackson to major general each serve to increase morale and a sense of well-being.

After the crisis of William's wound, John's diary resumes with details of camp life. The new Camp Harman is named in honor of brigade quartermaster John A. Harman who has chosen the favorable location.

August 1st. I am enjoying good health. Rains some. Get orders to be ready to march in the morning at 5 o'clock.

2nd. Begin our march at 6 and go to Camp Harman one mile below Centerville, 8 miles from the Junction.

3rd. Very well pleased with our new camp and find better water. No drilling today but have to clean up around our camp.

August 4th. Nothing of importance going on in camp more than our army is increasing.

9th/61. Our Brigade is drawn up with many others in line to salute Prince Napolean. Son of Louis Napolean.

JOHN — QUIET INTERLUDE

Aug 12th. Have a very hard rain; quite cool after the rain.

Aug 14th. Hear cannonading towards Alexandria and reported there was a fight, but only a few of our men killed; and 300 of the yankees. I am appointed orderly for the Col and adjutant.

In letters from Mary Ann (Mollie) Gander, 19, and her sister Frances Elizabeth (Fannie), now 17, we find more evidence of John's lively interest in the ladies and hints of something more serious between John and Mollie. Mollie's letter makes a point of how lonesome (and how available) she is in spite of John's rumor of her engagement. John P. Beaver, her reputed fiance, is a private in Co. H. Ella is Sarah Ellen Buswell, also John's frequent correspondent. David Coffman is in Co. E and "Elic" Rothgeb and Frank Yowell in Co. I of the 97th Va. Militia. Miss Barbara is Barbara Ann Rothgeb, just about 16 years old and a cousin and neighbor of Mollie and Fannie. The letters are undated, but they must be from mid-August, 1861, based on the context and the ripening state of watermelons. Well into the 20th century the Ganders are to grow watermelons on the island in the Shenandoah behind their farmhouse.

My Dear Friend:
I now seat my-self to answer your truly welcome letter which I received on the 8th instant, indeed I was glad to hear from you as it was the first letter that I received from you since you have been gone. You said in your letter that you had written one to me but never received and answer that was the first I knew of it. I never got it and was sorry that I did not for I would have answered it with pleasure.

John you do not know how glad I would be to see you you must get a furlough as soon as you can and come home for I would like to talk with you awhile and they are a good many more would like to talk with you besides myself. I was was up to see Ella last thursday evening she said that She had not received a letter from you since you have left Winchester and by that I know you have been corresponding with her. Alexander Rothgeb, Francis W. Yowell, David J. Coffman, all got a furlough and came home last thursday evening. they are meeting at mill creek to day and I exspect they will be there and then some of the girls will have a beau. it will not be quite as lonesome as it is other sundays. I tell you John it is the lonesomeness time here now that I ever saw in all my life.

John you ought to have been here last Sunday we had a very nice time in the evening after we came home from preaching they were eight girls and only one gentleman and you may know by that the boys are scarse. The girls was around him as thick as hops. Miss Barbera was here to I know you would of stood a pretty good chance if you had been here. now you must come soon for our watermelons will soon be ripe and I know you would like to have some. You wanted to know in your letter wether John Beaver and I are engaged. I will just say that we are not and when you hear from me again we wont be. Thats so and caint be rubed out. Do you not think so too.

I will bring my scribling to a close for I have no more news to write at this time but when I write again I will try and write a little more. You must write to me whenever you can for I am glad to hear from you at any time.

Come home soon for I want to see you so bad you must excuse bad writing for I was in a hurry.

Tell John P. Beaver the reason I did not answer his letter was that he left Winchester and I did not know where to write to and I think it his duty to write again before I write. No more at present write soon and give me all the news.

From your affectionate friend
Mary A. Gander

Fannie's enclosed letter makes an issue of Frank Yowell's visit which Mollie has passed over.

Dearest Friend John

I now seat my-self this sabbath morning, for the purpose to answer your kind and most affectionate letter which, I received on the 8th instant; I was extremely glad to hear from you once more as it was the first time I heard from you since you left Winchester, only I heard you was not hurt in that battle at the Junction.

John you said in your letter that you never received an answer from the last letter you written and you did not know why I did not answer it; the reason was that I did not write was that I heard you was agoing to leave Winchester, and I thought it would not be worth while to write, for you would not have got it know how, and I thought it would be in your place to write to me again. I would not mind writing if I knew what to write, if I had as much news as you would have to write I would write often. I was at Millcreek meeting to day, there was not a very many there like in old times past there were a good many women and girls there and a few young gentlemen, some of Jordan's company, and some of the militia that got furlough to come home, where there [sic].

John, Frank came home with Molly today and if you do not soon come home he will cut you out, he is here now yet; I reckon he will stay untill the morrow morning, as it is raining he can not get home to night, but however I guess he does not care nor she either.

You must come up as soon as you possible can for I would like to see you again, come up we have got some of the best apples, and watermelon there is not very many watermelons ripe yet but in a few weeks we will have plenty. I believe some of the militia would like to have some jelly bread, and milk, would you not like to have some too; if you would let me know and I will send you some.

I will now bring these few scribblings to a close as I have nothing more to write. Answer this immediately for I like to hear from you any time, if I can not see you, but I hope you will come home soon. This leaves me well, and I hope it will find you in good health and fine spirits. So no more at present.

From your sincere most affectionate friend

Fannie Gander

John's sister Mary Ellen (Ella) sends him news of home. David and Isaac Hite and Isaac Huffman are all home on furlough from the militia. William is still recuperating at Front Royal. Tom Spitler is of the branch of that family who moved from Page County to Indiana. A few of this branch actually serve in the Union army.

Luray, Va. Aug 22nd 1861

Dear brother

I will now try to answer your kind letter which I received few days ago and was glad to hear from you and hear that you was well, we are all well at this time. David got a furlow for six days to come home he started back last monday. he was well when he left here. he said he liked it very well down there though he said he would sooner be here than down there. I dont think there is any danger at winchester now.

Isaac wants to start to winchester to morrow. I wish he could stay here but he says he dont want to be called coward and have them to come after him as some dose. Isaac Huffman has not gone yet. they had come after him once and about the tim he was to start his child died and so he says he wont go till they come after him. you said tha[t] I should send you a box of provision by some of the soldiers. I will try to send you some if I cand [sic] but we never know when any body is going till after they have done gone. I wish you could come home and eat as much as you want once again for I know you would like to have some watermellon and some apples and other good things. but we have not many apples– Mary A gander sent William some nice apples. I would liked [to] have sent you some if could though mother says she is going send you some if she can get any. William has not come home yet I dont know when he will come he said he was coming this week but mother sent him word that he should be sadisfied untill the doctor says he can come. I have not saw him since he was hurt. Tom Spitler has come in from the west. he said he come a through the south. he tole them when he started that he was going to washington to get office under Lincoln.

I must come to a close. write soon for we are always glad to hear from you. good bey

Ella:Hite

About this time Col. Mann Spitler, Lt. Col. Thomas Buswell, and a sizeable number of the other militia officers, going over the head of General Meem, write a direct appeal to President Jefferson Davis on Aug. 23 and then to Governor John Letcher on Aug. 31. They plead for a dismissal of substantial numbers of the militia, pointing out that the men are needed to harvest wheat as there is little slave labor available in the area and, further, that only half their troops are armed and those with inferior weapons. Most, including Isaac Hite, Isaac Huffman, and Martin Gander, are discharged on Sept. 9, but will be recalled in early November. Among the regular volunteer regiments, many are feigning illness to obtain furloughs. John's sickness, likely contracted at Maggot Camp, is genuine.

August 22nd. I am taken sick with the camp or bone fever and sent to Narders Hospital. Feel very sick.

Martin Van Buren Kite, detached from Co. H to serve as a hospital orderly, writes home for the sick John Hite who is yearning for a visit from his father or his Uncle Stage (Modesitt).

JOHN — QUIET INTERLUDE

Manassa Junction August 24th
1861

Dear Sir

I have been requested by your Son to Inform you that he Is Still Sick and getting No better he has Now been removed to a hospital about 4 miles west of Manassa, they are five others from the Same Cum[p]any thair with him he Is well cared for and Shal be So long as I am permitted to attend to him. he Is complaining with the rumatism paines threw his limbs and back. he would be Exceedingly glad to See you or his Uncle Stage. Cum to See him if you can. Nothing More but remain your deutifull Son

John P. Hite
writen by M.V.B. Kite

John soon is well enough to write home for himself. Those named all show on the roster of Co. H except Surgeon Nicholson. John Francis Neff is a VMI graduate enlisted as lieutenant and later elected colonel. John's appointment as orderly to the regimental staff was noted in an earlier diary entry.

Aug. 31th '61
Dr Nicholson
Hospital under care of

Dear Father & Mother;

I believe I feel able to drop you a few lines this beautiful Saturday evening. I recieved your welcomed epistle yesterday, with five others from Page; they proved to be excellent medicine but some had went to the regiment nearly a week before I got them.

I have sent two short letters to you which you had not recieved yet when you wrote, one I got Martin V. B. Kite to write when I first came here, and was in bed not able to write. I was hauled to this place yesterday a week ago; over a rough road, distance about six miles from the regiment; and about 3 miles northwest of the Junction.

The names of the rest here from our company are W$^{\underline{m}}$ Webster Charles T. Chadduck A. H. Keyser Reuben Y. Coffman Soloman Lampkins & myself are the sick; and there is Martin Kite Cumberland G. Coffman & Woodford M. Lawrence here to tend us. Webster had the rheumatism very bad but is improving, Chadduck has the camp fever can walk about alittle, Keyser & Coffman same complaint, and can walk alittle; Lampkins has the rheumatism a good deal can scarcely walk.

The Painful News I Have to Write

I had been quite unwell for more than two weeks whilst in camp, and did not eat much, which I suppose was fever working on me. I was taken to bed on Monday after I wrote you the letter you answered and was very ill for more than a week, but began to get better several days since, and can now walk about out of doors a good deal. The Dr. called my disease Camp or bone fever as I had a great deal of pains in my bones, and a severe headache. I think the Dr. very good one that is here (Dr. Nicholson). I fell off a good deal whilst I was sick and got quite weak, but am gaining now, but think I would gain faster if they would give me enough to eat. I get a cup of tea or coffee, and two small biscuits for breakfast and supper, and rice for dinner.

In the letter that Kite wrote to you he told you or Uncle Stage to come and see me, but I know you are busy so; you need not come although I would be glad to see you; I put in the last letter I wrote that you need not send the box of provisions then, but now as I am better, and soon be able to go to camp I think; so you can send the box any time for I am down here where nothing is to be had. When I was taken sick; I told Adj. Neff, so he told me to appoint some one in my place of my company if there were any suitable, and then I could come back again as soon as I was able, for he said he wanted me. I don't get any more pay I don't suppose at least I heard nothing of it. I never had any news to carry further than 3 or 400 yards and not often half the distance, therefore I had no use for a horse only a couple times the Col. [A. C. Cummings] give his to go to Jackson's Head-Quarters. We have not recieved any pay yet, but the payroll has been made out several times. All the other regiments of the Brigade have been paid, but can't tell when we will get any. Give my best respect to Grand-Mother, and Write where she is. Yours as ever. Write soon.

John

John W. Kite of our company died at this hospital the day before I was brought here. He had Tiphiod fever.

Recovered from his illness, camp life resumes for John. The new camp near Fairfax Court House proves less desireable than Camp Harman.

Sept 13th. I return to camp again after staying at the hospital 3 weeks and having tolerably hard spell of sickness.

JOHN — QUIET INTERLUDE 31

Sept 16th. the whole Brigade march this morning very early down near Fairfax Court-house.

September 21st. The pickets have a fight nearly everyday, in which there are some few killed on both sides, but generally the most on the yankees.

25th. We get orders to cook for three days rations to be ready to march at a moments warning.

28th. We march early this [morning] down below Fairfax for a picket duty.

Fannie Gander writes again to John with more references to John Beaver, Frank Yowell, and cousin Barbara Ann Rothgeb. The unwelcome Martin Ruffner, 22, is later to serve in Co. D, 7th Va. Cavalry. Letter folded into a small square, sealed with wax, and addressed simply:

Mr John P Hite
Please hand this to the owner

At Home
September 29, 1861

My Dear Friend:
    as Sis is writing to J P Beaver I will write a few lines and put it in with hers. You must excuse me for not writing sooner, I had know news to write; nor I have know more now and you know what a task it is to write when you dont know what.
    I think you might do like John Beaver, write twice to my once, he generally writes twice to Sis once. To day was sunday and a lonesome sunday it was; Sis and me where at home all day, and know body much come, Mart Ruffner was here a little while but I have give him over to Cousen Barbra, I would sooner for it to have been you than him. you wanted to know wether I unriddled the puzzle or not: yes I did but I do not know wether that is any sign or not
    Well John as it is bed time I will bring my few scribblings to a close. I want you to answer this soon and I will write more next time. Oh I like too forgot, Sis looked for Frank to day but he did not come I do not know what was the reason he didn't.
    I believe that is all I have to say this time. So good by for the night

32   THE PAINFUL NEWS I HAVE TO WRITE

Yours sincerely
Fannie Gander
Please dont let any person see this

In margin: *Do not forget to write soon for I long to hear from you*

John's diary continues:

Oct. 2nd. Our company goes out on picket this morning. A good many of the men frightened in the night by the hooting of an owl.

3rd. Relieved this morning by another company.

Oct 4th. The whole Regt relieved and marched to out camp near Fairfax Courthouse. Get there 9 o'clock night.

On October 5, brother William finally returns to duty, believing himself fully recuperated from the wound received at Manassas.

Oct. 5th. Lt. Hite with others returned from home to Camp. We send away all the baggage that cannot handily be taken on a march also the sick but can't tell where to.

7th. Have a very hard rain about seven inches perpendicular water, and turned very cool after the rain.

8th. I stand guard from 11 to 1 o'clock also from 5 until 7 into the day, and 11 to 7 o'clock, also from 5 to 7 at night.

In the following entry, John describes the prescribed court-martial sentences for unauthorized absence. Since the regiment is seldom far from home, this is an increasingly common occurrence. Based on the wording of this entry, Lowell Reidenbaugh's regimental history says that John himself had been AWOL three times, but the time line from his diary effectively disproves that interpretation. The grand review on Friday of this week is a morale booster.

Wednesday 9th. Still quite cool and cloudy. Courtmarshalled for running off 1st to forfiet 20 days pay, also the 2nd, and to cut wood from 10 to 11 o'clock for six days; 3rd to forfiet 60 days pay and to cut wood from 10-to-11 o'clock A. M. and stand on a barrel from 2 to 3 o'clock P.M. for 15 days.

Thursday, Oct 10th. We see some sky rockets sent up in the air, supposed to be near Alexandria. Courtmartial trials today at Cols Hd Quarters.

Friday 11th. we hear near 50 reports of cannon last night; but don't know the reason of firing at night. Gen Jackson's whole Brigade goes on drill on a large level field in the presence of the following distinguished gentlemen: Generals Johnston, Beauregard, & Smith; also different staff officers Gen Jackson and Adjutant General Jones. The Brigade behaved remarkably well and was complemiented by General Smith for the Soldier-like appearance of the men. General Johnston was dressed with fine gray cloth coat, standing collar with stars on either side, gray cap and blue pants, rode a bay, horse. General Beauregard's dress was blue throughout rode a sorrel horse. General Smith wore citizen's clothes, rode a fine bay. A member of the British Parliament, and a French officer; also attracted attention from the admiring crowd.

Saturday 12th. Rains very hard last night, and turns quite cold, and cool all day. We don't have any drill in the afternoon, more than dress parade, on account of having to clean up in camp.

Sunday 13th. cool and very windy all day. Preaching at Head-Quarters to-day at 11 o'clock, also prayer meeting at Rippetoe's at night, which there is nearly every night.

Monday 14th. the Quartermaster draws liquor this morning because he can't get coffee, but can't draw any more on account of some of the men getting drunk.

Tuesday 15th. We have an alarm this morning at 3 o'clock and have the Battalion formed immediately; but don't march. We have orders again directly after roll call at night to cook; and that the revelle will be beat at 1 o'clock, and be ready to march at 3 o'clock.

October Wednesday 16th. We don't begin our [march] until 4 o'clock in the morning, neither do we get to sleep any. March very slow for

34 The Painful News I Have to Write

awhile on account of the wagons. Go half mile above Centerville. Soldiers get very tired from carrying large bundles. All our forces falling back near Centerville; the reason unknown. Has appearance of rain.

John receives a letter of an uncertain month, but probably written on Wednesday, October 16, 1861. The writer, Emily C. Judd, is the 18-year-old daughter of Daniel Judd. Her brother Samuel N. Judd is serving in Co. K, 10th Va. Infantry. John T. Johnston, the bearer of the letter, is in the Page Greys with John and has likely been home sick. The envelope reads:

Mr.. John.. P.. Hite
Manassa.. Junction

Kindness
of Mr Johnston

Wednesday evening 16th
Dear Friend
I received your letter afew days. I somewhat surprised on the receipt of your letter thinking you had forgotten me. I was glad to hear from you indeed. brother Samuel has been home. he spent 2 weeks with us he is now gone back he started back last Sunday. I was very sorry to see him start back again. Oh Mr Hite I know you have hard times. I am sorry for you. my sympathy for you is great. I would like very [much] to see you if you do get afurlow to come home you must be shure to call on us. Mr. Hite you wanted to [know] how I did to pass away the [time]. I will tell you how pass away the athinking about the Souldiers and talking about them reading letters from them. I read one letter about a dozen times. I must come to aclose. Jack Johnson is going start this evening. he is waiting. he came in just as I commenced writing. you must write soon. nothing more but remain your Friend untill Death. escuse me this time I will do better next time goodby   *Emma C. Judd*

John P Hite

Along margin: *I must tell you the girls are all tolerable well. I would like to see you a cooking and washing*

JOHN — QUIET INTERLUDE

John's diary resumes with news of skirmishes and impending battles. Some 200 Page County men are in Cos. I and K of the 10th Va. Infantry Regiment which he reports visiting.

Thursday 17th. Stand guard from 10 to 12 o'clock, also from 4 to 6 o'clock at night and from 10 to 12 o'clock also from 4 to 6 o'clock at night. The enemy within 5 miles from here. Expecting a fight everyday. Hear heavy cannonading during the day. Rains a good deal during the night. A great many troops around Centerville.

Friday 18th. Thirty barrels of flour, $600 worth of shoes left behind by one of US Regiments in their hasty retreat. The enimies pickets drove back to the Courthouse by our Cavalry. Hiram Trinty put in the guardhouse for selling liquor Saturday

19th. 25 of our Regiment sent down to Camp Harman (1 mile below centerville) on Picket. Recieve 26 letters from page. Wrote 41 to Page.

Sunday 20th. Went to the 10th Regt.; find most of the boys well and lively.

October Monday 21st. Very cool today and last night. Our Regt have marching orders. A fight at Leesburg today, in which four of our Regt Completely routed 11 of theirs; run a great number in the river that drowned, killed and wounded many, took 200 prisoners, 9 pieces of cannon; besides a great many other things. Our loss small when compared with theirs.

Reports from this battle of Leesburg or Ball's Bluff greatly raise the morale of Confederate troops. Federal forces (about five regiments rather than eleven as reported by John) crossing the Potomac toward Leesburg are forced into a disorderly retreat with many drowning in the river. Union casualties: 49 killed, 158 wounded, 714 missing and presumed drowned. Confederate losses: 36 killed, 117 wounded, 12 missing.

October Tuesday 22nd. Rainy and foggy all day. Got orders after dark to cook one days rations so as to go on picket early in the morning.

Wednesday 23rd. the whole Regiment goes on pickett three miles below Centerville. Our Regt relieves the 13th Virginia Regt.

Thursday 24th. Our Company goes on picket about 1 and 1/2 miles from the Regt, extends from 1 mile above Fairfax C.H. to a mile along the Little River Turnpike. Hear different kinds of noise in the night that we don't fancy. The enimy only two miles distance. I get some chestnuts close to our post, but not allowed to go and search long at a time.

Friday 25th. a very hard frost last night. Many complained of getting cold. Relieve of picket this morning. Go on a scout in the evening six miles from the Regt. We pass the enemies pickets and go to two yankies houses where the enemy had been the day before; mile distant from the yankee camp.

Saturday 26th. our Regt relieved by the 27th Virginia Regt. We go to our camp near Centerville. The whole Regt fire off their guns at once on their way to camp. 130 prisoners taken at Leesburgh last night. Pleasant weather.

October Sunday 27th. Have Battalion inspection as usual this morning.

Now John reports the beginnings of brother William's relapse, the final outcome of which is reported in the next chapter. Isaac Long is a Page County farmer, age about 30.

Monday 28th. Capt. Rippetoe and Issac Long arrive here at camp. Wm F Hite quite unwell, thinks he is getting the fever. 25 of our men sent to Camp Harman on pickets.

Tuesday 29th. Our company relieved of picket. Wm F Hite worse than yesterday, expects to start home in the morning with Mr. Long.

October Wednesday 30th. Wm starts for F. Royal this morning at 10 o'clock with Issac Long. I go with him as far as the Junction. A new flag presented to our Regt, also to rest of Virginia Regts by Governor Letcher.

JOHN — QUIET INTERLUDE

Bettie Hite writes to John with news of a cousin's wedding. The mother of the bride, Aunt Barbara (Grove) Yowell, an older sister of Rebecca (Grove) Hite, is a widow, age nearly 60.

Luray Va Oct 31st 1861

Dear Brother

As I have not wrote to you for some time I thought I would write few lines and send it by Mr Huffman as he is going to start in the morning. We are fixing a box of provision to cend to you and William but we heard this evening that he is sick in Ft royal so we will cend it to you. we did not hear whether William is much sick or not. we only heard he was braught there with 30 other sick ones. We received a letter from Isaac yesterday. he is well and he said they have come back to winchester. he also said they had orders to go to romney but I dont think they went. Cousin Ella Yowel and Elic Rothgeb was married to day. they had six waiters. thay was Barbera A. Rothget and Frank Yowel Cate Yowel Mart Gander Cate Strickler and Ambrose Rothgeb were they six. Aunt barbera did not ask no one but her children. I do not know who Isaac Rothgebs asked. They Malitia got orders to day to be ready to march next Monday to Strawsburgh. I do not know what the groom will do if he has to leave his lady so soon. Emma Young told me to tell you she cends her respects to you and that she would like to see you. I taken the letters you cent to me and read them all over and then put them away to take care of them. I almost thaught I could write a love letter after reading so many but I fear I could not. I will come to a close and let father write yet if he will. I wrote a letter to william last week and got father to back it and he directed it to you but it did not make much difference. no more but write soon and give all the news.

From your sister Bettie

On the back of this letter father Daniel adds:

Dear Son John

Bettie wrote a letter on the first page. I thought I would write a few lines to you, Mr Huffman is going to starte to the Junction in the morning, I thought I would send a small box of provitions to you and William but I was in town this evening and heard that William was at Frontroyal sick, I shall still send the box on to you, youre uncle Stage thinks you had better taken the over coat of Burners. he did not think he could get cloth to furnish you one this side of Christmust, the malitia are all ordered out again, and it is very douptful wether I can come down there this fall. we have got nearly all of yours cloths ready and are awaiting youre order. write soon and give us further directions, we have no Butter to send now to you. this leaves us all well, no more at presen[t] but remain your affectionate Father

Daniel Hite

we received your last long and interesting letter

John's diary continues with news of his reenlistment, unpleasant weather, and the arrival of Joseph Huffman with the promised "provitions." Gen. Jackson's farewell speech is to be widely quoted and credited with far greater impact than John's brief mention would imply.

Thursday 31st. mustered in service again for two months. The whole army goes on review in presence of our Generals and other officers.

November Friday 1st. It has the appearance of snow in the evening, but raining after dark and rains on; the wind blowing all the while. Our tents gets blown down about 12 o'clock at night, have a hard time putting it up. I have written 43 letters to Page, recieved 27.

Saturday 2nd. rains all day and the wind blows very hard all the time. Today being one of the most Disagreeable every experienced in my lifetime; a great many tents get blown down

Sunday 3rd. clears up after dark last night, cloudy and cool today. I paid 50 cts for a substitute to stand guard 24 hours.

Monday 4th. General Jackson bids his Brigade adieu. Makes a complementary address of ten minutes; starts for Winchester [to] take command of the valley.

November Tuesday 5th. Joseph Huffman with many others arrive here from Page with provisions; having one box for me.

Meanwhile, cousin Ella Buswell sends a long letter with another report of the Yowell-Rothgeb wedding. George is her brother, George Buswell. We recognize F.W.Y. as Frank Yowell and M.V.G. as Mart Gander, brother to Mary Ann (Mollie). Andrew Jackson (Jack) Kite is listed as AWOL from Co. I of the 33rd Va. Militia from November 4 to

Isaac Maggart, Later Martin Gander, Farm

View from foot of Daniel Hite farm lane.

12 and December 12 to 25 of this year. Martin Ruffner is later to enlist in Co. D, 7th Va. Cav., but we have no record of his reported enlistment at this time, apparently in Roberts, a village in Doddridge County, now West Virginia. Federal forces have taken Romney, some forty miles west of Winchester, with few casualties on either side. Col. Angus W. McDonald, Sr., of the 7th Virginia Cavalry, is an 1817 graduate of West Point. Due to age and painful rheumatism he soon resigns his field post but continues in military service. Wounded and captured in 1864, he is released only to die in Dec. 1864 as a result of mistreatment in Yankee prisons.

Leaksville Virginia
Nov 3rd/61

Cousin John
Yours of the 27th was received Wednesday; and although it is Sunday I must answer it; for if I put if off, it will not be written for a while; for if I <u>dont</u> answer a letter directly I generally leave them a good while; as you have seen: George came home last Wednesday; they were fifteen came up after deserters; they were thirty missing out of their company; the <u>deserters</u> are a great deal of trouble; they have ten days to get them in; though they are going to morrow if they can get them all together. the other <u>Draft</u> starts to morrow; I guess there are some Sad hearts to day; (it is not mine). F.W.Y. passed here a while ago I presume on his way to bid his girl farewell; I suppose you have not heard of the wedding yet; <u>Elic & Ella joined heart</u> & <u>hand</u> last Thursday; and he has to leave to morrow. I guess their joy will soon be over; for a while any how; I believe they did not have much of a wedding; had three sets of waiters; Ambrose Rothgeb & Cate Yowel, F.W.Y. & B.A. Rothgeb; M.V.G. & Cate Strickler; they pass here Friday. We were invited to neither place. I do not know how Frank got along at the <u>infor.</u> Cate & Mary Ann both and he had to tend to Barbara Ann. he and the Cates went by yesterday evenin; and he came down to the pike to day; so I think he took her home; & told her goodbye & is now gone to tell the other one goodbye. It seems as though war will not stop people from <u>marrying</u>. I think I Shall wait till war is over and take some of our good Soldiers if there is any left.

I heard Thursday Jack was very sick with the fever. David Johnston has gone to day to see him; he is very fortunate to get home before he gets sick. I am glad to hear you are so well satisfied with a Soldier's life; I though[t] you could be a good Soldier; if <u>you were little</u> it is not the largest people that are the best men; I wish your regiment would come to Winchester for Winter quarters; I do not *know where the Malitia will stay this winter they have been travelling about a great deal; You Speaking of your company. Scouting & passing the Enemy line of pickets. if you don't mind the Yankees will get you and then what will you do. What will we do with all of our <u>prisoners</u> if we get many more; they got so many at Leesburg; What do you think of our defeat at Romney & to think they got so much bagage wagons and horses; some think it was McDonal's fault; he ought to have the bagage moved; I expect they will try for Winchester now; if they were to get there now they would get in so few there; Should they ever get in there they would keep up the Valley and then we would be done for; As for my part I would (I believe) as soon be <u>dead</u> as live among them;*

Nov 5th. As you know it generally takes two trials for me to write a letter. I will see if I can finish now; as ten the Morning the Mail comes; I did not care to finish this Sunday as I wanted to wait till the Malitia started; They met (or rather some of them) in Luray yesterday, some started went as far as Burner's last night & stayed; they were so many missing that each company I beleive left five men to find & bring them on Thursday; Capt Aleshire left M.V.G. F.W.Y. John Modesitt <u>Elic</u> Rothgeb & Reuben Comer; they met here this Morning and started in different directions; Some of George's men did not come and Capt. Dovel detailed him & 4 others to <u>hunt</u> the men missing under his command here; till Thursday; so he started of this morning to met his company at Alma; and has not come yet and it is most ten Oclock; I know where he is perhaps riding yet; and it is so dark & cloudy I am afraid he will get lost as he is in a strange <u>neighborhood</u> up the river I expect; the Yankees put us all to a great deal of trouble; I think it would be better for them to go home and let our Soldiers come home; for the Winter as I do not see how you all will stand it laying out in the cold; more particulary those from far South. <u>Dont</u> you think <u>Martin</u> Ruffner; has gone to the Army in Robert's for a month; in Western Virginia; he is getting better;

George, Mary & I were going to the Hawksbill last Sunday but the Hawksbill was so <u>high</u> we were afraid we could not cross; So Mary & I would not go; George went; he said there were but a few there. <u>Uncle Booton</u> was afraid to venture over so there were no preaching and he went to Morgan Bidler's; next Sunday if nothing prevents I am going to Mill Creek, would like to see you there.

I heard a few days since Cousin <u>Will</u> was in Front Royal sick; the disease I did not learn; or if he was seriously ill; I have not heard from <u>Jack</u> since yesterday morning; he was no better. Some seem to think he will not get over it; the <u>Typhoid</u> fever is very bad when it gets a hold on any one and keeps them down so long; but still I think he will recover; I think he went out too soon after having the measels; We are all well except Willie he has not been so well since he had the measels;

I must close for I am sure this will weary your patience before you get through; it is the longest I have written you though it does not contain much news; Please excuse bad writing; & errors. Write soon to your little

Cousin Ella Buswell

P.S. I heard <u>Jack</u> was better.

Again, from John's diary:

Wednesday 6th. Election today. Page Greys vote for William H. Smith for Congress. We get paid for two months which is $22. Turn cold in the evening. Cousin Ellen Yowell was married to Alx. Rothgeb 31st of October.

Thursday 7th. All the Page militia ordered out the 5th of November. Joseph Huffman and Company start home. I send $22 home by Mr. Huffman. I buy an overcoat for $20.

John sends thanks for the provisions and urges his father to visit. Born November 14, 1840, he is conscious of politics this close to his twenty-first birthday.

$22.00 in this letter.

Nov. 6th/61
Camp near Centerville

Dear father:

yours was duly recieved yesterday evening, and the box of provisions, for which I feel thankful. You said that you did not expect that you could come down this fall, but I wan't you to in about two weeks for I know it would be worth the trip, but don't think I am homesick. If you were to buy several barrels of apples and bring down I could sell for $15.00 per. barrel with ease. We drew $22.00 to day, (two months pay). I send you $20.00 by Mr. Huffman. I have about $35.00 but my overcoat cost $13.00; made ten or twelve dollars on apples, enough to pay for my overcoat.

I wrote a letter to David and started it yesterday, so I'll not write much this time. Mr. Huffman can give the news.

It turned very cold since morning., The volunteers of Page are nearly all voting for W$^{\underline{m}}$ Smith for congress. I only lack 9 days of having a vote. The letter that Bettie wrote to W$^{\underline{m}}$ and you directed to me was not recieved.

From your affectionate son,
J. P. Hite

You can come with Mr. Huffman as he is coming again in a few weeks. Prices.

Apples $12 per. lb. [he means per bbl.]	*Liquor $10 per. gal.*
Eggs 25 cts. per. doz.	*Butter 30 cts. per. lb.*
Cheese 25 cts. per lb.	*Turkeys $1.50 each.*
Other things accordingly.	

Recognition by France and England is hoped for throughout the war, and John is not immune to optimistic rumors. Following his promotion, Thomas J. (Stonewall) Jackson sends for the 1st Virginia Brigade to join him at his new command in the Shenandoah Valley.

Friday 8th. Reported that France has recognized the Southern Confederacy. Four Regts of our Brigade start today for Winchester; ours have to in the morning at 3 o'clock. I hear that Wm Hite is very low at F. Royal.

Saturday 9th. Jacksons Stonewall [Brigade] leaves this morning at 9 o'clock. Arrive at the Junction at 10 O'clock, begins raining and continues until night, all of us stay out in the rain getting very cold. The whole of the Irish company gets drunk save a few; they get to fighting, in which swords, bayonets and knives are used; have a hard time tying them and putting them in the guardhouse. Several of both parties get badly wounded. I set up by the fire, all night; don't get to sleep but very little.

Sunday 10th. sun rises very pretty this morning. Leave the junction 9 $1/2$ o'clock, arrive at Strasburg 5 o'clock; a great many ladies on the roadside to see us pass. We stay all night on half mile below Strasburgh. I stand from 6 to 8, also from 12 to 2 o'clock at night, don't get but very little sleep for two nights.

Monday 11th. start for Winchester at 7 o'clock this morning. Camp three miles south of Winchester. Soldiers get very much fatigued from the march. [They had marched 18 miles to this camp at Kernstown.]

Tuesday 12th. some of the militia come up from Winchester to see us. I go to Winchester in the evening to see the page militia, find them generally well and in good spirits. Very fine weather.

Wednesday 13th. I return to my camp this morning. A great many ladies come up from Winchester to see us drill.

November Thursday 14th. It rains some in the evning. John P. Beaver arrives from home last naigt.

Friday 15th. I am 21 years ould today. Rains nearly all day. Wm F Hite still very low at F. Royal. Reported that the Yankees are leaving Romney.

Saturday 16th. Very cold and windy today. Several snow storms. The coldest day this fall. Doublequick it nearly all the time in drilling. A man to be shot at Winchester in a few days for shooting his Captain.

Sunday 17th. still cold and windy, I stand guard from 5 to 7 o'clock also from 11 to 1 oclock at night.

Leaving John in the snow, wind, and rain, we must now tell William's story, backing up to August and his recuperation in Front Royal.

CHAPTER 3

William – Recuperation and Relapse

"Do not mourn, for He that giveth him taketh away."

While John Hite has been coping with army life, William has been recuperating, first at Front Royal and later at home. We now return to August when, in the absence of both Capt. Rippetoe and of 1st Lt. William, responsibility for the Page Greys has fallen on 2nd Lt. Ambrose Booten Shenk. Both his friendship for William and his increasing personal burden are reflected in this series of letters. In the first he mentions other soldiers of Company H including John W. Kite, dead of typhoid fever on August 21, and Charles T. Chadduck and Alexander H. (Hamp) Keyser.

Camp Harmon
Aug 27th 1861

Friend Hite
I have concluded to write to you after so long a time & ask you to forgive me for not writing to you sooner as you are one of my warmest friends & I miss you so much here in Camp. I only wish you was well again so you could be with us, you & the Capt. both being absent & me having to take charge of our Comp. keeps us busy, as we have so many sick to see to attent, We Lost another one of Our dear Boys J^{no} W. Kite as you have heard ere this I expect, I attended his burying with six of our Boys.

I must tell you that I saw J^{no} your Brother on Sunday & he was quite sick at the Hospital & also Chadduck & Keyser are there complain[in]g considerable & we have several in Camp also, I tell you that we have had too Marches within the last week to Fairfax C.H. the Last one on Sunday we did not go but about 2 miles before we return, I did expect that we were Marching for another March fight, But the Enemy retreated back, I cannot tell when we May have to March again nor where to as you know, I am glad to hear you are improving so fast as I heard yesterday that you had been down to Dinner I only hope you May still improve and once more recover again as sound as ever. I am sorry to inform you that we now have not less than twenty three that are now sick here & the Hospital out of our Company, I feel *badly on A/c of our small compa[n]y when we go out on Parade, to see so small a number of our men present. we cannot get out more at any time than Thirty two or three out of our large Company as you know that to be so, I hope that it may be that you and all that are sick will soon recover & be with us again, I men [sic] are very much discourage yet and in a great degree on the Capt fault as they have not as yet become satisfied with him, I hope they may soon become satisfied or get Rid of him*

I tell you we are still encamp about 1 mile below Centerville But Cannot tell how long we will remain at this post. I must now close as I have a chance to send this to the Junction, Excuse me for not writing sooner to you but though[t] it best not in your situation. I hope you success. may you live to be a healthy man again, Shuler sends his respect to you & says he will w[r]ite to you soon Your friend
A.B. Shenk

write soon

In margin: *Excuse me as I have not time to look for mistakes*

Shenk is now sharing command responsibilities for the company with 3rd Lt. Michael Shuler, son of "Squire" John Shuler. Hamp Keyser's father, Alexander, and Charles "William" Webster's father, Samuel B., have come to visit their sons. Perry is Oliver Hazard Perry Kite. The Col. William Nelson Pendleton whose distant preaching inspires Shenk this Sunday morning is an Episcopal clergyman who is to become a brigadier general and commander of Lee's artillery. Envelope addressed:

Lieut Wm. F. Hite
Frot=Royal
Warren Couty
Virginia.
Politenys of
Mr. Cameron)

1861
Camp Harmon Sept 1st

Friend Hite
I was certainly very glad to hear that you were doing so well and hope you will soon be with us as I know it to be your desire to be with us but I fear that Camp Life will not suit you this winter & you will be compelled to remain at home, but if you can with safety to yourself be

William — Recuperation and Relapse

with us I hope you will soon gratify your desire, I am truly glad that I can let you know that John is improving finely & all our Boys but Keyser that was at the Hospital, I think if we can get our tents & then have dry weather for A short time that we will have a good Company again, we do not now when we go out to drill have over Thirty Men, I tell you that I and Shuler now has it very hard attending to the duties of the Company.

Mr. Keyser is now gone to the Hospital to see Hamp & will be back to night, also Wm Webster Father, Mr. K. said he met with you in Frot Royal & that you was doing well, I do not know what to think of P Kite as I understand that he is well. Sqr. Shuler wrote to Mike that Perry was well & some other boys are doing the same way I hope that they will soon report themselves here as we will be compelled to report them as deserters I heard Perry said he would be here the 1st of this week I hope he may, I do not want to see him or any of our Boys suffer. To day or now while I am writting on this Beautiful Sabbath Morning Gen Jackson has Preaching at Head quarters by Col Pendleton, He is a fine Preacher I heard him once but could not leave quarters to go to day. I can hear his voice from here but cannot tell anything I hear as it is so indistinctly heard from here, I heard that the Page Artillery was to pass by here to day if so I want to see them, But I do not look for them, I feel that we will soon take up the March to Washington City & I hope that if it will bring this matter to a close that we may soon go, as I would do anything to see it Brought to a focus. May Our Good Being direct our steps and tell us how & when to strike our blow to be effectual as I believe & trust he is with us & will remain with us in all our Battles. I look to him for our support & Eternal Welfare.

May all the south look to the God of Our Universe for Protection and Heavenly Blessings, May this find you trusting in Him who is Mighty to Save & when you & I come to die may we still look to our Good Being. Shuler joins me in regards. I must now stop as Mr Cameron is about to start.

A.B. Shenk

By the time of Ambrose Shenk's third letter, William has returned home to continue his recuperation. The messenger is Emanuel Strickler, a Page County farmer.

Camp Harmon Sep. 11th/61

Cousin Billy

As I rec your money on yesterday up to the 30st june I concluded to send it to you as you know how it is to keep money in Camp. The amt is Thirty Six dollars I think but cannot tell untill I look in my trunk. it is a draft on the Bank of Richmond. I send it By Mr. E. Strickler to leave at A.S. Modesitts & hope you may soon get it, so you can relive me of the uneasiness of a Part of the money, as you know it would be the case with anyone. I have yet about Six hundred dollars in my hand for those that are sick and absent, & if you see any person that is coming down try & get them to come so we might send it to those that are wounded & sick at home. But enougth as I have no time to write as Mr. E. Strickler wants to leave for home now and I must soon close. We are now getting along tolerably well & the men seem to be better satisfied now as the[y] have rec their Coats, Tents & Part of the Money for their services, I hope it may still keep something to encourage them, Our Capt is still at Home & I have written to him but cant learn anything from him, But I hope you & he may both soon be with us, But I do not wish either of you to come untill you think yourself able, as I have not time to write I must beg you to excuse me this time as this is a Hurried letter as you can see. I can tell you we have no news to communicate to. in regard to our marching as we are still at our old Camp & everything quiet here now But cannot tell how long it will remain so, I hope we may soon have the matter settled, and if we must fight I want to get at it if now I want it to see it settled soon. May this find you all well and you still improving in health. Oh if you see any chance to get any of our Boys do so, & secure them in jail if no other way & we will send for them & Bring them Back here.

I must now stop. My Respect to all enquiring friends, & also your self, you are due me a letter yet If you rec mine, sometime ago So farewell Cousin Billy.

A.B. Shenk

Before returning home, William has spent some six weeks of convalescence at the home of Gideon W. Jones, a Front Royal merchant whose home is attached to his store at the corner of Chester and Manassas Streets. In the 1860 census this family included Gideon and his wife Elizabeth, both age 40; children Henrietta (Bettie), 11, Gideon E. (Edgar), 10, and Earnest, 5; Gideon's mother Mariam Jones, 61; his spinster sisters Evaline, 38, and Jane C., 35; and three young clerks including William O. Rust, 19, who is now off to serve in the Warren Rifles, 17th Va. Infantry,

WILLIAM — RECUPERATION AND RELAPSE

and will later marry Henrietta. Here, young Edgar, now about 12, writes to report his safe arrival home after accompanying William on the return to Page County.

Front Royal September 7th 1861

Dear Friend
I arrived home safely yesterday about two o'clock found all anxiously looking for me. William Rust left us this morning for the Junction. he is much improved. left in fine spir[i]ts says he expects to fight. Thier were some 4 or 5 sick brought up to the hospital yesterday one is very ill his recovering is doubtful the rest are doing well. some will soon be able to leave. Thier was another marriage in town this week. Cousin Willie Dosh & sister left us for home yesterday. Sister will be home to day & we expect to start to school next week. I feel very grateful to you & all my kind friends for making my visit so pleasant I enjoyed it very much.
Ma grand ma Gaunts & Erna all join me in kind regards to you & all your fathers family. Ma says she will write to you in a few days.
your affectionately G E Jones

P.S. Mr Hite please return thank to the gentleman who came down in the Stage this morning for his kindness to Bettie. I do not know his name.   your friend in haste E A Jones

excus this scrap

Father Gideon encloses a business note on a separate small sheet of lined paper. Shams are heavy cloth jackets or coats:

Sept 7th 1861

Dear William
I send you a sample of the only Factory Cloth we have; it is $6/4$ wide. please send me word if it will answer & I will send it to you. We have nothing that will do for Shams & there is nothing in Town. let me hear from you.   Hastily & truly yrs. G. W. Jones

Starting a correspondence which is to reflect a family friendship lasting many years, Mrs. Jones sends more details to William. Front Royal has been designated a state hospital, and, before buildings can be erected, all available public buildings are put to use. Only a fortunate few like

William, perhaps because he is an officer, have found accommodation in private quarters. In the 1860 slave schedule for Warren County, G. W. Jones is listed as employer of a mulatto girl, age 14, owned by J. H. Carson. Kitty and Bet are likely this girl and the "old black woman" mentioned by William in a later letter.

Front Royal Sept. 15th

Mr. Hite

I am pleased to hear of your improvement. hope you will soon be well enough to make us a visit. <u>perhaps</u> the Ladys will consent for you to make a <u>visit,</u> I hope you have enjoyed Miss ......'s society. tell Mr Spitler he must <u>give me a full account</u>

Edgar was highly delighted with his visit. would be willing to go back. he thought it a short week, he should have returned thanks to Mr Modesitt for his kindness. his Papa intended paying his fare on his return, The Children Bettie Erny and Edgar return thanks for their presants. Bettie says tell your to tell your [sic] Sister the Apple was delightful. also for the presants which you left with me for them which they will lay it out in something that they can keep. also Kitty and Bet. tell your mother I enjoyed her cheese very much. and what aded to my enjoyment of it most the Other morning one of the Souldiers came in to the Store and ast Gideon if he could tell him where he could get some and I just had enough for him. one of the sick had asked for it

There is over 100 Sick in F.R. now. it has been made a State Hospittle. on Friday there was upwards of 90 brought from the Junction. now you may juge what Sort of a sight it was to behold those that were here when you left have nearly all recovered with one or two ecceptions. the 6 from Rockingham took supper with us on their way to the Cars. poore fellows seemed so <u>delighted</u> at the thoughts of getting <u>home.</u> (Oh how much meaning is sumed up in <u>that word Home</u>) they were very weak, they have taken the Baptist and Episcopal Churches and Court House and I suppose will take the Methodist to morrow

They say they say [sic] they expect 100 more to morrow. now it is very hard for them to suffer but it will be two many for such a place as this. they are North Carolinans. they say there is but 100 in their Regiment fit for duty. there was 13 taken out dead the day before they came up. had 2 deaths here last night. they were buried this evening with the honours of War. but Oh how sad me thought away from Home and Friends. G. and my-self went around this evening to see them. they look tolerably coffertable. many are improving. they got

WILLIAM — RECUPERATION AND RELAPSE

here before the Comissarys were ready for them. the Ladys have been providing for them since they have been here. I was very much pleased to hear from your Brother John. I hope he is well by this time

I heard from Mrs Caffroth the other day. She Spoke of Mr C's going up the Vally and would not be Surprised if you see him in Page soon. Willy Rust left last Friday a week and had to walk from the Junction to his Company. you will please burn this letter as soon as you read it. it is writen in in great haste

Mr Jones sent your Bundle by Mr Sowers as he mised seeing the Stage. hope it suited you   your friend E A Jones

Margin of second page: *dont show this to Miss ....*
Margin of third page: *remember us all kindly to all your family and receive a share your self*

Gideon Jones encloses a receipt with his wife's letter.

Front Royal Sept. 16th 1861
Dear William
   Yours is just at hand. Enclosing $ 6.^{75}/100 infull of bill. for which you will accept my thanks. the Pittsylvania money is not very current here but I will try and get the note off. as Mrs Jones intends writing I will slip this in her letter. remember us to all the family, and be assured of my wishes for your welfare
                    Hastily & truly yrs &c
                    GW Jones

Meanwhile, William writes to brother John from home, noting the thoughtfulness of neighbor Emily Coffman. Their younger brother Daniel S. Hite is now 12 years old. Joseph Johnston, a Co. H soldier, was killed at Manassas on July 21. Sometime during this recuperation period, William has received calling cards from Mr. & Mrs. M[ann] Almond and from Miss Susan M. Tyler, age 21 and residing with Baptist minister Richard N. Herndon.

Sunday Morning Luray Sept 15th 1861
Dear Brother
   As I have a convenient opportunity of sending you a letter by the boys that will start now soon I have concluded to write you a few lines. I written last week that you ought to have gotten it when you recd the

box from Mother but uncle Stage neglected to Send it. She also Started another by Mr Brubaker which I suppose you have got ere this time. I also sent a crock of Apple butter along by him for you and the rest of our boys that were sick in Hospital. Mrs. David C. Coffman sent it to me as Token of the high regard for a wounded Souldier in defense of our Country. I was so well that I could eat almost all kinds of victuals, and as it was intended for the sick and helpless that I felt as though I would be doing and act of kindness by sending it to you. I feel well as usual at this time, only a little week yet. I think I will be able to join you some time next week. I have been visiting a great deal since I came home. all are anxious to see the wounded souldier. I am going to hear the funeral of Joe Johnston preached to day. I wish the whole of the Co. could be there. Father's family are all well. Danl. S. got a letter from you last night. He was proud to read it. I am having my winter clothes cut by the tailor to be made up this week. Overcoat and pants. Write to me as soon as you get this. give me the news. People here have been expecting to hear of a fight near Alx for 2 weeks.

Your affectionate Brother Wm.

P.S. The last call of the Militia were released one week ago yestarday. Isaac is at home.

W.F.H.

John responds immediately to William's letter. The prisoner Mark Berry is fined by the court-martial for this absence, but this is not to deter him from two later desertions.

Sept 17th/61
Camp near Fairfax C.H.

Dear brother:

in obedience to your request I hasten to answer yours of the 15th which was received last night. You said I should give all the news, but I have none of much importance to write.

Several of the boys came in last night that had been in Page for sometime, bringing Mark Berry with them; he was sent to the Guard-House immediately, and suppose he will be kept there untill he is Court-martialed. We moved from camp Harman near Centerville to this place yesterday, which is 1 mile from Fairfax C. H. and 2 miles from Fairfax Station.

WILLIAM — RECUPERATION AND RELAPSE

There has been several skirmish fights near Alx. within the last few weeks, but whether there will be a general battle I can't tell. We heard over one hundred reports of the cannon, whilst on our march to this place yesterday, and understood there was a fight below here for a certain, but have not heard the particulars of it yet. The pickets fire at each other nearly every day. We dont have no more than about 30 men on drill. I heard the militia are recalled again, but I trust it is not so for I know they are needed at home. Tell Isaac I will write before long.

I can't write more for the present as the is a hard thunder shower will be here soon. I send my respects to you all.

John P. Hite

My address is now

John P. Hite
Fairfax Station
Virginia
33rd Regt. Va. Vols.

In search of deserters, Michael Shuler has also returned to Page Co., and Ambrose Shenk is now the only officer remaining with Co. H. Mark Berry, Joseph Berry (his brother), and Joel Knight are all on the AWOL list of Co. H. for this period. Return Nichols, Henry H. Griffith, and Irenus P. Printz are reported as absent sick. Martin Van Buren Kite (M.V.B.K.) is absent on detail and his brother Oliver Hazard Perry Kite absent sick. Calvin H. Cave and John J. Middleton are also on the Page Grey roster.

Sept 18th 1861
Camp near Fairfax Station

Friend Shuler & Hite
Dear Sirs

I am compelled to enclude writing to both in the same letter, in consequence of My duties now devol[v]e upon me, & in the first place I will inform you that Mark Berry is here in the guard house also Joel Knight and Returnd Nichols. & J. J. Middleton and as they did not get their coats I wish you to bring them with you

M. Berry's Coat was not made I hope you will get Bery Coat made & Bring it with you, M.V.B.K. & Brother are both gone & C.H. Cave since Shuler left. I suppose you have a list of all that left before Shuler left. But if you have not you will let me know and I will send you a list of the names immediately.

Friend Hite in regard to your Sword & other things I cannot inform you anything about them excep your Blanket that is here I think, John has it, and it may be your Gun that one of Jones Men have as they have one I understand he got off of the Battle field, it is a gun like ours, But I cannot tell you anything about it being yours,

As to your Sword I know nothing & the Col Says he does not know where it could be had as they are a very scarce article, here, & I think you had better try & get one before you come down for I fear you cannot find one here, Friend Shuler I hope you will succeed in getting those men that you went after & Bring them as they aught to be brought back.

I would like to see you both back as soon as you can conveniently & do justice to each of you I recevd a letter of Shuler from the Capt & took the liberty of opening it to see what it was & in reply to receiving his money &c, Do not forget H.H. Griffith & Printz that left together and so you ought to have taken a list of the names, But I hope you did taken a list of the names but cant tell whether you did or not as you left when I did not have the chance to tell or see you as you know. We have move our Camp down near Fairfax Station & C. Ho[u]se between the two places about 2 miles from the Station, we will have to go down on Picket in a day or two I expect— as I understand one of our Regiments in our Brigade has Receivd orders to go down, I do not know whether that is correct or not, Shuler Can tell about the Coats as he wrote to Mr. Yager about them,

My Very Best Respect to Both and hope to see you here soon, Yours &c

A.B. Shenk

Mrs. Jones soon writes again to William. Simpson Cubbage and Martin V. B. Judy (Juda) are on the AWOL list from Co. H. Sours is the Peter Sowers of Co. H who also was wounded at Manassas. Mr. Rippetoe, of course, is the ailing captain of the company.

Monday morning
[perhaps Sept. 30, 1861]

Mr. Hite

In addition to last nights Scroll all I will tell you there was another death at the Hospittle last night. I am a fraid they have kept them there two long.

Our Church was occupied yesterday by Mr Duncan the Episcopal Minister. gave us a very impressive discourse on the life of the Chris-

William — Recuperation and Relapse

tian and the happy change to life Eternal. Dr Hough preached last night. good as usual and I suppose the last time in Our Church for some time. there was a sick soldier taken through here not long since to your County or Town about which I felt some anxiety but could not learn anything. Mr Rippetoe was in the Other day. he was much better and spoke of going down this week but has not been so well since he is very week

I have just heard from William [Rust]. he has been on Picket Guard 5 days. Slept in the rain and Cut Corn all day Sunday to keep the Yankeys from hiding. had the pleasure of seeing Laws [Professor Thaddeus S. C. Lowe's] Balloon assend to take a view of the Army. they fired their Artilery at them

There has a circumstance taken place to day which has made me heart sick. 5 Soudliers came up on the Cars to[day] with out passes. were taken Charge of by the military and put under guard. 2 from Winchester, 2 of your men, Cubbage and Juda, the Others were from Shanadoah. I did not hear until late who they were. I should have gone to see them they are sick. I have a Cousin among the Guard. we have just sent them camp cots, but I am a fraid she will not get in. I wish Mr Rippetoe had been in Town. had another death at the Hospittle this evening. Mr Sowers is improving. Edgar send his particular regards

Your friend
E A Jones

Lieutenant
        Hite

The Ladys still
enquire

About the same time Capt. Rippetoe writes from Winchester explaining his absence and preparing to relenquish his captaincy to William. Mollie is his wife, Mary Rippetoe.

Mrs Miller's
Sept 28th 1861

Lt Hite,
My Dear Friend,

Your Kind & Truly Welcome letter is before me.

I perused its contents with great pleasure— You are under no obligations to me for what I did for you when you were hurt. I only did what it was my duty to do. And I feel in my heart that you would have done the very same for me had I been in your situation. I am sory that I was unable to do more for you than I did do–

My health is very feeble– and I begin to think my race on Earth will soon be run. I have had several hemmorhages Which in connexion with my debility from the fever & measles, unfits me even for social service– much more actual duty. I walk about a little, and have been to town in my buggy twice, but I could not walk two miles I believe in a day to save my life.

But since I received you letter I have determined to try to accompany you to Camp on a visit. I cannot remain there– But Shall deliver the Company into your hands and if my Health improves I shall take up my residence in Richmond City. I have proposals there in number from a government official received in the last ten days, Which he says shall be kept open for my acceptation or rejection until the 5th of December.

So there is plenty to do for those who have the qualifiat[ion] and the disposition to labor for their Country, in this her time of need.

I have a deep feeling of contempt for that man or woman who is not willing to give all and do all in his power to maintain <u>our blood bought</u> Liberty—and the Sacred Purity & happy comfort of our much loved fire-sides– I am sorry Lt. Shank is alone. I am sorry that it is necessary to send an officer after a Volunteer to fight for his country. I hope you & Shuler may get them– every one–

You speak of going Monday. I shall go down to Front Royal Monday Evening if nothing prevents– to take the cars on Tuesday morning– next. If you come down Monday see that the agent allows Jack to get on the stage, and if you do not come Monday tell Jack to be sure & come.

Present my kind regards to your Pa & Ma– & also to Stage Modesitt & Lady–

I am anxious to see you–

Very Truly
Your sincere friend
W.D. Rippetoe
P.S. Mollie sends kind regards to you.
W.D.R.

William returns to duty on October 5, but by October 28 has become ill again. The relapse is noted in these few entries from John Hite's diary, repeated from Chapter 2.

WILLIAM — RECUPERATION AND RELAPSE 57

Monday 28th. Capt. Rippetoe and Issac Long arrive here at camp. Wm F Hite quite unwell, thinks he is getting the fever. 25 of our men sent to Camp Harman on pickets.

Tuesday 29th. Our company relieved of picket. Wm F Hite worse than yesterday, expects to start home in the morning with Mr. Long.

October Wednesday 30th. Wm starts for F. Royal this morning at 10 o'clock with Issac Long. I go with him as far as the Junction. A new flag presented to our Regt, also to rest of Virginia Regts by Governor Letcher.

William then writes to his father from the Jones home on Tuesday, November 5. Isaac Long is a Page County neighbor who has been visiting the Page Greys.

Front Royal
Tuesday Morning Nov. — 1861

Dear father

   I suppose you have learned before this time of my illness at this place.
   Not very sick however and am improving. I was taken sick in camp on yestarday aweek. Was tolerably sick there until Wednesday when the surgeon said I would have to leave. I was finally put into the ambulance and taken to the Junction and came up on the Cars with Isaac Long that evening. I came on to my old home and the best Hospital in the place. I was to report to Dr. [Benjamin] Blackford immediately on arriving here But I concluded to stay one night at my old home Next morning I sent for Dr. B. he came examined my case and gave me permission to remain here.
   Dr. [James] Turner assistant Surgeon has been attending me. I have had intermittent fever. Have not been as sick since I reached here as I was in camp. I have kept my bed until few last mornings I would sit up awhile. I have been improving ever since I left camp. I feel this morning as if I could eat a hearty breakfast. My appetite has not been good. Nothing tastes natural. Mr Jones' were all surprised to see me, return so soon sick. The first word the old black woman said to me, was, Mr. Hite you ought not have gone down when you did. I thought she reflected the sentiments of Mrs. Jones. My sickness was caused by going on picket the week before. I got very cold at night.

I think I will be able to come up on the Stage in few days. The Dr gives me permission

Your affectionate Son
William

Daniel Hite

Just three days later Gideon Jones reports to Daniel Hite that William's reported improvement has not continued. Cover postmarked and addressed:

FRONT ROYAL VA NOV 8   Paid 5

>Mr Daniel Hite
>   Care of Mr Modesitt
>   Luray, Va

Front Royal V Nov 8th 1861

Mr. Hite
    Dear Sir
    I am sorry to inform you that William has been very sick for several days. he was so much better on Wednesday, that I hoped he would be able in a few days to go to see you, but since Thursday morning he has been very sick. He expressed a wish that I should write to you to come to see him. I fear he will have a regular spell of Fever. hoping soon to see you

I am yours in haste
G.W. Jones

Gideon's sister Jennie (Jane C.) Jones writes to John Hite about his brother. James W. Menifie is another Co. H soldier.

Front Royal Nov 12th
1861

Mr Hite
    I take the liberty of writing you a few lines to let you know how your brother W is; this day a week ago he was much better & walked down stairs & remained about three hours but he seemed to have some fever. he went back to his room & has been growing worse ever since. he was flighty from friday until sunday night he seemed to

WILLIAM — RECUPERATION AND RELAPSE

loose all conciousness has scarcely known any one or any thing since. his recovery is exceedingly doubtful. we hope & trust if it is the will of our kind Heavenly Father he may be restored to health & usefulness but we are fully convinced that he ordereth all things right though they seem strange & mysterious to us at times. His disease is a violent attack of Typhoid fever. Your Mother & father came this evening. he recognized them but dont talk any. he seems more composed since dark. we hope he will recover; The family are all well except Mother. she is suffering from a severe cold. they all join me in kind regards to you & Mr Menifee; please excuse haste as the gentleman is waiting.

Jennie C. Jones

David and Isaac are stationed at Winchester with the 97th Va. Militia, and by the following letter Daniel Hite informs them of William's condition. Envelope addressed:

In the ceare
of
Capt. Dovel
Col. Spitler

David C. Hite
Winchester
Va.

Front Royal   Nov 13th 1861

Dear Sons

I arrived heare yesterday evning, on last Sunday I received afew lines from Mr.. Jones stateing that Wm had got much worse and wished me to come down and se him, it was impossible for me to come on monday, yesterday morning I and mother started and got heare about sun set. found Wm very sick, eversience Saturday Mr.. Jones says he was like a deranged man. it was almost impossible to keep him in bed. entirely uncontious of anything that he said or done, his water and bowell discharges all went in the bed, and had a high fever, I and Mr. Petty s[t]ayed with him last night and had some difficulty to keep him in bed at times. but seem to know me and mother, this morning alittle before day he became quiet and went to sleep, and when he waked he seemed quite liked another man, he then knew me and mother quite well, to day he slept the most of the time and when awake was in his right mind, the doctor says he has not slept any for 48 hours. he thinks there has been achange fore the better so dose Mr.. and Mrs Jones if it continues. it is now sun down and he is still

The Painful News I Have to Write

resting very well. his Doctor is Blackford I know nothing about him, I am compellet to go home tomorrow, Mother will stay. I dont know how long. you know our situation at home. I hope he will continue to mend. I will try to get Mr.. Jones to write to you so you may heare from him. write to me often and let me heare from you all, be composed I feel entirely reconciled to his fait. he is in the hand of the Allmity, Miss Jane Jones wrote a short letter to John yesterevning. She expected to send it by Mr.. Summers but he did not call to getit. I enclose it with this. I am youre most affectionate Father

Daniel Hite

William F. Hite dies at the Gideon Jones home on Sunday, November 17, from typhoid fever complicated by the lung wound received on July 21. Uncle Stage Modesitt hears through Joseph Almond, a farmer from Cedar Point north of Luray. He sends condolences in a black-bordered envelope addressed simply: Mr. Daniel Hite

Luray Nov 18th 61

Dear Daniel
    Do not mourn, for he that giveth him Taketh away, for so it seemeth good in his sight. I have Just learned through amessenger from Joseph Almand. That William your Son, departed this life yesterday at 2 O,clock and will be sent up to your home this evening. your wife will be up early in the day. I will write to John David & Isaac, by this mail. From my verry Intimate acquaintance with William. Feel Strong hope he is far better off than those left yet to suffer what he has already Suffered, and his Soul is now at rest, and free from Suffering and death. Why then should we mourn

Truly your Bro.. inlaw
A. S. Modesitt

If you wish any thing attended to let me know by the Boys Return

John gets a furlough to attend the funeral. His pass gives a physical description noting his short stature. Lt. Col. John Robert Jones of Harrisonburg is a VMI graduate later promoted to brigadier general.

To all whom it may concern:
    The bearer hereof Jno. P. Hite a private of Captain Rippetoe Company H. 33 Regiment of Va. Vol. age 21 years 5 feet 5 inches high complexion toleraby fair, Blue eyes, light hair, and by profession a

WILLIAM — RECUPERATION AND RELAPSE

farmer, born in the County of Page, and enlisted at Luray in the County of Page on the 1st day of June 1861 to serve for the period of one year is hereby permitted to go home in the County of Page State of Va he having received a furlough from the 18 day of Nov, to the 25 day of Nov at which period he will rejoin his Company or considered a deserter,

Given under my hand at Camp Kearnston this 18th day June 1861.

Camp Kearnston   *A.B. Shenk 2nd Liet. Comd*
Nov 18th 1861   *Co. H 33 Rgt. Va. Vol.*

Approved
JR Jones Lt Col
33rd Va Vol

John's diary documents William's death and burial:

Monday 18th. stand guard from 6 to 8 oclock also from 10 to 12 oclock in the day. Hear of the death of my dear brother William whilst standing guard between 10 and 12 oclock. He departed this life on Sunday 2 1/2 oclock P.M. of the 17th of November. Brothers David, Isaac and I start home immediately on hearing of his death. Arrived at home at 4 oclock Tuesday morning. We are very much fatigued from our walk.

Tuesday 19th. Clear and still all day. Williams funeral preached by Mr. Booton. Text 103rd Psalm, 15th, 16th, 17th, 18th, verse. A large congregation at the burying. We have reason to believe that he has exchanged a life of toil and suffering for one of endless joy and peace.

The inventory of William Hite's small estate includes some $650 in cash and notes due, a revolver, and personal articles including a toothbrush, shaving brush, and razor. Several books of small value include a Testament, a dictionary, and two on military tactics, reflecting his position as an officer. His grave is in the Hite family plot, high in the pasture behind the farmhouse. Ambrose C. Booten, minister of the Mill Creek Church, preaches the funeral sermon from a familiar passage:

As for man, his days are as grass:
 As a flower of the field, so he flourisheth.
For the wind passeth over it, and it is gone;
 And the place thereof shall know it no more.
But the mercy of the Lord is from everlasting to everlasting
 Upon them that fear him,
 And his righteousness unto children's children;
To such as keep his covenant,
 And to those that remember his commandments to do them.

William Francis Hite 1838–1861

Grave in Hite family plot.
[Photo 1994, Robert L. Smith]

CHAPTER 4

The First Year Ends

*"Another wave upon the ocean of time
hath been hurled into an endless eternity."*

After William's funeral, John uses his furlough to visit with Page County friends and relatives including, surely, the young ladies with whom he has been corresponding. Thomas Buswell, mentioned in the Nov. 21 entry, once held a major general's commission in the Virginia Militia. As the war began he was named Lt. Col. in the restructured militia, and now he is variously titled Gen., Col., and Mr.

Wednesday 20th [November]. Cloudy all day and has the appearance of snow. I stay about home nearly all day; go to Rubin Rothgeb's in the evening, from there to Issac Shaffer's who is very low. Go to Uncle Abram Hite's after night and stay until morning.

November Thursday 21st. I kill two hogs in the morning, go to Mr. Gander's and Issac Rothgeb's from there to General Buswells in the evening; stay all night at Gen. Buswells, recieve very kind treatment at each place. Get plenty of apples to eat.

Friday 22nd. I go home from Mr. Buswells, from there to Luray, spend the day at Uncle Stage Modesitt and other places in town. Issac Shaffer died on the night of the 21st of November with the typhoid pneumonia.

Saturday 23rd. Go up to Mr. Shaffers burying, return home after the burying, Mary A. Gander and Frances also Rebecca Hite come to father's in the evning.

Sunday 24th. I start for Winchester this morning, stop a little at Abram Strickler's to get some letters that are to go to Winchester. Stay at John Burners till 3 oclock at which time we start again in a little wagon, arrive at Mt Jackson at 7 oclock.

THE FIRST YEAR ENDS 65

Monday 25th. Start from Mt Jackson on the cars at 2 oclock at night. Arrive at Strasburgh at 3; take stage to Winchester arrive at 7 oclock A. M. Have my Amborotype taken. Cold and cloudy get to camp at 3 oclock P.M. find the boys well.

Unfortunately, this ambrotype and another taken in December have not been found. At the conclusion of his furlough, John returns on time to the camp, now at New Centreville, about four miles north of Winchester. In the company reorganization after the loss of both 1st Lt. Hite and Capt. Rippetoe, Perry Kite loses twice in the elections to lieutenant, both to Charles T. Chadduck and to Harrison B. Jones.

November Tuesday 26th. I stand from 5 to 7 oclock and also from 11 to 1 oclock at night.

Wednesday 27th. stand guard from 5 to 7 oclock P.M. Very cold last night ground freezes hard. Rains some during the day while on guard. A.B. Shenk elected Captain without opposition. M Shuler 1st Lieut. without opposition; C.T. Chadduck 2nd Lieut and Majority over O.H.P. Kite H.B. Jones elected by majority over Kite.

November Thursday 28th. Rains a little. Get the baggage that had been sent to Manassas Junction about two months since.

Friday 29th. Hear heavy cannonading. Cloudy and raining all day. No drill but have to clean up in camp.

Saturday 30th. The enemy in six miles of ours at the junction. Expecting a great fight there, and at Acquia Creek; also in Kentucky.

Sunday 1st [December]. Court-martial was held at the Colonel's Headquarters all last week.

Monday 2nd. The whole Regiment detailed to cut wood and haul it to camp. I stand guard from 5 to 7 o'clock also from 11 to 1 O'clock at night.

Tuesday 3rd. I stand from 5 to 7 o'clock A.M. also 11 to 1 O'clock P.M. Very cold last night whilst on guard. Still wind & cold this evening.

Leaving John for a short time, we hear about activites of the militia in a letter from Isaac. Also serving in this 97th Regiment are David Hite and Samuel Miller, now 45 and soon to be discharged for his age. Envelope addressed:

Miss Eliza E. Hite
Luray
Virginia

Politeness
of
Mr. Samuel Miller

November 30th 1861
Camp Flowing springs Two miles
north of Charlestown Jefferson
County Va

Dear Sister Ellen
    As I have not written to you since I have been in Camp I will drop you a few lines. We are all well at this time of your acquaintances. We are now encamp in a beautiful piece of woods a few hundred yards East of the flowing Springs, the place we were encamped when we were here before.
    We arrived in camp Monday about dark, We would have got here about 10 OClock but the Cars had just left Winchester when we got there so we had to foot it to Charlestown distance about 21 miles. We left John in Winchester. When we got to Charlesto[w]n we found the regiment encamped in town in school houses, meeting houses, &c. They waited there on account of the tents not being ready. We received the tents on Tuesday, and on Wednesday we marched here through rain and mud from Charlestown distance 2 miles, Lieut Col. Buswell gave orders for us to pitch our tents in the field where the mud was about shoo deep but the orders were not obeyed by officers nor men. The tents we received are very small. It was said that they were to be large enough for eight men, but three fills them very well. Our mess of seven has three tents – in two of them only two stay. We have got a way of building floo[r]s to them which adds very much to our comfort. Capt Dovil's Company have large tents where they can have floo[r]s large enough to cook, and stay in all together. It is very wet here. To day it is raining by spells.
    Sam Miller and several other men have gone down to Harpers Ferry to day. The Cavalry that are stationed here say they go down nearly every day, some of them, where they can see the Yankees camp on the Maryland heights. They say they can see but few tents over there any more, though whenever they see any of our men in the Ferry

THE FIRST YEAR ENDS

they mighty apt to shoot at them. The soldiers of this regiment seem to be tolerably well satisfied at this time more than some of them are badly in need of money and would be glad to get that which is promised them. I think it is likely we will camp about this place the time we will have to stay if it is until spring.

Your affectionate brother Isaac

Mary Ellen Modesitt sends a note to her cousin John. Virginia, the beautiful daughter of widower John Lionberger, is just 14 years old. Envelope reads:

Mr. John P. Hite
Winchester
Va.

[Note in pencil: Rec'd Dec 5th]

Urbanity of a Soldier

Luray Dec. 3rd /61

Cousin John

As I just heard of a member of your company going down this morning thought it would be a good opportunity of writing. Don't you think I have <u>diptheria</u>! I assure you it is not a very pleasant disease, though my throat does not pain me at all now, & <u>has</u> but very little since [I] have had it, though it was very painful before. it is almost well now have not been out of doors for almost a week. It is very cold here the ground is covered with snow. I feel sorry for the poor soldiers, suppose some of them have now seen something they never before have seen, that is snow. Have not heard from Uncle Daniel's since last week. they were all well then. A great many persons in town & in the country have diptheria, and many a common sore throat. almost every one you see have their neck rapped up. Ginnie Lionber[ger] died with it last Friday. was buried Monday. she was the most beautiful corpse I ever saw, there was a smile on her mouth just as though she was going to speak. Tis said they are expecting a fight at the Junction every hour, but I still think they will not have one shortly though I am afraid I am mistaken. There is no news of importance here now. they say the stage is ready to leave, so I must close. excuse mistakes and bad writing as I have written in great haste. Write very soon & often we are always delighted to hear from you.

From your little
Cousin Mary Ellen

THE PAINFUL NEWS I HAVE TO WRITE

John's diary continues with December events. Upon his appointment as brigade commander, Richard C. Garnett gets a garbled spelling by John and a mixed acceptance from the troops. But he soon is spelled right and wins both confidence and affection. Joseph Benton Huffman and Charles William Webster are both privates of Co. H.

Dec. Wednesday 4th. Our troops have several skirmishes with the enemy near Fairfax Court-House. Reported in one that over 100 of the Yankees were killed & wounded and only a few of ours wounded.

Thursday 5th. Recd. 36 letters from Page.

Friday 6th. Benton Huffman & I go to Winchester. I have my ambrotype taken. Get orders to wash our clothes & bodies every Saturday morning. General Thomas C. Garter takes command of the 1st Va. Brigade by order of Maj. Gen. Johnston.

Saturday 7th. General Richard C. Garnet takes command of the 1st Va. Brigade by orders of General Johnston.

Sunday 8th. Have inspection of guns cartridge boxes and knap sacks etc. This morning as usual.

Dec. Monday 9th. Very pleasant weather which it has been for the past week.

Tuesday 10th. The militia from Page starts from Winchester towards Romney. A Maryland Regiment comes on our side at the junction. Have a general review this morning in the presence of Gen. Garnett and aids also a large no. of citizens. Garnett rides a large fine Bey horse.

Dec. Wednesday 11th. Rains a little in the morning. Clears up in the evening, and gets very cold.

Thursday 12th. Eight Yankees taken near Harpers Ferry and brought to Winchester. Wm. Webster arrives at camp with some of the absentees sent for; also hats sent for by the company.

Welcome provisions are often brought to camp by **Page County** friends and relatives. This time they come by Trenton Graves of the 7th

THE FIRST YEAR ENDS

Va. Cavalry who is recuperating from wounds received at Manassas. Peter Long has also been in that unit, and Morgan Biedler is a 47 year old farmer of Page County.

Friday 13th. Have guns and accoutrement with knapsacks haversacks canteen etc inspected by Gen Garnett. Peter Long, Morgan Bidler & Trenton Graves arrives at camp with a great deal of provisions.

Saturday 14th. Wash our clothes again today.

Sunday 15th. Get orders early this morning to cook one day's rations. I go to Winchester and [send] Wm's things home by Mr. Bidler. Get orders in the evening to strike in the morning at 3 o'clock.

Jackson's aggressive operations and forced marches, described in entries over the next several days, are intended to disrupt Yankee cargo shipments by destroying Dam No. 5 on the Chesapeake and Ohio Canal. A sizeable breach is finally effected with the loss of only one Confederate artilleryman, but it is repaired after only a short interval.

Monday 16th. The whole of Garnett's Brigade begins their [march] toward Martinsburg this morning at 6 o'clock. Stop in the evening 8 miles south of Martinsburg; distance marched today 16 miles. Get orders to cook another day's rations though we are all very much fatigued. Major Gen. Jackson with his staff also comes down with us.

Tuesday 17th. Gets orders to cook another days ration. Start again at 12 o'clock toward the Potomac. March on untill 9 o'clock at night stop $1/2$ mile of the Potomac; distance March 14 miles. Leave our tents and knapsacks behind.

Wednesday 18th. We go back $1/2$ mile to cook some. I go out in the country; get an excellant breakfast. Two companies of our Regiments go down at the river on the dam and pull it down. The enemys shoots at our men all day. Kill one, whilst our men kill a good many of them. The whole Brigade move again within a quarter mile of the river. Our company go on picket along the river. I stand on post from 2 o'clock to 4.

Thursday 19th. The enemy open fire at us with two pieces of artillery, and a great many infantry cannon balls and shell fall very near us, and drive us back to the Regiment. One man of the 27th Regt. gets killed. We go back again near the river and stay behind hills. I crawl to a strawback near the river and shoot at Yankees on the other side, make them run; they return the fire. Jackson shoots bumshells in a barn on the other side of the river. Firing kept up all day. Relieved of picket this evening.

Friday 20th. Still fire some during the day. Several of our men get wounded; also some of the Yankees. Two of our company missing since yesterday, supposed to be killd or taken prisoners; their names W.M. Lawrence, F.M. Baley.

Official Co. H records report that the absences of Woodford M. Lawrence and Francis M. Bailey on December 19 are due to desertion rather than military action. Neither of these men appear in the 1860 Page County census, and they may be among the few Page Greys recruited elsewhere.

Saturday 21st. Our men finished pulling down the dam in the river. The whole brigade starts for camp at 6 o'clock this morning, arrive there 11 o'clock A.M. Distance 14 miles. I am very much fatigued when we arrive at camp, also have sore feet. March the distance without breakfast. Get orders to cook a days rations.

Sunday 22nd. Begin our march at 6 o'clock this morning arrive at camp Stephenson 4 miles below Winchester at 3 o'clock P.M. pitch our tents where they were before we left.

Monday 23rd. Rains and hails all night last night. Very cold and windy all day; can scarcely keep warm or do any cooking.

Dec. Tuesday 24th. Still cold and windy today I have recd 38 letters from Page and written 58.

Wednesday 25th. A very dull Christmas here in camp. A fight at Drainsville near the junction, in which 50 of our men were killed & 130 wounded, 300 of the Yankees were killed & wounded.

The dull Christmas has been brightened a little by an overly-optimistic report of the Dranesville battle on December 20. Official casualties are

THE FIRST YEAR ENDS 71

43 Confederates killed and 143 wounded and just 5 Union troops killed and 61 wounded.

Thursday 26th. J. P. Beaver & I go to Winchester, to take the mail up.

Friday 27th. Turns cold & windy again. Dr. J. K. Smoot visits us today.

Saturday 28th. We get paid yesterday for two months service. I stand guard from 8 to 11 o'clock in the day; and from 8 to 10 o'clock also from 2 to 4 o'clock in the night; have several in the guard-house for getting drunk.

Sunday 29th. Joseph Huffman arrives at camp this evening brings a box for me from home.

Just before the New Year, Lt. Harrison Jones, Corp. Andrew Rinica, and Pvt. James W. Menifie are sent home after runaways.

Dec. Monday 30th. I have a disagreeable cold. Lieut. Jones, Corp. Rinica & private J. W. Menefee sent to Page after the boys that run off.

Tuesday 31st. Very pretty weather. Get orders to keep a days rations ahead cooked.

As the year ends, Mary Ellen Modesitt exercises her creative writing skills in this letter to John. William and Elizabeth Chapman have a large family in Luray with children near the age of Jennie (Lucy Virginia) Modesitt, now 12. Grandmother Susannah (Spitler) Hite, 81, has apparently been living with several of her children in turn. At 1860 census time she was with her son Martin Hite.

Tuesday night Dec 31st
1861
Will cousin John pardon me for not writing sooner, but if you know all preventing circumstances. I know you would. In the first place I heard you had left Winchester and knew not that you had

returned until a few days ago so that I would not have known where to direct.

'Tis now near the close of this year. On fleet wings another twelve months have passed away, another wave upon the ocean of Time hath been hurled into an endless eternity. The bright visions which spread themselves upon fancy's canvas when the last twelve months dawned upon us have fled; like the cloud passes over the noon-day sky, so have those rainbow tints faded from the horizon of anticipation. Little did many of our soldiers dream that they would spend their next New Year day in camp.

Hope you have spent a pleasant Christmas though I know it was not so much so as the last was when you were at home with relations and friends. We have had a very dull Christmas here, though the very small girls & servants have had a merry time; they have had several parties. Sister Jennie is now at one at Mr. Chapman's. she was anticipating a delightful time hope she may realize it: But poor I have had to spend the whole week in doors, was in the dining room to dinner yesterday for the first time for almost 3 weeks, have had diptheria ever since I wrote you before, was just getting over it when I had a second attack much worse than the first. Oh! you have no idea how unpleasant it is having your throat cauterized twice a day when 'tis so sore you cannot swallow without its raising you almost off your chair. I will ever have a perfect horror of caustic, or even the name (diptheria). Have not heard from Uncle Daniel's for some time but when I last heard they were all well. Grand-Ma was there the last we heard from her, as well, as usual. Don't you think four of our family had sore throat at the same time but they are all well except Willie & myself though W. is almost well & mine too I think. I have had a very pleasant time in the house. have company every day. some girls dined with us yesterday so you see I could not withstand the temptation of going to the table as I have been so often deprived of that pleasure. Hope you are well.

Heard yesterday they have had another fight on Aquia creek and that it was a greater victory with us (of course) than that of the 21st, hope we will hear more about it to night. What do you think of the Mason & Slidell affair. I think there is every prospect of the enemy's having to fight England too; they will yet be taught to rue the day they ever took up arms against our glorious south. It is getting very late almost New Year so I must close. Please excuse bad writing and mistakes, I have such a miserable pen, I am ashamed to send this, but please tear it up as it is blotted up so badly. Write very soon

to your cousin M.E. Modesitt

CHAPTER 5

Winter 1862

*"Rains nearly all day and night.
Have a good many dispatches to carry."*

The year of 1862 begins with a campaign by Jackson's Valley District troops to disrupt Union communications and to reinforce the Confederate position in western Virginia. The initial objective is Bath, now Berkeley Springs, West Virginia, a short distance above the key Federal post at Hancock, Maryland, on the upper Potomac. John Hite's Co. H is guarding the wagon train which is laboring to keep up with the troops. Without blankets and supplies, the soldiers spend two nights cold and hungry. Riding up during the the long-awaited hot breakfast on the morning of January 3, Gen. Jackson demands to know who has ordered the delay. Excuses are met with his sarcastic comment, "I never found anything impossible with this brigade," and Gen. Garnett quickly orders the march resumed. And we resume with John Hite's diary.

Wednesday Jan 1st. The whole Brigade takes up line of march this morning at 6 o'clock; Start in the direction of Romney. I am left back to stay with provisions, untill they can be hauled. We don't get off with the provisions untill about 7 o'clock. We travel till about 1 o'clock in the night; stop 2 miles behind the Regt. Distance traveled 14 miles.

Thursday 2nd. Cook a day's rations. Drive up to the Regt. Start again at 9 o'clock A.M. go as far as turnpike that leads from Martinsburgh to Romney; late in the night when we get there with the wagons on account of it being such a rough road. A great many stall some upset. It is mountainous country the whole way, we travel through deep ravines and over high hills. A force of 15,000 here together, with between 20 or 30 pieces of artillery, also some cavalry.

Friday 3rd. I march with the Regt., today I have a bad cold. March 8 miles. Stay all night 5 miles of Bath. Snows some during the night. We lay in the brush without tents. 8 Yankees taken & brought to the guard house of our Regt.

Saturday 4th. Another Yankee taken & brought to our guard house. We take the town of Bath in the evening, but the Yankees all leave about 1 hour before we get there; their number 1,000. Find a few things in Bath that the Yankees leave. An Arkansas Regt. get in a fight near Cacapon after night, get 5 killed and about 30 wounded; only a few of the Yankees wounded. About 30 of the Yankees taken prisoner. Our company stay in a fine house all night in Bath.

Sunday 5th. Gen Jackson riding day and night. Very cold last night. Don't thaw any during the day. Take two pieces of artillery from the Yankees. We move down 5 miles below Bath, 1 mile this side of Hancock which is the other side of the Potomic. Our men tear up the railroad all day. Some heavy cannonading done during the day.

Monday 6th. Snow last night to the depth of 4 inches, we had to lay out in the snow all night. We move back about 4 miles from the river. Don't get anything to eat today until after night. I go up to Bath and buy a meal and victuals. The Yankees throw bumbshells at our men; kill one. A great many overcoats taken from the Yankees that they left in their retreat, I get three letters from Page.

Tuesday 7th. The whole Army moved back towards Winchester, start today at 2 o'clock PM, march till 11 o'clock at night. The roads so slick that we can scarcely get along. A great many fall and hurt themselves, also many horses get cripple. Distance marched 11 miles.

Jackson's troops have succeeded in tearing up miles of track and destroying, after a fight, the railroad bridge over the Great Cacapon. Then, finding it impossible to bridge the Potomac at Hancock and fearing Federal reinforcements, they begin a southward movement beset by severe weather, first heavy snow and then mud. Meanwhile, on January 7 the 97th Virginia Regiment of Page County, together with other militia units, has been surprised and humiliatingly routed by a Federal foray east from Romney. Capt. John D. Aleshire of Co. I and some fourteen others are killed in this battle of Hanging Rock Pass. In their incursion Federal troops also burn a number of private houses and kill cattle, a conduct criticized as uncivilized by commentators both from North and South. Letters in this collection express the feelings of some Page County residents about both the battle and the vandalism.

WINTER 1862

Jan Wednesday 8th. We stay here at the Cross-Roads all day. We cook two days rations. Send some of the baggage to Winchester; also several loads of leather and a great picks, spades, etc that were taken from the Yankees. A fight near Romney a few days since in which 'tis said that Captain Aleshire was killed and several others from Page wounded.

Thursday 9th. Last night the coldest it has been this winter. The snow melts a good deal today. My cold begins to get better.

Friday 10th Jan. We move about $1/2$ miles Northeast. Thaws today: so muddy that we can scarcely travel. The mud about shoe depth.

Saturday 11th. I wash my clothes today. Still warm. I stand guard from five to seven o'clock also from 11 to 1 o'clock at night.

Sunday 12th. I stand guard from 5 to 7 A.M. and 11 to 1 o'clock noon. Three deserters of the yankees come to our camp who say that the yankees all left Romney. We get orders to cook a days rations after night.

Monday 13th. Reveille beats this morning at 4 o'clock; we take the line of march at 6 o'clock; start in the direction of Romney. Stay all night near Blooming Furnace. Distance marched 12 miles.

Tuesday 14th. Start this morning at 11 o'clock. Snows some late night and this morning; depth 2 inches. Distance marched 9 miles.

Jan Wednesday 15th. We start this morning at 6 o'clock arive in Romney 2 o'clock P. M. Distance 14 miles. Snows last night to the depth of 4 inches; rains today a good deal. I get very wet. I get to see the militia from Page who have started for Martinsburgh; find David and Isaac well. Our Company Headquarters in Jail in Romney.

David and Isaac of the Page militia must enjoy their reunion with brother John. Welcome supplies are captured at Romney, and during a stay there of more than a week, the energetic Jackson prepares for a further march to destroy bridges upstream on the Potomac. While plans are made and debated, Harrison B. Jones, recently promoted to 2nd Lt., brings some of the runaways back to Co. H.

Thursday 16th. Six yankees taken and brought to this place (Romney) A great many tents, crackers, etc taken that the yankees left in their retreat.

Friday 11th. 200 barrels of flour, 6 sides of bacon, and some other things taken from the yankees. Martial law prevails in town. We get orders this evening at 6 to be ready to march at 8 o'clock P.M. but countermanded afterward.

Saturday 18th. A few more yankee prisoners brought in town. Begins raining early this and continues until 12 o'clock. A man of our Regt. shoots himself accidently in the leg.

Sunday 19th. rains all night last night and today until 12 o'clock. The waters get very high. Very mud[dy]. I go to meeting in town this evening.

Monday 20th. Rains nearly all night and a good deal today. Waters very high; nearly all the creeks past fording. Lieut Jones return with a good many of the boys sent for. I have received 44 letters from Page and wrote 60.

Tuesday 21st. It rains nearly all night and today again. We get orders to cook two days rations and be ready to [march] in the morning at daybreak; countermanded at 10 o'clock at night.

Reluctantly responding to the weather and resistance from both officers and troops, Jackson finally orders a retreat to winter quarters for most of his force. The Stonewall Brigade takes up the march to Winchester. Capt. Litman and the nature of his dispute with Capt. Shenk have not been identified.

Wednesday 22nd. we get orders this evening to be ready to march at daylight in the morning.

Thursday 23rd. Garnett's Brigade take the line of march this morning towards Winchester. March 14 miles. A controversay occurs between Captain Shenk and Capt Litman.

Friday 24th. Start again early this morning. March 12 miles over mountainous country. See about 30 houses that were burnt by the

WINTER 1862

yankees and a great many livestock that was killed by them. Very cloudy and has appearance of snow.

Saturday 25th. we start again at 6 o'clock this morning. We stop two miles west of Winchester; we travled 14 miles. Snows last night to depth of three inches; nearly all melts today. Gets very cold and windy in the evening.

John's father Daniel Hite writes with a humorous account of the rout of badly frightened militia troops. Reuben Rothgeb's sons include Emanuel, 27, Franklin, 25, and Martin, 20.

Page County Va.. January 25th 1862

Dear Son John

We received your kind and interesting letter yesterday and was truly glad to here from you, you mentioned in that you had not received any letter from home this year. I wrote you a letter just before Christmust I am anxous to know wither you got it, when you write again let us know wether you received it, it is true since we have not wrote we often heard from you, and that you was allmost constant moving and thinking it douptfull wether you would get it, but as you said before we should allways direct to Winchester and you will get them, we dont considder it of as mutch importance for you to heare from us, as what it is for us to heare from you, if any thing of mutch interest was to take place of course we would write to you, and you are where there is allways changes taking place, and of course we are anxous to get all the information we can, and to heare of your wellfare, I have nothing of mutch interest to write to you at this time, I wrote to you in my last concerning Williams esstate if you received that you have all the information necessary. I was appointed administrator and have a power attorney, ready to send on to you at any time when you think the money could be received, but would reather send it by some safe privet hand,

Many of the militia are still at home and seem to be slow in going back, from all accounts many of them ware very mutch frightened. hardly any two told the same tale. all seemed to be confused and got away the best way they could, some of them I dont belief stoped untill they got home, I heard a letter read last week that was sent from out there stating that the deer and rapits could not near get out of the way fast enough, some of the militia runn a round them, but I suppose that is camp news,

We had a greatteal of cloudy, rainney wether for the last week, and mud allmost impasably, yesterday about twelve oclock it commenced snowing and hailing, and continued until some time last night. this morning it was about 3 inches deep, to day was a very fine day, and it has melted very mutch. the wind is blowing verry hard to night. but not very cold, but it has the appearance of getting cold, I often have to think of you poor souldiers, when the nights are cold and the wether is bad, and try to pray fore you to that God who alone can save you from the enemy, and be a shield in every kind of trouble.

We have not got in all our corn yet. there is some four or five loads out yet. it is all shucked that is in the barn. This leaves us all well and o how thankfull should we be fore that blessing, the people generally are well, Reuben Rothgeb boys are all four at home and complaining and not able to go in service now, I must close my sheet is full, write soon as we are very anxious to heare from you as you was complaining when you wrote, I as ever remain your affectionate Father

Daniel Hite

John's diary continues from the camp near Winchester. Joseph F. Stover and William A. Brubaker are both promoted to sergeant as of February 1, 1862.

Sunday 26th. still cold and very windy.

Monday 27th. Has appearance of snow. We get orders in the evening to be ready to march at 8 o'clock in the morning.

Tuesday 28th. Rains a good deal last night and this morning. J. F. Stover, Wm. Brubaker, and others arrive here from home. A fight near Summerset, Kentucky in [which] we had about 500 killed and wounded besides a good deal of baggage taken.

Here and elsewhere John often exaggerates the casualties of distant battles. In the battle of Somerset or Mill Springs on January 19 and 20, officially reported Union losses are 38 killed, 194 wounded, Confederate losses 190 killed and 160 wounded. The winter quarters soon to be built are named in honor of Confederate Gen. F. K. Zollicoffer, killed in this engagement.

WINTER 1862

Wednesday 29th. We move about five miles Northwest from Winchester to build huts for winter quarters. Very cloudy.

Thursday 30th. Hails and snow some last night and this morning.

Friday 31st. we begin to build a hut for winter quarters. Get orders to stop about 12 o'clock as we expect to move away from here.

Saturday 1st Feb.. It snows and hails last night to the depth of four inches. I have received 45 letters from Page and wrote 66.

Of the total reported in this, the last count of letters in John's diary, eleven of those received and four of those sent have been found and are included here. Soon John receives another from young Cousin Jennie (Lucy Virginia) Modesitt with news from home and the first mention of David Hite's illness which causes him to be sent home at the end of this month. Bettie and Mary Ella are Jennie's sisters. William Townsend Young is captain of Co. K, 10th Va. Infantry, and Gabriel Jordan, a wealthy Luray resident, has died at the age of about 69.

Luray Feb 2 1862

Dear Cousin

I hope that you will excuse me for not writing sooner, but the others have been writing and I thought it was not worth while, Bettie received your letter and was glad to hear from you. We are all well and hope you are enjoying the same health. Uncle Daniel was out to day he says that they are all well at home, I am sorry that Cousin David is sick but I hope he will soon be well enough to come home.

I heard that the Militia have moved away from Martinsburg to Winchester, the people says that the Yankees were coming through Luray in less then two months, but I do not believe it until I see them coming. I do not think that I would be afraid of them, it seems as if they are going to surround us, the Militia met here yesterday to be reorganized, there are a great many of them here, there were a great many of Captain Young's company here about two weeks ago and I suppose they are here yet. I should like very much to see you, I hope that you will come home soon, Papa came home from Richmond Friday. It has been a hard winter for the soldiers though it has not been a very cold but it has been so much rain, it snowed here to day. Old Mr. Jordon died last week in Lynchburg he will be brought home to day, I have no news of any importance. Bettie says she will write

soon. Mary Ella wrote soon after she received yours. it is getting late and I must close write soon. from your affectionate Cousin
Jennie Modesitt

The day on which John's diary continues, February 2, 1862, is the twentieth birthday of Mary Ann Gander, the "Miss Mollie" whose "very affecting letter" is received at the end of this week. Meanwhile John gets a visit from Susan Coffman, the well-chaperoned "Miss Sue" of whom we are later to hear much more. She is the 17-year-old daughter of David and Emily Coffman, neighbors of the Hites. This does not deflect his interest in a new acquaintance, Miss Jennie Johnston. Gideon B. Long is a comrade in Co. H, but his relationship to Mrs. Susan Long is not known.

Sunday 2nd. Very muddy.

Monday 3rd. Snows last night and this morning: depth of 3 inches. Captain Shenk start to Page this morning. Mrs. Susan Long and Miss Susan Coffman came to our camp in a carriage, bring some provisions for me. Gideon B. Long and I go with them to Mr. Coffman near Newtown.

Tuesday 4th. I get aquainted with Miss Jennie Johnston. Gideon and I leave Mr. Coffman's at 2 o'clock P.M. get to Camp at 7 o'clock. I enjoyed myself very much at Mr. Coffmans.

Wednesday 5th. I stand guard from 6 o'clock P. M. to 12 o'clock midnight.

Thursday 6th. I stand guard from 7 to 12 o'clock A.M. weather very good this time of the year.

Friday 7th. Several of the Company enlist for two years. Very muddy.

Saturday 8th. The weather cloudy and cold. I receive a very affecting letter from Miss Mollie.

Sadly, Miss Mollie's letter which apparently includes an impertinent note from sister Fannie is missing from this collection. But now we hear

Winter 1862

from Cousin Sarah Ellen Buswell who uses a Sunday afternoon for a long letter to John with another account of the rout of the militia. Mary, Wesley, and Abram are her sister and brothers. The soldiers mentioned by initials are Gideon Long, David J. Coffman, Edmund J. Rothgeb, and Martin VanBuren Gander. Daniel Judd and Arthelia Kibler have indeed been married on February 4. Franklin Rothgeb who has been serving in the militia, will recover and later enlist in the Page Greys. We have no letters from reported correspondent Martha R., probably 16-year-old Martha F. Ruffner.

Leaksville, Virginia
Feb 9th 1862

Cousin John

I received your kind letter last Friday, and was very glad to hear from you once more, and that you had gotten back to Winchester again; I know you must have had a hard time of it while marching, so much bad weather; but hope you can remain where you are now a while; I wonder that more of the Soldiers are not sick though it seems as though you all can stand allmost anything, since in the Army that which you thought would have kill you at home;

You said you looked for a letter from me so long in vain it was not because I did not think of you; I commenced writing once and I heared you had marched & did not expect you had time to read a letter if you got it; you said you dreamed of me, but you know you must allways reverse dreams those enyhow; I dreamed of seeing you last night with with a lot of girls. Mary Wesley Abram & myself was at Millcreek to day. I saw Sue Coffman; she said she was to see you all; I would like to come in & see you cooking; you have not forgotten how to wait on the ladies as Sue said you & G.L. came home with her; There were several of our Malitia boys there to day D.J.C. E.J.R. & M.V.G. all home on sick furlough; There were some deserters I don't count them; they ran away when they thought they would be a fight; and leaving only a few to whip the Yankees and doubling their duties; such men I believe if the Yankees should come through here would join them.

We received a letter from Pappa a short time since in which he said that most of the men that went to Romney and saw the destructive work of the Vandals concluded it was better to go from home to fight than to let the enemy come through here; I agree with them though I very much hate to see the men go away; yet I would tell [no] one to stay that I thought was able to go; I have been hearing the Malitia was coming home but I will believe it when I see them; I wish they could come home a while for some of them lost nearly all their clothes,

Pappa has not been home for 4 months about as long he ever stayed away; I think you are getting spunky sure enough talk about Volunteering again; I thought you would be a good Soldier.

There are still some weddings a going on about here I suppose you have heared Joe Spitler was married after so long a time he & his lady rode by here to day, he looked as though he had a wife; I heared Daniel Judd & Miss Arthelia Keibler were to have been married last Tuesday I have not heared if they were or not but suppose they were; Jack Johnston were to be one of the waiters; I have been looking for him but fear he has not come yet. he stayed all night here about a month ago; it is the same Jack it used to be. Mary & myself have been trying to get out on that Hawksbill for sometime; the weather has been so bad and we have but one horse and no person to drive for us; if we take Wesley Mother & the two little boys will be here by themselves; so you see it not only takes the men away, but makes the girls stay at home; it makes girls do a great many things they never was used to; I am willing to do all I can & stay home [if] you will only whip the Yankees and drive them from our land; I think they can not stand it much longer; I think from what I can get from the papers they are making preparations for a grand sweep but I hope they may meet with with the same success they did at Manassa; We can not expect to be successfull every time but if we get whipped once we must not give up but try harder next time; Dont you think our Militia made a miraculous escape at Hanging Rock; that they got none prisoners. I think they showed themselves a barbarous Nation their. I do not think the Indians ever did a much worse act; considering one always passed for a civilized & enlighten people while the other we know were not. We lost a good officer out there; J.D. Alshere; he had made himself very popular with his men and the Regt.

Franklin Rothgeb is very sick though the Dr thought him a little better yesterday; he has Pneumonia; I suppose from cold taken in camp.

I was to stay overnight with Bettie since you were home; it looked a little lonesome not to see you about; Fannie and Sarah Gander & Barbara A Rothgeb were [here] a few Sundays since; Fannie was asking if I knew where your Regt was; she wanted to write to some of the Regt and did not know where to write; but I guess you have let her know it before this time; I suppose you & Miss Martha R. carry on a regular correspondence; I have not seen her since xmas she looked about as usual; I guess the light has not shined much for you this year; for it has been too cloudy,

WINTER 1862

I received a letter from Millie Kagey a short time since in which she sends her love to all her friends; & as I suppose you claim to be one I send it to you; I suppose Mag has forgotten us all she never writes any more; I must close this scribling it is a right long letter though not much news in it; please excuse error or bad writing; Mary joins in sending love to love to you; No more at present; will try and do better in future.

As ever your Cousin Ella

February provides an opportunity for reenlistments and a liberal leave policy in addition to social visits to Winchester. Jackson soon withdraws his remaining force from Romney. As John's diary continues, he describes the Roanoke Island battle of February 8 in which Col. H. M. Shaw, acting for the ailing Gen. Henry A. Wise, is forced to yield to an overwhelming force of Federal troops and gunboats under Maj. Gen. Ambrose Burnside. He surrenders 2527 men and 30 guns and loses this important coastal postition. In the follow-up, most of the Confederate gunship fleet is destroyed. In the West, Maj. Gen. Sterling Price's Missouri campaign is little noted in the runup to Grant's advance on Fort Donelson in Tennessee.

Sunday 9th. 20 of our company reenlist for the war.

Monday 10th. The 20 that reenlisted yesterday get their $50 and start home. All of Gen. Loring's force leave Romney and come to Winchester.

Tuesday 11th. I have the reumatism in my neck; can't turn my head. Great disaster at Roanoke Island, North Carolina, about 3000 of the Wise Legion Taken prisoners. Snows a little this evening.

Wednesday 12th. Squire Shuler arrives at camp. Gen Price has another great battle in Missouri; rout the enemy, though with a considerable loss.

A letter on small note paper, embossed with an elaborate flowered border, comes from Emily C. Judd, 19. The marriage of her brother Daniel may have put her in a Valentine mood. Brother Samuel N. Judd serves in Co. K, 10th Va. Infantry.

*Hawksbill February 11th
1862*

Dear Friend
 I this evening seat myself to acknowledge the reception of your very welcome letter which I received. I was extremely glad to hear from you once more. I should have answered it sooner but we have had great deal of sickness in the family. we have all had the mumps when I received your letter we was fixing for an infaiar [infirm?] brother. Daniel is married he was married the 4 of february. we had a nice time although it is no time for weddings now, I am looking for Sammy home soon. he has Volunteered for 2 more years he has a furlough of 30 days. I believe all the company have. Oh, I do wish you all could come home. I would so much [like] to see you all. it would afford me great pleasure but I hope the time will soon come when you all will be permitted to return to your much loved homes there to spen[d] the remainder of your days with whom you love and cherish and for whom you are now undergoing these many awful dangers. oh: we did not know how to appreciate peace liberty and independence. but if we are ever so lucky as to conkur every opposing foe then will we know how to appreciate our homes. I will close by asking you to write soon for I am glad to hear from you at any time. it gives me great consolation to think that the souldiers think enough of me to write to. I get letters from a great many of them. nothing more at present but remain your sincere friend until death. give my love to Perry Kite. tell him I said he must be a good boy. please let no person see this letter

*from your friend
E.. C.. J..*

Mr.. John P.. Hite

Though the initialed signature on the following letter is scarcely legible, it is likely that of Mary [J?] Rothgeb, 16, whose brother Edmund J., has been serving in the militia but will later enlist in the Page Greys. After an ironic opening, she mentions soldiers Joseph Benton Huffman, Henry Aleshire, David Coffman, Martin Gander, and Capt. William T. Young of Co. K, 10th Va. Cav. No service record has been found for John Morris, son of Simpson Morris of Waverly PO.

WINTER 1862

To J P Hite

                Achorn Hill Page County Virginia February the 12.1862
Dear Cousin
    I will try to answer your eight lines that you wrote to me in John P. Beavers letter. I received your few lines last friday and have been reading at it ever since that time, and have just now got over it; I tell you John it was a big letter for the first one that you wrote to your cousin and then never signed your name but the hand right is just as good as the name would be, and you never said that I should answer but I reckon that you thought I couldent answer such a long letter as that but I will try to answer it. Martyn V. Gander is here now he come here just as I was finishing Bentons letter it was nearly sundown. I stoped writing then and got supper as he said that he couldent stay all night. I though[t] that he could stay till after supper so he is here yet but he talks of leaving. he just come out to see Ed about going back to camp he and Ed was going to start back Tomorrow but Martin come out to tell Ed that he wasent a going. he said that the Militia was all a comming home the last of the week for they wouldent pay them and they was coming home with out there pay. they stacke arms last thursday and talked of comming home but they concluded to stay a little longer. they though[t] maby that they would get there pay but I reckon that they think they have served long enough with out getting payed. I do wish that they would all come home for they dont treat our Militia fair, but Ed still talks of going Tomorrow if Martin dont go he said that he can go by hisself he is so keen to get back to camp as they have all stacked arms. I am agoing to send this letter with Ed but if he dont go I will send it by Maile. Martin Gander is gone but David J. Coffman is here now we never lack for company for we have company most evry day but I am glad to see any of our soldiers come here. Henry Aleshire and Johnnie Morris landed in page yesterday. I do expect that they will be another wedding in Page since John M. has landed. they are a great many of the Volunteers a comming up. nearly all Capt Youngs men has come home. I must close excuse this writing and spelling and write soon from your friend   *M J R*
To John P. Hite

Fannie Gander reports again to John of Franklin Rothgeb's illness. Man and Mart are his brothers Emanuel and Martin Rothgeb.

The Painful News I Have to Write

Thursday evening
February 13th/62

Dear Friend:

It is with pleasure that I seat my-self this pleasant evening to answer your very kind and interesting letter, which I received yesterday and read with great pleasure. I was glad to hear from you and would be more so to see you again. I heard that you was coming home the first of March.

There has been a good many soldiers come home this week, thouhg [sic] not many from a bout here, Henry Aleshire is one that has come and was to see us a few minutes yesterday, though I did not get to speak to him. I hope it will not be long before you can all come home and stay though I heard yesterday that the Yankees gained victory down in the south some where. I do not know exactly where, and if that is true it dosent look much like peace.

I was out at Millcreek last Sunday as you guessed. I was there a listening at Uncle Booten preach. I was to see Frank Rothgeb he has been very sick but he is a little better though the Doctor says he is not out of danger yet. Cousin Barbra Rothgeb and my-self are a going out there this evening to set up, they have to set up all night with him. If I gou [sic] I will get to see Man and Mart. We have a good many malitia boys here now but the most [of] them are deserters. I think they will will have to bring the balance back to take them back again, for it will take all that is down there yet. I think I will have to close or else you cannot correct all the mistakes, you will find them plenty. I reckon you thought that smart to send you such a piece of paper as I did. The reason why I sent you that was Sis and B.A. Rothgeb was writing letters and I had none to write and I just written that for fun and put it in with Sis'es and she said that if I did not take it out she wouldent. I would not of cared so much if had of been on other paper but I hope you will excuse me.

As Sis wants to go to store yet this evening I will have to close for it is most night. This leaves me well and hope it will find you enjoying good health.

Please excuse all mistakes. Write soon as you can, or when it is convenient for you to do so.

From your sincere friend
Fannie

John's diary reports another of those rumors of European recognition which buoy Southern hopes throughout the war. In the reported battle of Bloomery Gap, Union losses are 11 killed and 5 wounded, Confederates

WINTER 1862

13 killed and 65 missing. The roundabout he buys on February 17 is a short, tight jacket.

Thursday 13th. Reported in the paper that England has recognized the Southern Confederacy. I stand guard from 4 to 9 o'clock P. M.

Friday 14th. the Yankees drive the militia from Bloomery. We get orders to get the no. of rounds of cartridges and rub up our guns, and be ready to march at any time.

Saturday 15th. Snows to depth of 3 inches.

Sunday 16th. Have inspection today for the first time for several months.

Monday 17th. Go to Winchester and get a roundabout for $13..

Tuesday 18th. Quite pleasant today.

Wednesday 19th. Raining all day. The Yankees take Nashville Tenn.

Thursday 20th. Reported that the Yankees take Fort Donelson, Tenn. Our loss 11,000.

In the battle and capture of Fort Donelson on February 14 through 16, Gen. Ulysses S. Grant establishes his fighting reputation and captures a reported 13,829 Confederate prisoners with Union losses of 500 killed, 2,100 wounded, and 200 missing.

The Rev. Ambrose C. Booten (Uncle Booten) sends some avuncular admonitions to young John. He has been minister of the Mill Creek Church since 1846. This Baptist church at Hamburg was founded about 1800, taking over the log building from a Mennonite congregation. Ambrose Booton was born 26 June 1789, and, though his hand is shaky, his spelling and punctuation reflect his good education.

Page County Va 15 Feb 1862
My highly esteemed young friend John
Yours of the first Inst has been most gladly rec'd & carefully read several times; your father's family that are at home have all seen it, &

were enjoying common health last sunday, when as usual I dined with them.

Yours was the first letter I have received from any of the page soldiers, & I read your brief history of your privations and suffering from fatigue and exposure to wet & heat in the summer, & cold, rains & sleets and snows & winds in winter, as well as the several battles you have been in with heart felt sympathy and gratitude to that Almighty being in whose hands are the destiny of nations, and of individuals, And when I reflect on your remarkable preservation the words of the Poet come i[n]to mind with force:

"Plagues and death around me fly,
Till he bid I cannot die;
Not a single shaft can hit,
'Till the God of love see fit."
Oh thou gracious wise & just
In thy hands my life I trust.
Have I somewhat dearer still
I resign to thy will."

Your beloved father informed me sometime since of the interesting fact that you discovered a marked difference between the preaching of the hirelings in the Army and that which you had been accustomed to hear in page; and I consider it a good omen, for it is impossible for an unenlightened person to believe the truth as it stands recorded in the bible and as it is preached by gospel ministers, they know not their right from their left in things divine and are said to take darkness for light & light for darkness "Bitter for sweet and sweet for bitter" I hope the Lord intends to make you instrumental in gaining a just political cause, and also in promoting his spiritual kingdom. I will say to you that I believed all the time that the north especially the black republican party who with one consent voted down in congress all the peace propositions which were made by the South are wholly to blame for our prese[n]t Civil War & all its horrors, and should feel no misgiving about the final result, if the souther[n] people were humble and prayerful and all united and determined by divine assistance to gain an honoral [sic] independance; but alas! when so many who have means to supply the needs of the poor soldiers extortioning on them, and making themselves rich by swindling the government, soldiers, and every unfortunate person that comes within their grasp, add to that the unwillingness of so many both volunteers and malitia to be in the army & the deception practiced to keep out of it, can but feel misgivings, and to honor true

WINTER 1862

hearted men like your self. We had a rumor afloat this week that their has been recently been two considerable battles fought in the south in both of which the yankees were victorious. I hope to be reliably informed tomorrow, this being a verry snowy day prevents my going to church meeting at Luray – I hope never to want a heart to sympathize with, reverence & minister according to my means to true hearted suffering soldiers.

The health of the people on Mill Creek has been good this winter, with a few exceptions you have no doubt been informed of the death of our neighbor Isaac Shaffer and the extreme illness of one of Reuben Rothgebs sons, he at last accounts was thought convalescent. the dipther[i]a & scarlet fever has taken off quite a number of children especially near the heads of the two Hawksbills –

And now in conclusion I must thank you for your kind remembrance of me and I do assure you that my hearts best wishes for your safety both here and hereafter shall go with you wherever it may be his pleasure to cast your lot. farewell dear John.

A.C. Booton

my sight so dim & my hand so nervous that it will [be] a task for you to read.

In his next letter home John refers to this letter from Uncle Booten. John Henry Lionberger and James William Walter are in Co. D, 7th Va. Cavalry. Henry Aleshire is with John in Co. H. Camp Zollicoffer, near Winchester, is occupied by the 33rd Regt. from January 25 to March 12, 1862. The power of attorney is required for John to collect back pay due William. Reenlistments earn a furlough and a $50 bounty.

Feb 20th 1862
Camp Zollicoffer

Dear Father:

I recd. a letter from Ella a few weeks since; answered it a few days after its reception, no I am mistaken I have not written since the receipt of her letter. She said that Col. Buswell had injured himself in the estimation of the people & that they thought the militia could come him [home] if it was not for him. But I assure you it is not his fault, but believe it is in the power of Gen. Meem to release them at any time, as the governor says he did not order them out. As to their getting thier pay, I believe it is the fault of their officers.

She said she heard John Lionberger & Billy Walters was to be hung, for giving a false alarm at a methodist meeting. It is true they

Mill Creek Church

Built as Mauck Meeting House.
During the Civil War period had
shingle roof and white weather board exterior.

WINTER 1862 91

gave a false alarm & were drunk, but as to their being hung is altogether false; though they have been Court-Martialed in Winchester, have not heard their fate, but nothing very serious I am confident.

I had wrote to some of the family for you to send the Power Attorney by Capt. Shenk but he arrived here yesterday, said he did not seen & of course you could not send it by him. I think you better send it by Henry Aleshire he is to be here till the first of march then I can get the money & bring it home as I expect to be there by the 5$\underline{th}$ of March unless something prevents:

There is 1342 already reenlisted in the Stonewall Brigade & ere the expiration of the year, it will be as formidable as at first. No more at present as I expect to see you soon. Yours as ever.

J. P. Hite

P. S. I recd. a highly interesting letter from uncle Booton day before yesterday, which I carefully perused & will preserve as a criterion.

J.

John's diary continues. The "victory in Arkansas" reported on February 25, is the battle of Sugar Creek, in which Union losses are just 13 killed and 15 wounded.

Friday 21st. Cold and windy all day

Saturday 22nd. I stand guard from midnight till 7 o'clock A. M., also from noon till 4 o'clock P.M.

Sunday 23rd. Things dull in camp.

Monday 24th. Thunders a good deal this morning, turns very cold and blustering after 9 o'clock A.M.

Tuesday 25th. Very still today. Gen Price gained a victory in Arkansas.

Wednesday 26th. We get orders to cook one days rations and keep it cooked until further orders. I am detailed orderly at Gen. Garnett's Headquarters.

Thursday 27th. Very cold and windy all day. Am riding all day carrying dispatches. Garnett's Brigade move near Winchester. The militia run out of Martinsburgh by the Yankees who are there. Expect a fight soon at this place.

Friday 28th. Still cold and windy. D.C. Hite starts home on sick furlough.

Saturday March 1st. Things very active in camp.

Sunday 2nd. Snows to the depth of 3 inches.

Monday 3rd. Rains nearly all day and night. Have a good many dispatches to carry.

Carried by John in his duty as orderly to the adjutant, these many dispatches are the harbingers of a spring campaign soon to begin.

CHAPTER 6

The Valley Campaign

*"We marched 35 miles today,
the hardest marching on record."*

In March of 1862 the armies slowly begin to stir from winter camps. John Hite's reenlistment is to be for the rest of his life, but far short of the war's duration.

Tuesday 4th [March]. I reenlist for the war.

Wednesday 5th. Very muddy.

Thursday 6th. Expecting to move all day. Everything active.

March Friday 7th. The enemy come within six miles of Winchester. Jackson's command, whole command, go below town to meet them; they come contact; several wounded on each side; the enemy falls back to Bunker's Hill.

Saturday 8th. A great excitement prevails during yesterday and today. Move near Winchester this evening to our former camp.

In a Sunday letter, John describes the skirmish in which Jackson's offer of battle is refused by Union Gen. Nathaniel P. Banks.

*March 9th
Camp near Winchester*

Dear Father:
I will endeavor to write you a few lines again. There was great excitement here in about an hour after Isaac left. The yankees came within about 6 miles of Winchester, with about 5 Regts. infantry, 4 pieces of artillery & 400 cavalry. Jackson soon had his whole force a few miles below Winchester in line of battle awaiting the attack. [Col. Turner] Ashbey with several companies of his [7th Va.] cavalry routed them. The yankees fired their cannon about 12 times. There were

several of them killed & wounded. One Col. horse shott under him. One or two of ours wounded.

If the yankees had come up they would have met with a warm reception, for the boys were keen for a fight as the yankees had been victorious in other places for sometime; so they wished to try them. They are about 10 miles from here at present, & we are expecting an attack here soon as they have been re-enforced, I feel as if I can fight them with the determination of conquering.

I presume Isaac told you that I could not draw Wm's money here, also the incidents thereto. I am sorry that I can't succeed in getting the money here as I understood it. I had the promise of it by Major [G.D.] Mercer [Quartermaster, 2nd Corps, ANV] before I had the Power Attorney; but after getting it he looked in his book concerning it, & said I could not get it without sending to Richmond, so I'll send you the Power Attorney again.

We expect to get paid some time during this week, if there is no move. Our Chaplain is preaching again in a few yards of our tent. The first time for several months. I thought to be at home to-day a few weeks since, & would have been had not things turned up as they did.

When I come home I'll try & get some necessary writing to get the money due Wm. if there can be any got from Shenk or any one.

J. P. Hite

As John's diary continues, Jackson's army begins a retreat up the valley before the Union forces, now under Gen. James Shields. The Missouri battle reported on March 14 is the battle of Pea Ridge, Arkansas, fought on March 6-8, 1862, in which Gen. Sterling Price's Missouri state guards under Confederate Gen. Earl Van Dorn inflict heavy casualties on Union forces but eventually are forced to retreat, largely ending southern ambitions west of the Mississippi. The naval victory is the damage to Union ships at Hampton Roads on March 8 by Confederate ironclad *Merrimack*, now rechristened *Virginia*. The celebrated but inconclusive first battle of the ironclads takes place next day upon the arrival of the Union's *Monitor*.

Sunday 9th. Several Yankees Taken prisoner yesterday. Get orders to be ready to move at a moment's warning.

Monday 10th. Rains a little this morning. Very high wind in the evening.

THE VALLEY CAMPAIGN

Tuesday 11th. We are roused early this morning, but remain at camp until about one oclock when I am sent along the Romney Road to bring in the picketts. Our force go below town to the Yankees. The picketts keep firing at each other until night. Several wounded on each side. Our forces keeps falling back till sundown; and then all leave and go above town six miles where the wagons are. The Yankees about 25,000, which tebbles ours. I don't sleep scarcely any. I get very near the Yankees while I [am] riding around with General Garnett carrying dispatches.

Wednesday 12th. Our whole force falls back near Strasburgh save Ashby's cavalry. The enemy continues to advance. They take possession of Newtown. Great excitement among the citizens of the Valley.

Thursday 13th. We remain at the place we came yesterday evening. The Yankees fall back several miles beyond Newtown.

Friday 14th. Reported another great victory gained by Gen Price in Missouri, also a Naval Victory near Norfolk.

The army continues to retreat up the Valley until Shields begins a withdrawal on March 21, intending to join McClellan at Manassas. He is soon pursued by Jackson. On the afternoon of Sunday, March 23, having just marched 36 miles in two days, Jackson's army meets and engages Shields's division at Kernstown, four miles south of Winchester.

Saturday 15th. Our whole force falls back 3 miles south of Winchester. Rains a good deal during the day.

Sunday 16th. Still go further South. Start nine oclock A.M. stop 8 miles north of Mt Jackson. Great excitement prevails among the people of the county on account of our forces falling back.

Monday 17th. A good many of the boys of my company leaving without permission.

Tuesday 18th. Quite warm and pleasant.

Wednesday 19th. We [halt] three miles this side of Strasburgh, expect something great to be performed in a short time, but can't tell anything about its nature. Rains some in the evening.

96   THE PAINFUL NEWS I HAVE TO WRITE

Thursday 20th. Our whole Brigade strikes tents early this morning but don't move until about 3 oclock in the evning, move three miles south of Mt Jackson. Very foggy, cloudy and rainy all day. Rains, snows and hails after night. Great excitement prevails among the people on account our falling back.

Friday 21st. Pack up early again this morning but don't move until about 1 oclock, go down the road in the direction of Strasburgh. Stop 2 miles below Mt Jackson, Very wet and muddy. G. D. Buswell joined A. B. Shenk's company for the war.

Saturday 22nd. The Yankees evacuate Strasburgh in double quick time, also Winchester and start for Maryland. Reported that 13,000 Marylanders have taken up arms for the South. We start this morning again march 24 miles till night. Great rejoicing from the citizens as we pass down the road. Yankees destroy a great deal about Strasburgh. Gen Johnston gains a great victory near Fredericksburg.

Sunday 23rd. Start again early this morning, stop about 3 miles below Newtown, where the men get orders to load their pieces. The fight begins about 1 oclock with the cannon and continues till after dark. Our men fight gallantly through much fatigued from hard marching. Have many of our best men and officers killed among which is Adj. General Genkin [Maj. Gen. D.C. Jenkins, Jr., Adj. Gen. Dept.].

John Hite's transcribed diary ends after the March 23 entry, not to be resumed until April 21. The entry of March 22 must be based on a totally false rumor as there is no report of any such action near Fredericksburg. But the battle at Kernstown is all too real. In the diary of George Daniel Buswell, who has left home and enlisted in Co. H just two days earlier, we find this more complete account:

Sun. 23rd. At an early hour we continued the march. About 1 pm the army filed off the road near Kernstown & prepared for an engagement, having come upon the enemy. I had no gun, and as I could not procure one from the Ordnance Department, I, with the consent of Capt. Shanks, stayed back until a member of the 37th Va. Regt. came out wounded by a piece of shell. I got his gun & started in pursuit of the 33rd. When within 3/4 of a mile of the regt., I heard the rattle of musketry, which plainly told that our army was hotly en-

THE VALLEY CAMPAIGN

> *gaged. I then fell in with the 5th Va. Regt., which was just going into the fight. I remained with them through this, my first battle, & came out unhurt. The enemy very largely outnumbering Jackson's Band, which when all told was small, but now considerably reduced by straggling, it was compelled to fall back, which it did without any considerable loss. The command collected & bivouaced for the night a few miles above Newtown. In our Company the good & noble Capt. Shank & Private John J. Smith were killed; Sergt. Joseph Stover, severely wounded in the thigh & left on the field; Privates Wm. A. Brittan, wounded in arm, & Eli M. Frazier, in ankle, both of them got off the field. Return Nichols was captured. Col. Echols, of the 27th Regt., was severely wounded in the arm.*

Confederate casualties at the battle of Kernstown are officially reported as 80 killed, 375 wounded, and 263 missing or prisoners compared to the Union's 118 killed, 450 wounded, and 22 missing. Jackson's army retreats in some disorder, but the Federals find it necessary hereafter to maintain a strong force to counter Jackson in the Valley. Accused of withdrawing without authorization, Gen. Garnett is relieved of command and forced to prove his bravery with tragic results more than a year later at Gettysburg. His replacement is Charles Sidney Winder.

Having lost the first captain, William Rippetoe, to disease, and his potential replacement, William Hite, to his wounds at 1st Manassas, the Page Greys now lose another captain, Ambrose Booten Shenk. An oral tradition in the Buswell family is that friends remove the coat from his corpse, leaning against a tree on the battlefield, and send it to his widow, Mary Ann. She is able to make positive identification from the lining of this coat which she made for him.

Of the other Page Grey casualties, Smith first enlisted on March 15. Stover, Britton, and Frazier never return to the company, though Frazier is later to enlist in the 7th Va. Cavalry and is mortally wounded in June, 1864. Return Nichols is exchanged and does return—in time to receive a mortal wound at Chancellorsville the following May.

George Buswell's diary reports for April 3rd:

> *...went down the pike to within 2 or 3 miles of Edenburg ... Here we remained a week or more, without tents, the weather very rainy. Lt.*

Chadduck, Sgt. Kite & John Hite were sent home to arrest absentees from the company. The rest of our men being absent, Gideon Long & I built a small bush shelter.

Rejoining the Page Grey company, John Hite resumes his diary. Though catching runaways has proved tiresome, John succeeds in getting his brother David, now recovered from his illness and discharged from the militia, to enlist in Co. H as of April 22. On April 23 the Stonewall Brigade undergoes a reorganization as required by Virginia's new conscription law. Col. Arthur Cummings of the 33rd Regt. resigns in a disagreement with Jackson and is replaced by John Francis Neff. A VMI graduate, Neff at age 27 becomes the Brigade's youngest regimental commander. In Company H, Michael Shuler is elected captain to replace Shenk, and Charles T. Chadduck, Oliver Hazard Perry Kite, and Harrison B. Jones are elected 1st, 2nd, and 3rd Lts. John Hite is elected 1st Sgt., and James W. Menifie, John T. Johnston, and George W. Koontz 2nd through 4th Sgts.

April 1862
Monday 21st. I have been at home for sometime hunting up the runaways of the company & bringing them back; find it a hard task. The yankees taken full possession of Page (my native Co.) a few days since. Gen. Johnston gain a victory at Yorktown a few day's since.

Tuesday 22nd. Hear that the yankees are destroying a great deal in Page, & arresting many of the citizens. Very wet for the last several days.

Wednesday 23rd. Elect Shuler Captain, Chadduck 1st Lieut., Kite 2nd., Jones 3rd. Hite elected 1st Serg. Menefee 2nd. Johnston 3rd. Koontz 4rd. About 6,000 yankees in Page.

Thursday 24th. Rains all day, waters very high. Ten yankees taken in Page, 3 of them at Isaac Rothgeb's. 6 yankees taken dinner at my father's last Monday.

Friday 25th. Still cloudy all day, but don't rain any.

Saturday 26th. Only about 2,000 yankees in Page instead of 6,000.

The Valley Campaign

Sunday 27th. A skirmish take [place] near Magahasville; a few wounded on each side. We move up the mountain hollow about 2 miles.

Monday 28th. No news of any importance transpiring.

Tuesday 29th. We move down near the bridge.

On April 30 the Stonewall Brigade resumes the series of long marches, skirmishes, and countermarches which give them the nickname "Jackson's Foot Cavalry."

Wednesday 30th. Have reveille this morning at 1 o'clock, Start at 3 o'clock. Go about 3 miles west of the bridge, where we remain till about 11 o'clock A.M. then go back on the east side of the bridge, & go southwest in the direction of Port Republic. We march till 9 o'clock at night. Rains a good deal in the evening. Don't get any sleep scarcely on account of not getting any of bedding neither do we get anything to eat. Ewell's division over from the east side of the ridge.

May Thursday 1st. We march again today 'till about 11 o'clock at night through the mud & water about knee deep. Rains again to day. Don't have anything to eat since yesterday at dinner. I get lost in the woods in the mud & water & briars so thick that a rabbit could scarcely get through.

Friday 2nd. We remain here, (about 1 1/2 mile east of Port Republic) all day.

May Saturday 3rd. Jackson whole division crosses the Blue Ridge into Albemarle Co. in eastern Va. Ewell's division remains in the Valley. We cross at Brown Gap.

Sunday 4th. Great dissatisfaction among the soldiers on account of having to carry all our bed cloths. We stay near Michel's Station [Mitchum's Station per Buswell's diary] about 10 miles distant, from where we stayed last night.

> *Monday 5th. We go to the [Greenwood] station near the great tunnel through the Blue Ridge, & get on the cars; get off about 2 miles from Stanton.*
>
> *Tuesday 6th. We stay 2 miles of Staunton all day. Cook one day's rations. The yankees taking & destroying a great deal in Page.*
>
> *Wednesday 7th. We start this morning & go 14 miles west of Staunton on the road to the Shenandoah mountain.*
>
> *May Thursday 8th. We start again early this morning. A battle fought between the rest of the command & the yankees. A great many killed & wounded on both sides. Our Brigade taken near the battlefield twice, but get orders to go back about 2[?] miles both times; 3 o'clock in the morning when we get to the wagons the last time. The men entirely worn out, & broken down from hard marching & loss of sleep. We marched 35 miles today, the hardest marching on record. Col Gibbons of the 10 Va. Regt. killed. We stay at the Shenandoah Mountains. The fight begin about 4 o'clock A.M. last till 9 o'clock P.M.*
>
> And in an undated note from end of diary: *The battle of the 8th of May 1862, fought at the* ~~Shenandoah Mountains~~ *In the battle of McDowald fought the 8th of May 1862. Our loss is estimated at 60 killed & 250 wounded. The yankees losses thought to be equally as many, besides many tents, cooking utencils, knapsack, commissaries, horses, wagons &c captured.*

As rear guard, the Stonewall Brigade is not engaged in this Battle of McDowell or Bull Pasture which forces a Federal retreat. Confederate casualties reported at 75 killed, 424 wounded and missing; Union casualties 28 killed, 225 wounded. Albert W. Whitestone, the deserter, is listed in the 1860 census as a distiller, age 23, born in Prussia, and living alone in Page County.

> *Friday 9th. We start in pursuit of the yankees again early this morning. They keep falling back. Capture a great deal of their baggage at their encampment. A Whitestone of my company desert, & starts for to go to the yankees, but caught. G.D. Buswell & myself left back to guard him. We go from Staunton (Augusta) to Highland Co. then get in Alleghany The yankees turn off from the main road; go in*

The Valley Campaign

the direction of Winchester. reported that Gen Ewell has had a fight below Harrisonburgh & taken 900 prisoners. We travel 11 miles.

In his diary, George Buswell gives this report of the same incident:

Fri. 9th. Marched 1 or 2 miles beyond McDowell, all pretty tired. John Hite and I stopped in Yankee camp to rest, were put to guarding a Sutler wagon, that had been left by the Yankees, & 2 deserters who had been caught, one of them was Albert Whitestone, a member of our co.

Again from John Hite:

Saturday 10th. The yankees go due north through Pendleton; we still follow in pursuit We go about 10 miles. Our company go out on picket all night, don't get but very little sleep.

Sunday 11th. The yankees make a stand in Pendleton at Franklin the County seat. We put out skirmishers, they get in contact with the enemy; kill one of our men. We kept in line of battle till about 10 o'clock at night only a few hundred yards of the yankees.

Monday 12th. The yankees have such a good position that it is impossible for our troops to get to them without being very much exposed; so we fall back 6 or 8 miles.

Tuesday 13th. We continue to fall back. A fight in Page about a week since, near Liberty between 2 regts on our side & several on the yankees. Two of our men killed, & several wounded; 14 yankees killed 29 captured.

Wednesday 14th. We move back 15 miles farther. Rains all last night & some this morning; we get very wet from having to lay out in the rain. Very muddy travelling.

Thursday 15th. We move back to the Shenandoah; distance 15 miles. Rain some again.

102   The Painful News I Have to Write

Friday 16th. We lay still all day. to day set apart as a day of fasting & prayers by president Davis. [in thanks for the victory at McDowell]

Saturday 17th. Jackson's whole army of 10 or 12,000 take the road that leads to Harrisonburgh. Our whole rout is a mountainous one first over mountains then through deep ravines. I am taken sick & sent to the Hospital in Staunton, find about 1800 sick & wounded at the Hospital.

May Sunday 18th. I still feel very unwell, Don't like being here as there are so many, neither do we get proper care. Rains in during the day.

Monday 19th. About 15 dies here every day. The Regt (33rd) I belong to is near Harrisonburgh, Va.

Tuesday 20th. I go to a cloth factory which is a great curiosity to me. Rains some agains this evening.

Wednesday 21st. I leave the hospital this morning, & start for my Regt. which is near Harrisonburgh; get to Harrisonburgh about 3 o'clock P.M. I get my things on a wagon. Stay all night at Mr. Jennings.

Thursday 22nd. I start again this morning for Page, as Jackson's whole army has crossed the mountain, & gone in Page. Get to John A. Burner's 'till 4 o'clock. See a great deal the vandals have destroyed. I get shot accidentally through the hand, from falling in getting over a fence.

Friday 23rd. I go home this morning from J. A. Burner's then go to Luray, & have my hand dressed. Jackson's whole army go in the direction of Front Royal. A big fight expected every day.

Saturday 24th. [blank, no entry]

In the battle of Front Royal, Union losses are reported as 32 killed, 122 wounded, and 750 missing. Confederate losses not available.

Sunday 25th. Jackson's whole army below Winchester. Capture about 300 wagons a great [many] small arms, battery ammunition baggage, commissaries &c. several thousand prisoners &c. &c. worth millions of dollars. My hand very sore.

Monday 26th [no entry]

This date with no further entry ends John Hite's diary, and we have no further day-by-day record from him or from his brothers. We do not know how his hand has healed, but he is reported back on duty by June, 1862. These notes appear on the last page of his diary booklet:

Mess account
2 lbs butter 2 dosen eggs. $1.12
3 lb lard 50 cts.

1 Serg. Hite
2nd Menefee
3rd Johnston
4th Koontz

1 Corp Robertson
2nd Long
3rd
4th

Due D.J. Abbott $4.30 [probably Daniel B. Abbott]
Due H.P. Strole $4.00
Due G.W. Koontz $9.00

CHAPTER 7

Distant Battles and Yankees in the Valley

*"I could freely give up all
if I had my horses back."*

After his discharge from the militia at the end of 1861, Isaac Hite has joined the Dixie Artillery, a Page Co. unit first formed in June, 1861. Its first captain was John Kaylor Booten who resurrected a moribund company given to firing 4th of July salutes with its two old iron cannon. After Booten's election to the state legislature in November 1861, he is replaced as captain by William Henry Chapman. Isaac and others have been recruited while the company is in winter quarters near Manassas.

When this letter is written, the Dixie Artillery is in reserve at Blakely's Mill Pond, near Richmond. The battle described is that of Fair Oaks and Seven Pines fought on May 31 and June 1, 1862. Reported casualties: Union– 790 killed, 3627 wounded, 647 missing; Confederate– 980 killed, 4749 wounded, 405 missing. As a result of Gen. Joseph E. Johnston's wound, field command is given to Robert E. Lee, who soon proves his tactical skills.

*June 2nd 62
Camp near Richmond*

Dear Parents:-
*Again I have an opportunity of sending a few lines to you. When I last wrote to Bettie (a few days ago) I though[t] I would hear from you before writing again, but as their was a hard battle fought some five miles East of Richmond, on Saturday and Su[n]day last, I have no doubt you feel some anxiety as to the result. There have been so many different rumors about the fight, neither does this mornings papers contain any correct account of it, therefore I am unable to give any correct account of it whatever.
This much I believe is authenticatid that our forces suceeded in driving them back, even beyond one line of their breast works, though with a very heavy loss. Our loss is beyond a doubt very heavy, perhap equal to that of the enemy, by they having their fortifications to shield*

them. *The Yankee is said to have fought well—stubbornly resisting every foot of ground as they fell back. The battlefield is a low marshy place; our men were often in mud and water two feet deep. Many fell, though not mortally wou[n]ded, yet it is said they strangled in the mud and water for want of help.*

Gens Johnson and Longstreet both received slight wounds. It is unnecessary for me to write more at present as I cannot give reliable information. Our company is a reserved battery, therefore was not in the fight.

Yours as ever I. M. Hite

We received our bounty a few days ago.

With McDowell threatening Richmond, Jackson's division moves from the Shenandoah Valley to the support of Longstreet and A. P. Hill. Shortage of rolling stock on the railroad and, later, swamps and ravines in the unfamiliar terrain delay his arrival and participation in the famed Seven Days Battles, of June 25 through July 1, 1862. We take up the fortunes of the Page Greys in excerpts from the diary of 1st Lt. George Buswell.

Wed. 25th [June, 1862]. Started early, did not march very hard. We are now in Hanover. Encamped tonight near Ashland....

Thurs. 26th. Finished cooking & lay down this morning at 2; got up at 3 am. Started early & marched through swamp & wilderness until 11 pm. Had just gone to sleep, when an order came for our company to go on picket. Officers had a hard time waking up the boys. I having the colors, was exempt from such duty & slept on.

Fri. 27th. Were aroused by distant artillery & musket firing. Marched early. We are now within 10 or 15 miles of Richmond. We passed Brig. Gen. JEB Stuart's Cavalry, I saw the Gen. for the first time.... In the evening we heard the rattle of musketry & were hurried towards the front through fields, brush & almost impassable swamp. The rattle & roar of musketry could, by this time, be heard as far as the ear could reach, I think they were 18 or 20 miles in length. The Yanks were driven back & their position taken by our troops just as our brigade was going on the field. We followed on at a double quick until sometime after dark. Col. Neff captured a Yankee major. Vedettes were then thrown out, & we lay down to sleep, and here we rested on the field, where had just been fought the "Battle of Cold Harbor."...

Sat. 28th. Moved a short distance & back to the same place. Co. H was taken out to guard some Yankee prisoners at Gen. Winder's Hd. Qrs. ...

Sun. 29th. Lay still until about 12 noon, when Co. H rejoined us, & we moved down to the Chickehominy, where we remained until evening, waiting, I suppose, for the bridge to be rebuilt. We then moved back to where we lay yesterday. The sun shone excessively hot today & no water could be found fit to drink. ... Rained a very heavy shower this evening. Just as we were ready to retire for the night, the long roll beat in the other regts., but by the time the order reached our regt., it was countermanded.

Mon. 30th. We were aroused at 3 am. by the long roll. Moved about $1/2$ mile & lay still until after sunrise. Then crossed the Chickehominy, passed over the battle-field of yesterday—saw a good many of our dead & a great many Yankee dead. The Yankees scattered their knapsacks, clothes, wagons, etc. all over the country. We met more than 100 prisoners & several hundred horses & mules. Considerable cannonading this evening. We moved quite near the line.

Tues. 1st [July]. Moved about 6 or 7 am, passed 2 or 3 Yankee hospitals and a great many Yankee prisoners, wagons, etc. Our brigade, now commanded by [Lt.] Col. [Wm. S.H.] Baylor of the 5th Va., was ordered to the front. We waded 2 small streams, climbed a fence and became engaged about 8 pm. About the first round I received a flesh wound in the right arm, near the wrist. I then handed the colors to Benj. F. Coffman, & went off the field under a very heavy shelling; the Yankees using the guns on their gunboats. I stopped at a hospital about $1^1/2$ miles from the battlefield & had a Yankee prisoner to dress my wound. This was the "Battle of Malvern Hill." Casualties in Co. "H"; James N. Alger, killed; Benj. F. Coffman, slightly wounded in side by ball; David C. Hite, in right arm by shell; Willis Cubbage, ball through hand; & Jessie W. Riley, in left hand by shell. Joseph Perry of Co. "I", was mortally wounded & Samuel Switzer, of same co., severely wounded in right [illeg.].

Wed. 2nd. Rained nearly all night. David Hite, Benj. Coffman, Jessie W. Riley & myself started about 2 pm for Savage Station. Got there about dark, took the cars for Richmond, reached Richmond at midnight. Arm pained me very much.

Thurs. 3rd. Slept until day on the floor at the depot. Got a pass to to to Staunton, but were too late for the cars. Papa found us. We put up for the night at the Monument Hotel. I went to a hospital & found Ambrose Rothgeb, who, alas!, had lost his left hand in the fight of Monday. Hunted for Daniel Brubaker, who had lost his right eye, but could not find him. We looked through the state capitol this evening. ...

Remarkably, George Buswell's father, Thomas, in government service at Richmond, has learned of his son's wound and has been able to locate him. At Malvern Hill, the final battle of the Seven Days, the Union threat to the Confederate capital is finally ended. Of 129 rank and file in the 33rd Va. just before the battle, four are killed, including James Alger of Co. H. Of the 29 wounded, four are from Co. H including David Hite and Ambrose Rothgeb, who is later to become school teacher to Bettie and Ella Hite. Total casualties in these Seven Days' Battles have been: Union- 1734 killed, 8062 wounded, 6053 missing; Confederate- 2820 killed, 14011 wounded, 752 missing.

Isaac's account of the campaign, from the perspective of the Dixie Artillery, is written in a letter to his young brother Daniel S. Hite. The unit has fired its first shots of the war at Frayser's Farm on June 30. Daniel Brubaker loses an eye to a shell at Malvern Hill on July 1. He is later to marry Fannie Gander, thus becoming a brother-in-law to Isaac. John Keyser, killed on June 30, is listed on the rolls of Co. D, 7th Va. Cav., rather than of the Dixie Artillery. Martin Coffman and Isaac Maggart are near neighbors of the Hites.

Camp Near Richmond July 8th '62
Dear Brother:
Having just returned to Camp once more, after two weeks fighting the Yankees, I will write you a few lines. To attemp to give anything like a full detail of all that transpired in this grand movement, would consume more time and space than I feel willing at present to give, knowing that you already have heard the most of them. I have yet been spared while hundreds have been hurried off. The Casualties in our Comp. are slight comparitavely speaking, though the best men in

the Comp. were the ones that were hurt. Ambrose Rothgeb, Daniel Brubaker, and John Keyser were the only ones that were badly wounded, the latter died the same night. Ambrose Rothgeb had his left hand blown off, and Daniel Brubaker was wounded along his right side from head to foot. His right eye is thought to be out. Besides these there were several others that were bruised slightly by fragmens of shells. This was done in the monday's fight, being the only one that we were in, though in the Friday's fight shell bursted all around us—several of the boys run very narrow escapes.

Upon the whole this is though[t] to be a great victory for us and no doubt will add greatly to our cause abroad. McClellands army is very much demoralized beyond a doubt. It has been estimated that he lost at least some 35000 in killed, wounded, deserters, and prisners. Our loss has also been enormous. David was wounded through his left arm on tuesday which I suppose you have heard of if he has not got home. There are many other things that I might write, but I will stop for the present.

I hope some of you will write to me as soon as you get this, and tell me what mischief the Yankees have done in Page. I learn that they have nearly ruined Isaac Magart, besides many others. Tell me whether they burnt much fencing for father. Col. Buswell told me that the Yankees caught you knapping in Martin Coffman's wheat field, though they payrolled you.

Yours as ever
Isaac

A few weeks later Isaac's father writes with details of the "mischief the Yankees have done." Henry Gander's house is on the Shenandoah, south of the "White House". The bridge at the White House has been destroyed earlier this summer to prevent the joining of Union armies under generals James Shields and John C. Frémont. David has been at home recuperating from his wound, but as of August 12 has returned to Company H. John also has been at home recuperating from the accidental gunshot wound reported on May 22 in his diary.

Page County, Va.. August 17th 1862

Dear Son Isaac,

I received a letter from you yesterday and was glad to hear from you and that you was well, you wish to know what the yankees have done. our damage alone here is near $1000. we have not got ahorse *any more. we have got the two yearlin colts and the sucklin colt that fan had in the spring, the following is a list of the property taken,*

Barney and fan $200 each	$400
28 Barrels of flour $6 per bbl..	168
125 Bushels of corn	125
11 head of hogs $6 each	66
6 head of sheep 2..50 each	15
1 steer	30
300 hundred weight of Bacon	60
100 hundred bushels of oats	50
	$914

besides the butter and milk and bread they eat at the house sometimes 10 to fifteen eat in one day, they dug near all our irish potatoes cut off some bridle rains and carried them off some buckets and some bags, David's bea hive, many other things too teagieous to mention, Barney was taken when Shields was here the secont time out of the field, fan was not interrupted until a few days bfore the third army went away, when they first came in which was directly after harves. David was here then he taken them up on top of the ridg stayed about one week. we though[t] they ware leaving he came home, the yankees still did not leave, he took them up the secont time stayed a few days and brought them back again, thinking there was mutch danger of them being taken up there, the yankees in stead of leaving mooved their camps in to Daniel Rothgbs. David then went over the mountain to get out of their way, I and John went to hauling in grain. hauled in all the grain and hay and plowed over a good part of our corn, the yankees often meet us in the road and was all round us in the field and at the house and barn but never interrupted us nor our horses. we then heard they ware taking horses from the Hawksbill, Reuben Rothgeb and others had taken their horses over the mountain, we got a little alarmed and we though[t] we would better send them over the mountain Mann Rothgeb said he would take them. when Barney was taken we got a coalt of Mr.. Tobin that had been worked some to haul in our hay and grain. he said we could have it all the fall. I said I would take all the pains I could but would not be responsible if it was taken, so Mann Rothgeb took the two work horses and the colts went as fair as Mr.. Ganders. the next morning he was to start by day light. Alexandria Rothgeb concluted to go with him. they did not get off soon. the yankees that morning crossed the River at the white house which they ware not in the habit of d[o]ing. Mann crossed at Henkels did not se them till he meet them at Mr.. Shearleys sawmill where he and Alexandria ware taken prissoners and the two horses. the colts they left. I heard of it the next morning went to town to try to get the horses back but could not. Mann and Alex.. boath had to take the oath to be released, had I kept my horses at home they would not been interrupted I am satisfied the yankees left the next day, John Lionberger loned me an old horse is all my dependanc to seed with. ther was a good many horses taken out of the County. the most of them were sent off and found by the yankees and cused of being bushwackers, and of course taken. very few were taken from home. many of the sitisens from the Hawksbill and out towards the Ridg ware taken up and carried to town and forsed to take the oath. none from the River nor the creek, we had no fencing burned, Shields men the second time ware camped on both sides of the Creek at Corbins and the sawmill, and burnet many rails for Megard [Maggart] and Young, many ware camped over at David Kiblers and from there out several miles the other side of town. there was mutch damage done to the farmers near Luray. Mr.. Chapman has suffered very mutch. a greate many negroes have left and gone off. they also camped at the uper road at your uncle Abram Hite bunned many rails for him and others. Millrun has suffere[d] very mutch from one end to the other Isaac Megard has but one colt in the horse line, uncle Abram Spitler has but one horse, I could freely give up all if I had my horses back. the corn look very well considering the tending it had. we have not heard from David since he left. I suppose he is gone to the army, this leaves us all well. I am as ever your affectionate Father

Daniel Hite

From early maps we can visualize the area Daniel Hite has described. Martin Henkel's farm is just upriver from Henry Gander's. Martin Shirley's sawmill is just over a mile up Massanutten Creek on the west side of the river. Corbin and Kibler are on Mill Creek near Hamburg, and Isaac Maggart is Daniel Hite's nearest neighbor, just across Mill Creek.

Perhaps it is near this time that Bettie Hite, now just 19, has the experiences reported nearly 100 years later by her daughter Mary R. Brubaker [*Page News and Courier*, October 19, 1961]:

On the opposite hill from the house was a big woods in which some Yankees were camped. One evening my mother went to the barn-yard to milk when a Yankee walked up, took her bucket from her and began to milk. In those days all farm girls wore sunbonnets.

DISTANT BATTLES AND YANKEES IN THE VALLEY 111

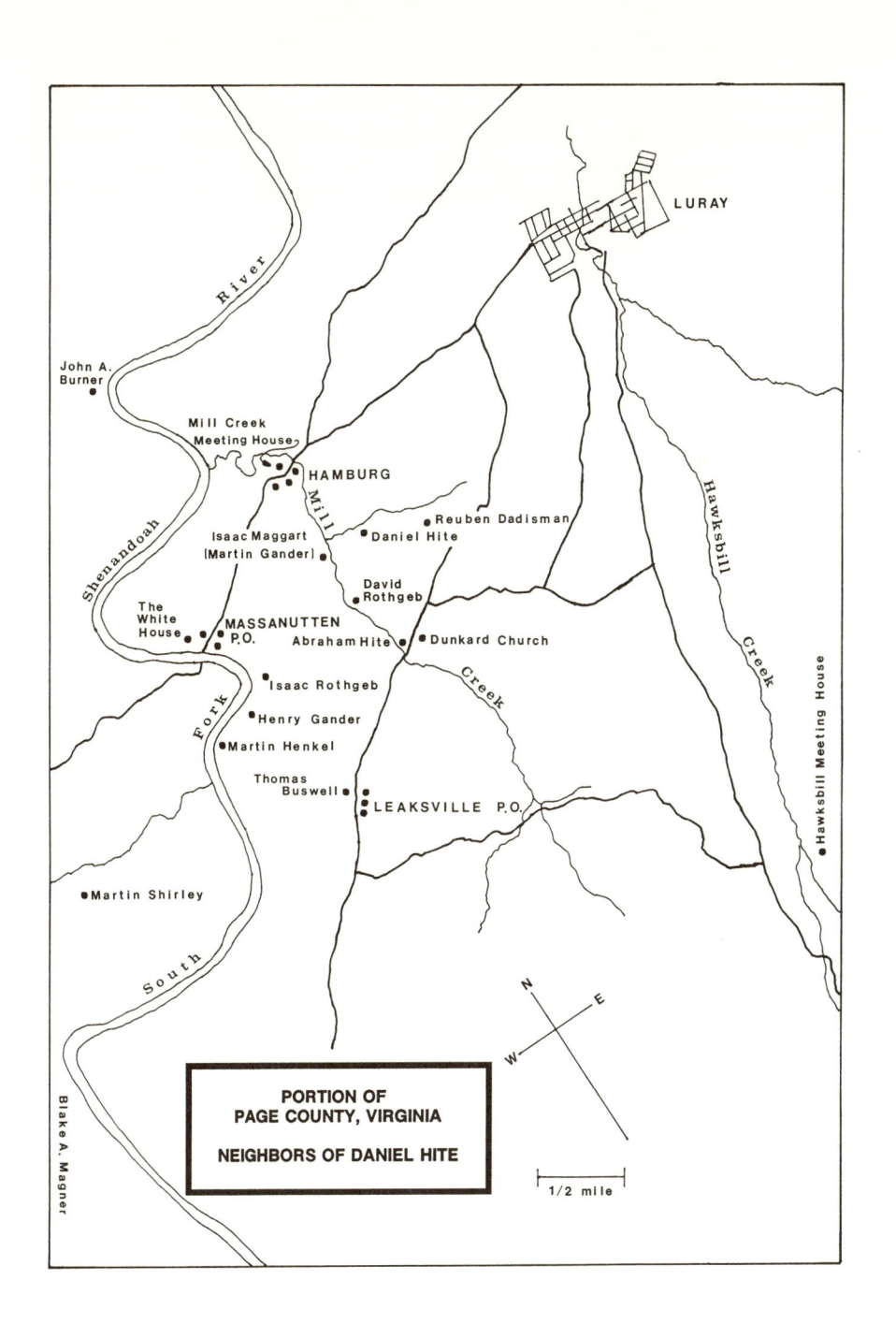

PORTION OF PAGE COUNTY, VIRGINIA

NEIGHBORS OF DANIEL HITE

There was a drizzling rain that evening and her bonnet got wet. Every now and then she would take off her wet bonnet, slam it in the Yankee's face, telling him to give her the bucket. After so long he grew tired of that and gave her the bucket. She finished milking the cow, and started back to the house. When she set down the bucket in order to open the gate to let the cow into the field, the Yankee, who had lingered nearby, picked up the bucket and started away with it. She ran after him, grabbed the handle of the bucket and held on. The Yankee also held on to the bucket and dragged her down the hill, across a little stream and up another hill toward the Yankee camp. Her father was in the yard, watching these proceedings and when he saw that she was still holding onto the bucket as the Yankee neared camp, he sent one of her brothers to bring her back.

On another day a Yankee, apparently planning to steal whatever he could, came to the house and went rummaging through the rooms. My mother and one of her sisters followed him and saw him go upstairs into my mother's room. In this room she had a little chest in which she was putting away some things to keep. Among these things was a beautiful home-woven bedspread. My mother had locked this chest and the Yankee ordered her to open it. She did so and when he saw this beautiful spread he picked it up and started down the steps. She was determined not to let him have it and went after him. She grabbed one end of the spread and begged him to let her have it back. He went on down the steps with my mother still swinging on the spread. He dragged her all the way downstairs and across the living room. As he went out the front door he threw the spread back to her and told her to "take her old blanket."

With George Buswell wounded at home and no word in this period from John or David Hite, we take up the narrative of Company H from the diary of its captain, Michael Shuler. In the Battle of Cedar Mountain which he describes below, the 33rd Regiment is led by Lt. Col. Ned Lee, Col. Neff being under arrest in a dispute with Gen. Winder. Union forces under Gen. Banks are driven back in this opening round of the 2nd Manassas campaign. The Stonewall Brigade's commander, C. S. Winder, hated by the troops for his harsh discipline, is mortally wounded. Casualties reported: Confederate– 229 killed, 1047 wounded, 31 missing; Union– 450 killed, 660 wounded, 290 missing.

DISTANT BATTLES AND YANKEES IN THE VALLEY   113

Aug 9. We were in line this morning before day, thought we would have the enemy upon us, it was nothing but their scouts. Marched by sun up in direction of Culpeper C.H. It is very hot [yet] today. The men suffer a great deal by the heat. When we arrive within about 8 miles of C.C.H. rested and found our artillery getting in position. Canonading commenced about 12 M. We were soon advancing; from the hill we could see the yankee line. Our batteries soon advanced from the hill. Ewell's division on the right. Hill's in the centre. Ours on the left. We lay under a very heavy fire of shell before going in the fight. Not more than 10 minutes after the Musketry Commenced upon our Right we were ordered to advance. Col [Samuel H.] Reynolds [31st Va. Inf.] in advance of the Brigade (he having command after Gen Winder fell). We had not got far before he came galloping back [to s]ay 1st Brigade prepare for a charge bayonets. The Brigade charge with a terable yell the Yanks fled. The men fought well I had two wounded. Captured a great many prisinors The enemy were driven from the field leaving their killed and wounded and a great amt. of Arms. We encamped on the Battle field. ...

Aug 11 Monday. The wagons left last night about 12. Father came to camp this morning. ...

Aug 12th Tues. Did not march until after sun rise. Road was very good. Lieut. Kite was away with the prisenors. 'Tis very warm. Marched very hard. Had a very heavy rain when we got this side of Orange C.H. Got to camp about an hour by Sun. find Nichols there who had been exchanged. Hite & Cullars had also returned.

Return Nichols has indeed returned. David Hite and Joseph L. Cullers come in just two weeks before the 2nd Manassas battle in which both are wounded, David for the second time. Two days later three more come in, including Robert Aleshire and Reuben Comer from being AWOL. John Wilson is killed at Groveton just a fortnight later. Shuler continues:

Aug 13th Wednes. Father started home today. I sent by him $510.00. I drew $493.00 this morning. Every quiet [sic].

Aug 14th Thurs. This day has been set apart by order. Gen. Jackson for prayer and thanksgiving for the late victory at Cedar Run. I have for the first time the duties of field officer of the day to perform. Robt Aleshire, Jno S. Wilson and Reub Comer came in today. ...

114   The Painful News I Have to Write

The battles of Groveton and 2nd Manassas, described below, halt Union General John Pope's Virginia campaign and permit Jackson's invasion of Maryland just a week later. The Dixie Artillery, with just two guns, is engaged on both August 28 and 30, being credited on the 30th with breaking up the attack of Fitz-John Porter's Federal force. The Stonewall Brigade, beginning with just 635 effectives, is heavily engaged in both battles. Not reported by Shuler is the death on Aug. 28 of Lt. Col. John Francis Neff, popular young commander of the 33rd Regiment.

Aug 28 Thursday. We rested a little north of the old Battlefield of Manassa. Shifted positions often during the day and had nearly given out the idea of a fight as the sun was just sinking in the west. About an hour by Sun we heard distant canonading in the direction of Thorough fare Gap. We were ordered forward to the Right of Grafton [Groveton]. lay in the woods a short time advanced just at sun set and fought for about an hour and a half the severest infantry fighting I ever saw. drove the enemy back upon the Battlefield at night. I went to see my wounded. I had one killed and 8 wounded in my Co. viz. Killed Jno. J. Wilson. Wounded Serj. [James W.] Menifee, prvts [Charles W.] Webster, Ambrose Huffman, David Hite, Geo. Kite, Jos. L. Cullars, Silas A. Somers, I. P. Printz. None, I think dangerously.

Aug 29th Friday. I went early this morning to the Hospital to see my wounded when on the Road the Yankees Run in upon our Ambulance nearly getting me. I was not able to get to my Regt. this day. The Regt. was again engaged. My Company lost 2 killed, Hiram Strole, Jno. W. Modesitt. fell back a short distance and were not able to get the dead off.

Aug 30th Saturday. Got with the Regt. about 10 A.M. We lay in line of Battle untill 3 P.M. when the greatest Battle of the war commenced in earnest. Regular skirmishing had been kept up all day. The Battle opened Right in our front. we were ordered immediately forward. We met a desperate fire but pushed forwards until we gained the old Rail Road. Soon got the Yanks in full retreat. Longstreet closed in upon the Right and did some desperate fighting. finally got them to Running. We followed in pursuit about an hour after dark encamped right near stone Bridge. We had in today's fight the following wounded: Serj. [Edward C.] Mauck, Corp. D[avid] Stomback [Stombaugh], pvts. Chas. A. Young, Robert Cubbage, Jno. L. Good & Joseph Decker. I am not left with not over 15 men present in My Company.

DISTANT BATTLES AND YANKEES IN THE VALLEY

Joseph F. Decker dies of his wounds on Sept. 14. Total causalties to the Stonewall Brigade over these three days are 67 killed and 348 wounded of an initial strength of 635 men. Reported losses for all forces total: Union– 1747 killed, 8452 wounded and 4623 missing; Confederate– 1090 killed, 6154 wounded. After this disastrous Virginia campaign of Aug. 23 to Sept. 1 the pompous General Pope is relieved of his Union command. His defeat gives Lee an opportunity to send Jackson on the Maryland incursion perhaps best remembered from John Greenleaf Whittier's poem, "Barbara Frietchie." Both the Dixie Artillery and the Stonewall Brigade join Jackson's march to Frederick, where Shuler's description of the welcoming citizens does not apply to Whittier's heroine:

> *"Shoot, if you must, this old gray head,*
> *But spare your country's flag," she said.*

Rather, in the light of Shuler's note of long marches and short rations, the poem's opening stanzas seem more apt:

> *Up from the meadows, rich with corn,*
> *Clear in the cool September morn*
> *The clustered spires of Frederick stand*
> *Green-walled by the hills of Maryland.*
>
> *Round about them orchards sweep,*
> *Apple and peach tree fruited deep–*
> *Fair as the garden of the Lord*
> *To the eyes of that famished Rebel horde.*

Sept. 5th Friday. Marched very early. Got to the Patomac River at 1 P.M. We forded the River at Hollin Ferry. Marched on Frederick City Road about 6 miles. Marched about 16 miles.

Sept 6th Saturday. Didn't get our Rations last night. Marched before day towards Frederick City. Marched by Monocacy Junction. passed through Frederick City about 1 P.M. and encamped 2 miles North of city on Baltimore & Frederick Cty Road. Remained in Camp 3 days. Everything quiet. Citizens welcome us in Maryland. Many flocking in to join us. Soldiers conscious to purchase at the stores in town. not many open after Saturday. We are treated very kindly by the citizens.

116   THE PAINFUL NEWS I HAVE TO WRITE

Strict orders in regard to interrupting citizens property. Geo Griffith, Benj. F. Beahm, & Israel Shaffer returned to Company Sunday also [blank] Printz joined Company. A. J. Stoneberger was discharged Monday 8th by order Col. Grigsby sent a letter home by him.

Griffith and Shaffer have been AWOL and Beahm sick. It is little wonder that Shuler misses the first name of Isabias A. Printz who enlists this day. The reason for Andrew J. Stonebarger's discharge is not known. By mid-week the troops march west from Frederick, passing through Braddock Heights on what is now Route 40A.

Sept 10th Wednes. Marched 3 A.M. this morning passed through Frederick City before day light to the F. City & Hagerstown Road. Marched through Middletown crossed the Blue Ridge into Washington County. encamped at the foot of the Mountain near Boonsboro. Cooked three days rations. Marched 16 miles today.

Sept. 11 Thurs. Marched out the Meadow by day light. passed through Boonsboro and took the Williams Port Road, passed through Williams Port, crossed the Patomac into V^a. after marching some 2 miles on the Martinsburg Pike we took a road leading through Heyersville. Marched within a mile of North Mountain Station. The Regt. was on picket at the Station. Marched about 20 miles. All very nearly broken down.

Sept 12 Friday. Marched by day light passed through Heyersville, took the Martinsburg Road arrived within sight of Martinsburg in a woods. Was exceeding warm marching. The Yanks left town 2 this morning. Marched 8 miles. Hill & Ewells' divisions have passed on. We had orders to March but has been Countermanded. Wrote a letter home.

Sept. 13. Saturday. Marched out Camp at 4 $^1/2$ this morning. passed through Martinsburg by day light. took the Road to Harpers Ferry. Marched by the Cross Roads. Left the direct Road to harpers Ferry to the left and took a road leading to the Charlestown & Harpers Ferry Pike about 2 miles below Charlestown. Encamped in a woods about a mile & half from the pike, in sight of Bolivar and very plain view of the enemy's Camp. Shelling Commenced about 12 M. and kept up until dark. Marched about 16 miles today.

Distant Battles and Yankees in the Valley

Sept. 14th Sunday. Shelling commenced before sun up this morning. We marched out Camp about 9 A.M. Marched to the left of Boliver near the Railroad and lay there until P.M. when we marched across the rail road and took position on a hill to the left of Boliver. Two of Capt. [Arthur L.] Rogers [Louden Artillery] pieces opened about 3 1/2 P.M. and kept firing until dark about 9 in the night. we still changed our position farther to the left and nearer the Ferry. posted pickets and lay upon our arms [all] night without blankets. Marched in all to day about 5 miles.

Sept. 15th Monday. Marched back to the same position we had late last evening. before day this morning Canonading commenced on the Right of our line. before sun rise the enemy reply from Boliver. Capt. Page opened two parot Guns on Boliver but the enemy do not Reply. Moved to the position we held last night when the white flag was discovered on Boliver. Soon recd. orders to advance that the enemy had surrendered. We were not permitted to go on Boliver. The no. of Prisinors is estimated at 12 thousand, great many Wagons &c. Were ordered back to the wagons to Cook rations. Jno Hite & Jno Decker Returned to the Co. Marched about 6 miles to day. orders to March as soon as we get Rations.

John Decker's return is from an unauthorized absence, and John Hite has been recuperating from his wounded hand. David is still at home from his second wounding. In the surrender of Harpers Ferry, Union losses are reported at 44 killed, 173 wounded, and 12,520 missing and captured. Confederate losses are 500 killed and wounded. More importantly, the Confederates gain a strategic position (to be lost again just four days later) and a vast supply of food, artillery, and small arms. Shuler's diary continues:

Sept. 16th Tuesday. Reville about 12 in the night, marched at 1 A.M. passed through Shepardstown a little after sun up. waded the Patomac again and are again in Mayerland. Canonading commenced in our front very early this morning. Marched to a woods but a short distance from the Canonading and rested. Marched to the left of Longstreets line of Battle, took position in line about sun set. The yankees opened a very heavy fire of shell upon us. Infantry skirmishing to our Right. Marched 15 miles.

> *Sept, 17th Wednes. We lay on our arms all night in line Battle. Skirmishing kept up all night to our right. day light heavy firing commenced. The enemy advanced upon our line about sun up, the fighting was terrible. we have possession of the Battlefield. The fight has been general to day and very hotly contested. I am feeling very ill this evening. Went to the rear.*

Michael Shuler's brief account gives only a glimpse of this Battle of Sharpsburg or Antietam in which the Stonewall Brigade is heavily engaged. Though they are not directly engaged, the Dixie Artillery in which Isaac Hite and Martin Gander are serving comes under artillery fire as they approach Sharpsburg on September 17. Total casualties for this, the bloodiest day of the War, are reported as: Union– 2010 killed, 9416 wounded, 1043 missing; Confederate– 1890 killed, 9770 wounded, and 2304 missing.

The parole and exchange routine noted in John's following letter is common practice in this period of the war. The official agreement between the warring parties, known as "The Cartel of July 22, 1862," is here quoted in part:

> ARTICLE 6. *The stipulations... to be of binding obligation during the continuance of the war, it matters not which party may have the surplus of prisoners, the great principles involved being, first, an equitable exchange of prisoners...; second, that... officers and men of different services may be exchanged according to the same scale of equivalents; third, that all prisoners... are to be exchanged or paroled in ten days from the time of their capture, if it be practicable to transfer them to their own lines...; fourth, that no officer, soldier, or employee... is to be considered as exchanged and absolved from his parole until his equivalent has actually reached the lines of his friends; fifth, that the parole forbids the performance of field, garrison, police, or guard, or constabulary duty.*

John Hite's letter to sister Bettie indicates he has been captured in unknown circumstances on the eve of the battle and immediately paroled. Even on this, the bloodiest day of the War, his own officers will not permit him to take up arms until officially exchanged. Curiously, John's letter paper is embossed with the single word "UNION" under the stars and stripes. Envelope addressed:

Distant Battles and Yankees in the Valley

Urbanity of
Col. Buswell

Miss Bettie Hite
Page Co.
Va.

Sept 21st/62
Camp near Martinsburgh

Dear Bettie:
As I have an opportunity of sending you a letter I embrace it. We are now about 6 miles below Martinsburgh on the road that leads to Williamsport. Since I last wrote I have been in Maryland 4 day not there long enough to form an opinion about it. On Wednesday last there was a hard battle fought near Sharpsburgh M.D. Some parts of the battle field we repulsed the yankees, whilst in others they repulsed us, neither party can claim much of a victory to my opinion. We captured a good many prisoners they also done the same. The next day after the battle I went over a good deal of the battle field; found the dead yankees at least twice as thick as ours. We were taken in the evening before the general engagement. I went in with them but as I have not been exchanged yet to a certainty the Capt. sent me to the rear. I went out under a heavy cannonading, had many shells to burst all around me, one solid cannon ball rolled between my legs; supposed it would have broken my leg if it had struck it. The ball passed on some distance struck a solid fencerail which stoped it, I then went to it. Capt. Walton will make out a report of my being captured, will send it to Jackson, then if I have not been exchanged I will be released immediately. I have not taken a gun yet, of course the officers will not let me untill they know I have been exchanged.

John T. Johnston, George Griffith, A.H. Keyser are the wounded my company. G. B. Long missing supposed to be killed or badly wounded & captured. The Capt. told me this morning, that he expected I would be appointed Serg. Major of the Regt. you need not let the news go out of the family for the present. We captured the whole yankee force at Harpers Ferry about 13000 strong with every thing that is necessary to equip such an army which of course was a great deal.

I don't [hear if?] the Dixie Artillery was in the recent engagement. Col. Buswell & son got to us this morning. If you see B. F. Coffman or any one that is coming to our company tell them to enquire at Winchester Post Office for a letter or letters for me individually. If you answer this send it by some one for I can't tell where we will be soon.

John

Service records report John T. Johnston and Alexander H. Keyser wounded in action, Gideon B. Long taken prisoner, and George A. Griffith absent sick from Sept. 17. Capt. David H. Walton of Co. K has been wounded at 2nd Manassas on August 28 and is now on administrative assignment in the rear. Benjamin Coffman of the Page Greys has been at home recuperating from wounds at Malvern Hill in July.

There is little to report for the balance of 1862—no letters and no personal diaries of the Hites. The Dixie Artillery is disbanded on October 4 and all its men and equipment transferred to Cayce's Company. The Stonewall Brigade spends two months in the lower Shenandoah Valley, moving from camp to camp and tearing up railroad tracks near Martinsburg. On November 21 they begin the march to join General Lee in the vicinity of Fredericksburg. Michael Shuler's diary reports an amusing incident enroute.

> *Dec 2nd. Marched by 7 A.M. to the Fredericksburg - Richmond Road the Road leading to Guinea Station. Encamped in a woods to left of road about 2 miles of station. Marched about 10 miles to day. I was ordered under arrest by Col. Lee for shooting my pistol at a squirrel when we stopped this evening*
>
> *Dec 3rd & 4th. We lay in camp quietly was relieved of arrest the evening of the 3rd. Jesse Riley & D[aniel] B. Abbott came on the 3rd.*

Shuler's arrest by Lt. Col. Ned Lee is quickly resolved. Throughout his diary, which ends a week after this incident, he has kept careful note of returning troops. In this case, Riley has returned from wounding at Malvern Hill, and we have no explanation for Abbott's absence.

At the Battle of Fredericksburg on December 13, the 33rd Regiment comes under fire, but is never closely engaged. Col. Ned Lee, Robert E. Lee's distant kinsman, resigns command of the 33rd Regt. due to ill health, and, shortly before Christmas, the Stonewall Brigade goes into winter quarters at Moss Neck near Guiney Station.

CHAPTER 8

Winter and Spring, 1863

*"I hope you may get home soon,
for I have a crow to pick with you."*

As 1863 begins, the Stonewall Brigade is in Camp Winder, their winter quarters south of Fredericksburg at Moss Neck, the Richard Corbin plantation. The camp streets are muddy, and fires in the crude log huts are smoky, but camp life is not too uncomfortable. John Hite starts the year with a letter home.

Jan. 7th 1863
Camp Winder Caroline Co. Va.

Dear Father:

I presume you all begin to think that I am not going to write any more. The reas[on] I did not write sooner, was because I have been waiting to see whether I'll get the position of Quarter-Master Sergeant of the Regt. or not. I have not the appointment yet though Capt. Martin says I will, with Shuler's recommendation which I have; so you will please send me the comfort back, I sent home by Martin Kite, as I'll get it hauled & a horse to ride besides. The revolver I sent back by him, told him to keep it 'till you or some of the family called for it. It got out of fix on the way down, couldn't be stiched from what cause I know not. The boots I had made were too tight in the instep, sold them, and bought another pair; would be glad if you would send me leather to have them halfsoled, as they will need it in several weeks. We arrived here safe with our prisoners on Sunday before Christmas who were immediately conveyed to the guardhouse there to await their trial. Three of the number have been Court-Martialed, their sentence not known; am confident they will be severely punished. Some 8 or 9 have been shot for desertion since the army came this side of the Ridge; many others being put to hard government labor in chains for different periods, then branded with the letter D. from three to four inches long, have half of their heads shave, then get a dishonorable discharge. Our present camp is ten or twelve miles south of Freder-

icksburgh near the Rappahannock; a nice camp ground only we have sorry water, a great objection.

The yankees are said to be in large force on the opposite side of the river, & down towards Acquia Creek, presume they will remain there 'till spring; unless the weather remains mild as it has been. This Brigade during the past year, was in 9 engagements victorious in all save one; had 1220 men killed & wounded, had on the 1$\underline{st}$ day of the present year 1200 men present for duty, marched 1500 miles averaging over 100 miles per Month. The fight at Murfreesboro Tenn. (which I guess you have heard of) resulted in the rout of the yankee army with heavy loss in killed & wounded, the capture of many prisoners 200 wagons 24 pieces of artillery 5000 stand of small arms; & considerable quantity of commissary stores, so says Bragg's official report. The company number at present about 25 for duty. John [N.] Koontz's son was sent from here a few days since very sick, had the fever I believe, was going to Richmond provided his illness would admit of it. Tell Reubin Rothgebs that Frank. is well and hearty. There has been a detail made from the whole Brigade to go to the Valley to hunt the deserters, two from the company, Ambrose Huffman & Alfred Kite.

I close hoping to hear from some of you soon. I send my kindest regards to you all.

Yours &c.
J. P. Hite

P. S. I'll give you my full address in order that yours will come direct.

Jackson's Division Paxton's Brigade
Com. H. 33rd Regt. Va. Vols.
Guinea Station
Virginia

There is no record that John ever was promoted to quartermaster sergeant under Albion Martin, the Commissary Captain. From the 33rd Regiment, there is a total of 33 courts-martial between January and May of 1863, including 30 for desertion. Of ten sentenced to be shot, at least eight escape this fate through technicalities. The report of Brigadier Frank Paxton confirms John's figure of 1220 men killed or wounded in 1862. Of a nominal 1000 men per regiment, he reports a total of just under 1700 men present in the brigade's five regiments. The Battle of Murfreesboro on December 31 to January 2 is not Confederate victory but nearly a standoff with about equal losses on both sides. Alexander H. Koontz, only 15 years old, is to die of his illness on January 18 at Guinea

WINTER AND SPRING 1863

Station just three miles from Camp Winder. Franklin Rothgeb, the Hite neighbor who was reported so ill last winter, has enlisted in Co. H as of September 23, 1862.

Cousin George D. Buswell has been elected 2nd Lt. of the Page Greys in September, 1862. These excerpts from his diary give a further picture of life in winter quarters, including some fine dining. He reports on an excursion for picket duty along the Rappahannock and sends more news of courts-martial, including the calling of John Hite and others as witnesses.

Thurs. 1st. [January] This, the first day of 1863, finds us at Camp Winder, a good & well arranged camp near Moss Neck. Capt. [Michael] Shuler & Lt. [Perry] Kite walked out of camp & came back with a very fine turkey for which they paid $8.00. We cleaned & cooked it. Very fat.

Fri. 2nd. [Benjamin F.] Beahm went to Guiney's Station, brought us 1 gal. oysters, paid $10.00. Cooked half of them just before we retired for night. Capt. Martin & Benny Wierman ate with us. [Benjamin B. Wierman of Co. G is later promoted to commissary sergeant under Capt. Albion Martin, perhaps in place of John Hite.]

Sat. 3rd. Sent A. H. Koontz away sick, to the hospital at Guiney's Station. Ate the remainder of our oysters. Wm. Brubaker ate with us. Lt. Chadduck on guard. ... [William A. Brubaker, once sergeant, is on detached service as wagoner to the company.]

Tues. 6th. The <u>boys</u> are making a hominy mortar.

Wed. 7th. We are busy beating & cooking some hominy.

Thurs. 8th. Capt. Shuler's father [John], Mr. [Mark] Ruffner & Mr. [John N.] Koontz came to camp. Mr. Shuler brought us a new mess chest full of provisions. Mr. Ruffner brought me a box & a letter.

Fri. 9th. Papa came to us from Richmond. Orders to cook 1 days rations, to go on picket tomorrow.

Sat. 10th. Reveille at 6 am, moved at 8 am. Capt. Shuler & Lt. Kite stayed in camp to attend a court martial, as witnesses. 4 or 5 miles from camp we came to a halt, pitched our tent-fly & built a large fire, had a merry time. It rains.

Sun. 11th. Somewhat cloudy, but no rain. I scouted around the river, saw a few Yankees, nothing of interest. Orders to cook 2 days rations; to go on out-post tomorrow.

Mon. 12th. Went on post on the river bank. Saw a few Yanks across the river. Lt. Chadduck is in charge of parts of Cos. C & H on a post at a house on the river's edge. Have good quarters.

Tues. 13th. Sergt. [John W.] Rosenberger, [Benjamin F.] Beahm & myself went down the river 1 1/2 miles & back; saw couple Yankee pickets. ...

Wed. 14th. We were relieved from post & went back to the wagons. E[dmund] J. Rothgeb, B[enjamin] F. Coffman, J[ohn] P. Hite, Geo. T. Wilson, Willis Cubbage & myself were ordered back to camp as witnesses in court martial. Found all our cooking utensils stolen. ...

Tues. 20th. Capt. Shuler & myself went to see a review of Brig. Gen. Lee's Brig. of Cavalry near Gen. Jackson's Headquarters. Gen. R. E. Lee, the old Gen., was reviewing officer. Gens. Jackson, Stuart, A. P. Hill, Pender & Jones were present. The review was something grand. Some ladies present. Inspection in our Brigade. Lts. Chadduck & Kite on guard. Rainy.

We leave George Buswell's diary with this account of the grand review of Fitzhugh Lee's cavalry brigade. During this quiet interlude, John Hite gets several interesting letters from home, this first from Mary Ann (Mollie) Gander, who frequently alludes to John's relationship with Sue Coffman.

River Dale Virginia Jan. 15/63

My Dear Friend:-

I will now try to scrible you a few lines, in answer to your kind and interesting letter which I received on the 12th inst, and indeed it was perused with great pleasure, as it has been a good long while since I have received a letter from you or any one else. Well indeed I was surprised though when I got that letter from you for I thought that you would occupy the most of your time writing to Sue, heard that you and Sue were a going to get married shortly. I suppose you will be one of the boys that will get a furlough to come home.

Winter and Spring 1863

Mary Ann (Gander) Hite 1842–1943

From ambrotype circa 1862.
The "Miss Mollie" who corresponded with John and married Isaac Hite.

I hope you may get home soon for I have a crow to pick with you; and I guess you will have a bag to hold the feathers.

*John I,ve saw the best holydays this chrismas than I saw in my life only wish that you could have been here   I know that [you] would have enjoyed yourself very much   (will you turn over)
            (indeed)*

I was at three parties and I tell you we had a jolly time. We had a nice little time here Chrismas day Sue Bettie and Ellie were here they were the only strange girls and they was a boy for every girl I wont mention the boys names for it will take up to much room. there would have been room for you too if you would have come. Sue would liked very much have [to] seen you on that day as well as myself, but I hope and trust in our Saviour that we may have the pleasure of meeting again soon and have a happy time. Oh: could there be peace again I would be as happy as a bird. You said that you wouldn't be surprised of hearing that somebody and I would be joined in wedlock. I do not know what for lock that is but I suppose when it is locked it can not be unlocked again. he has not gotten home yet. Well indeed I must close or else I will get so far off the track that you will not see any sense in it. I would sooner talk to you than to write if it could be so. this is such a sorry letter that I am ashamed to send it you always write such interesting letters that I never get tired of reading them. I hope I,le do better next time. Please excuse bad writing and mistakes (my love to all)

From your true friend Mollie A. G.

In margin: *Write soon and give me all the news. Please do not let any one see this. it's too bad to let you see it.*

At top of second page in a curlicue cloud: *Good night and pleasant dreams be thine. a kiss for you I have*

Cousin Ann Huffman writes the next letter to John with more rumors of his unconfirmed engagement to "Sue." By this date Isaac Hite has been enrolled in Lee's bodyguard, but apparently has not yet been posted to his duty station.

Winter and Spring 1863

Locust Dale
Feb the 6/63

Dear Cousin

Your kind and welcome letter came to hand a week or two ago with pleasure; it came very unexpected to me as I thought of receiving a letter of most any person but you as I thought you ocupied all you leasure moments in writing to Miss Sue, but glad to see you thought of your unworthy cousin whilst your are in camp. Cousin you spoke of the pleasant times we had during the holidays. that is true but we could of enjoyed ourselves much better if this everlasting war would of been ended or that was the way with myself, some of the ladies enjoyed themselves, there was some few gentlemen in the neighbourhood but not all that I had a desire to be here.

We had a nice time at the wedding at Mr Joseph Grove,s a few weeks ago, Cousin I know you would of enjoyed yourself for there was quite a nice little crowd there about a equal number of ladies and gentlemen. Miss Mary F. Grove and Mr Thompson Brubaker was their waters. There was a great many persons at the infor. I had a invitation but did not attend as the weather was very cold and disagreeable. You said you thought Lt. Kite is a going to get married shortly. I heard he was to be married the first of the month; I do not think he will as his lady is in the hands of the Yankees, but probly she will come across the line if they have made arrangements to get married. he is at home but have not seen him yet. I read a letter the other day that Cousin Ambrose Hite written a few days ago he spoke of the disagreeable weather that has been down there. said you all keept very comfortabl in your camps I am very glad to hear you have warm camps to stay in. there has been a greateal of cold weather and snow this year. I do not see how you all keep from freezing. Cousin I must tell you I have had one sleigh ride this year and I had the promise of one last sunday but the snow did not last so I had to ride horses back to preaching. the roads were awful mudy

I heard cousin Isaac is agoing to start next monday. Cousin John don,t you think he has not been to see us yet he promised to come out this week but has not come yet. I am fearfull he will not come. I forgotten to tell you you ought to of been at home during the holidays for Miss Sue spent the most of them at your fathers. I know you would of had a nice time. There was two refugees here this week from Fredric Co. they said the Yankees were treating the people very badly. I wish old Jackson would make haste and drive them away for I think they are staying two long.

This is the second letter I have written to night. I think it is time for me to close. this leave me and the rest of the family well and also

your fathers family is well as far as I know. I will close. write soon and give me all the news.   From your true cousin Ann Huffman
To John P Hite

One of the very few mentions of slaves appears in the following letter to John from brother-in-law John A. Burner. In 1860 Page County had a total of just 850 slaves, both black and mulatto, amongst the free population of about 6950, which included about 75 free blacks and 350 free mulattoes. The Hites and their closest neighbors did not own slaves, but in 1860 John Burner owned nine including a mulatto male, aged 53; black males, 45, 28 (probably the Charles who has been drafted), and 24; a mulatto female, 31 (probably Charles's wife); and four mulatto girls (their daughters), ages 6, 4, 2, and 2 months.

In the bloody battle of Fredericksburg on December 13, Gen. Burnside has failed to gain a foothold across the Rappahannock. Union losses are 1180 killed, 9028 wounded, and 2145 missing. Confederate losses are 579 killed, 3870 wounded, and 127 missing.

Massannutten Page Cty Va February 15th 1863
Dear Brother
Your letter has reached us some days but on account of close confinement to business (partly) and of haveing Rheumatism in my rist and arms (which I now scarcely can form a letter from the effects) I have neglected to answer your letter, Your kind favor found my family in a sickly condition. I myself had been housed up about three weeks with a severe attack of Rheumatism, have got partly over it, but oweing to have the Mill to attend too and all my feeding to do myself in all sorts of weather it goes very tough with me. I can scarcely get a hand to do anything, on account of the scarsety of hands, and Charles was taken to in the draft from this County to Richmond to throw up breast works fo[r] 60 days but his time runs out tomorrow then I shall look for him home. his wife has been sick three months or upwards, Tomorrow I shall have to bury her, And the Children has been complaining a good deal with the earache. Sue had to stop her school three or four days the past week, on account of sickness. But I believe they are all right again, with the exception of myself (as above stated)
    We have had some hard Wintry weather the last of January and the first of February, But for the last week has been and is fine weather, I have been plowing some little whenever I could get a hand,

WINTER AND SPRING 1863

I have not been able to do anything with my Cloverseed yet, have some of my cornstuble to cut yet, No firewood choped, But the present prospect for peace makes me forget all that, the most I fear is that we will be disappointed in our anticipations, There has been a great many Yankee deserters passing along this way, they say the reason they are deserting so fast is that they have just found out what they are fighting for, as they have seen quite lately in Old Abe,s proclamation, I had a Yankee all night with me night before last from the State of New York, that had belonged to the regulars, by the by, he was a pretty shrewd fellow, he told me there had 30000 deserted since the Battle at Fredericksburgh, he said it was all a lie, of their men haveing orders the third time to Cross the River and refused to do it but said they would of Crossed had they not stuck fast in the mud, he said there next attack would be at three different points, And then he says there is lots of Yankees just waiting and wishing for the next Battle, for an opportunity to ground there arms, which they declare will do the first opportunity, he told me too that he had received a letter from his woman a short time ago, she wrote to him the people of York, was getting very tired of the War, Old Abe might draft but can get no person to respond to his call, And the folks there Call Fredericksburgh, Burnsides slaughterhouse. And thinks when Hooker makes the attempt it will be no better than Burnside, that is the opinion of the Soldiers generally, they declare they never can take our position unless they had some siege guns to bear upon us, John answer soon I will close for the present as it goes hard for me to write, The family joins me in love to you.

No more but remain Yours &tc J. A. Burner

John's niece, Sue, adds a concluding note which mentions her cousins Caroline, Sarah, and Emily, the daughters of John H. and Nancy Rhodes (or Roads). The names drawn include Capt. Daniel A. Grimsley, Co. B, 6th Va. Cav.; 1st Lt. Peter C. Reid and 2nd Lt. Lafayette Rhodes, Co. D, 7th Va. Cav.; and Capt. Charles T. O'Ferrall, Co. I, 7th Va. Cav.

Dear Little John,

As Uncle John is tired of writing and has left a little vacancy I will fill it though he just now said he was going to plague you about getting a furlough to get married, says he has heard people talk before you about living old Bachelors. I just came from Uncle Rhode's the girls were inquiring after you. We had a Ticket drawing among ourselves that is Cousin Lina, Sallie, Emma, and I. I drew you Cousin

Fayette & Capt. Grimsly three times, Cousin Lina Lieut Reed and others I forget the others. O yes Em drew Capt. O'Ferrel and Brother John. Cousin Hamilton left last night. I am sorry, when he is gone I get so lonely. It is getting quite cloudy. The river is being forded to day it has not been for several days. You must write often I will always be glad to hear from you,

Good bye little one, Sue

Meanwhile, Isaac Hite has arrived at Lee's Headquarters, also near Fredericksburg. Isaac and his future brother-in-law, Martin Gander, have been assigned as of January 9 to Company C, Lee's Body Guard, of the 39th Battalion, Virginia Cavalry, also known as Richardson's Battalion of Scouts, Guides, and Couriers. The unit is not officially mustered into service until March 9.

Camp Lee Feb. 23rd 1863

Dear Father:-

We arrived here after a march of seven days. We got to Stanton the second night, where we only stayed until the next morning. It snowed and rained several days on the march, and the roads were very bad. Yesterday, and night before last the snow fell about ten inches deep here. We have tents to go in, though our horses have to stand out. My horse stood the trip very well, and is now improving some. Broadus brought the horse with him that he got of me, and since he got here one of his eyes has gotten very sore again. We get a gallon and a half of corn, and about 12 ^{lbs} of hay per day for our horses. Our rations are very slim; a small piece of bread, a little sugar and rice, and a very small piece of bacon is our daly allowance. Yestarday we elected our officers which resulted in [Samuel Bradford] Brown Capt. [Albert H.] Pedigrue [Pettigrew] 1st Lt. [John H.] Lionberger 2nd Lt. [Clarence L.] Broadus 3rd Lt. There were a great many office seekers here which created some little disturbance before the election. Although we have organized we cannot be mustered into service until we have some 73 men present. We have about 58 men here now. Lionberger started to Page this morning, and Brown to Stanton to get the full number as soon as possible. Last Saturday there was a man shot here for desertion. Some six balls passed through his body—he fell, and died without a struggle. I inquired of Bettie paper at Harrisonburg; the editor has gone to parts unknown. He will not resume his editorialship there again. *Yours &c Isaac*

Winter and Spring 1863

In margin: *The company will draw all things needful as soon as mustered into service.*

Soon, Mollie Gander writes again to John Hite and explains the "crow pick."

River Dale Virginia. March 1/63

Dear friend,

After a long delay I will proceed to answer your very kind and interesting letter which was read with great pleasure. To day is sunday suppose you enjoyed your self finely in camp. I know that I was very well pleased. went to singing at Mill Creek. Ambrose Rothgeb was the teacher. had very good singing considering the crowd that was there. came home after singing. brought Fannie Bettie John Grove and Mr Doran home with me had quite a lively time. wish that you could have been here with us. I know that you would have enjoyed your self. but not so well as either because Sue was not here. I think if I were in your place I would come home on a marriage mission. Sue would be very glad, from what I can learn she would be right in for it, You told me once that you could not love another girl I think that you spoke before you thought that time for you have done engaged your self to another. I knew at the time that you did not mean what you said. Although I am satisfied if you are and I rather guess you are.

You said that I must tell you all about the crow pick. suppose you recollect one sunday night when you were here and F was here at the same time. you know too what you ask me that night and I told you all about the circumstances and you went and told Sue and Isaac all about it. suppose that you did or they would not have said you did. I don't care much if you did tell them so you dont tell any one else if you did tell them. I guess you will tell me or write wether it is so or not.

Well I believe I will stop on that subject and begin another, it has been very windy and cold to day hope it wont last long though as it is getting the time of the year to be warm and pleasant. it snowed last sunday about eight inches deep. did not get one sleigh ride. I think that if some of you soldier boys would have been here I would have gotten one or two sleigh rides, wonder if the soldiers sleigh any in camp. When you answer this letter I want you to tell me all about them deserters where was to be shot and whiped. Oh! is'ent that awfull to see that I could not look at one shot if it was to save my life I believe.

Well indeed I must bring my scribling to a close or else you cant read it for I get worse and worse the more I write the worse it gets. I hope you will excuse me for this time for my pen is so sorry I can scarsely write at all. if you cant read this send it back I want you to burn it up as soon as you read it if you can read it at all. I believe I will close and go to bed for I am getting sleepy. Please write as soon as convenient to do so for I am glad to hear from you at any time.

Please do not let any one see this letter but commit it to the flames as soon as you have read it.

Good night and pleasant
dreams be thine is all I have to say.
Your most affectionate friend
Mollie A. Gander

Ambrose Huffman, a cousin and a Page Grey comrade, is detailed to look for deserters which he calls the "Blue Ridges Regiment." Some other implications of this letter to John Hite remain a mystery. Outer cover:

Mr. John P. Hite
Co. H thirty

Politeness of a friend   third Regiment

Walnut creek March Third/63

Dear friend

I this morning seat my self to let you hear from me. I am well and hope these lines may find you enejoying the same blessing. I have not received aletter from camp sins I left and I should like very mutch to hear from you and to hear the centanse of those that is in the guardhouse. I will inform you that we have had quite atime with the petty coat tribe in some few instances but we are threw with the worst cases. we have all so had some nise times.

I would like to stay in page but am tired runing after they old blue Ridges Regement. they boys sayes they is aregment in the ridge and so we call it colonel blues Regment. Well I will say that I have seen your Darling onst sins I have bien hear. She looks quite well. at the time I will try and bring aletter from hir when I come for I will have an excuse for going after it. I understand that you have strange reports from what Ambrose M Hite rights. well you can think as you choose about it. I will close for the time. Wright soon. Nothing more but Remaining your Friend

Ambrose C. Huffman

N.B. excuse bad wrighting and spelling

WINTER AND SPRING 1863

Cousin Jennie Modesitt sends John more news from home. Her uncles are Daniel and Abraham Hite, and grandmother is Susannah (Spitler) Hite, a widow for the past 38 years who will live to age 89 in 1869. Frances A. Long, aged 30, and widow Naomia G. Keys, aged 52, were Luray neighbors of the Modesitts. William Asbury Keys, 25, only child of the widow Keys, saw earlier service in the 97th Va. Militia, but there is no record of the enlistment reported here. John H. Grove has enlisted as of February 24, 1863, as corporal in Capt. John H. Grabill's Co. E, 35th Va. Cav.

Luray Va
March 12th 1863

Dear Cousin

Mary Ellen received your kind letter the other day, We was very glad to hear from you. We are well and hope you and Cousin David are the same. Ma and Papa were out at Mill Creek Sunday. Uncle Daniel and Uncle Abe were there, they both said they were all well. Grand Mother is at our House now, she says she is not very well now. Mrs. Peter Long was buried Monday where Mr. Graves used to live. Mrs Keys died last week too, Asbery has been at home all the time waiting on his Mother, no one knew he was at home until a few moments before his Mother died, he says he is ready to anything for the army now, he went over to Newmarket the day his Mother was buried and joined a company.

I started to school last Tuesday a week to Cousin Lucy Marye.

I suppose you have heard that Pappa has quit merchandising. I miss the Store very much. John Grove started to the army wednsday. he joined Captain Grabel,s company. I am very sorry that some of our Page men had to be shot but I hope that will be the last one. It is getting late and I must close. Give my best respects to Cousin David, Write soon for we are always glad to hear from you.

From your affectionate Cousin
Jennie Modesitt

Cousin George Buswell writes from his Company H post to Bettie Hite. The cavalry attack at Kelly's Ford near Culpeper is one of the first engagements of this spring campaign. Union forces withdraw with some 78 casualties to the Confederates' 133.

> Camp Winder
> March 20th 1863

Dear Cousin:

After some delay I proceed to reply to your kind favor which I recieved in due time. I have been kept pretty busy since I recieved it or I would have answered earlier.

It is now 2 o ck P.M. & has been snowing nearly all the time since day light though the snow is not very deep. If I were in Page now & there were as much snow there I think I would sleigh some person. Capt. S[huler] and Lt. C[hadduck] have got safely back. I guess I am entitled to a furlough next. I do not know when I will get one. I think they have quit granting furloughs for this winter. Yesterday was four months since I left home & then was only at home a week & did not [see] any one scarcely.

Day before yesterday morning we thought we were going to leave Camp Winder & commence the Spring & Summer Campaign, revellie was beat at $3 \, 1/2$ A.M. & we were ordered to cook 1 days rations & be ready to move by daylight, fortunately for us we did not move & all has since become quiet; The cause of the stir was this; A force of Yankees crossed the Rappahannock at Kelly's ford in Culpepper County. I suppose for the purpose of making a reconnoisance. Gen. [J.E.B.] Stuart with his cavalry drove them back across the river with considerable loss.

They may make an advance on Richmond in a short time. I think Gen. Lee is prepared for them.

You, in your letter spoke of a very nice valentine you recieved two years ago and accuse me of sending it. I guess I had as well acknowledge that I sent it. how did you find it out?

At our ticket drawing here on the 14th I drew three names three times, all Page girls, I am sorry I had no Valentines to send them.

I wish you were here now to see us cook, we are just going to get dinner, so I must close.

Write when convenient, to your well-wishing friend and cousin.

> G.D.B.

To

> Miss Bettie Hite
> Page County
> Virginia

Isaac Hite writes home from camp near Richmond. Lt. John H. Lionberger has served with Isaac in the Dixie Artillery and now in Richardson's Battalion. Mann Spitler, formerly colonel of Isaac's militia regi-

Winter and Spring 1863

ment, is now serving in the Virginia legislature. The lower (northern) Shenandoah Valley is controlled by Federal forces who are now pressing Gen. John M. Jones's Confederates. Isaac's "sham" is some sort of light overcoat.

Camp Lee March 21st 1863

Dear Father:-

I received your letter sent by Lt. Lionberger, and had expected to write to you again shortly, but as we were not mustered into service until a few days ago, I concluded not to write until after that time.

As yet we have not received our equippments, though we will get them in a day or two. We received our bounty on the 17th and also pay from the time we enlisted in the Company up to the 1st of March for ourselves, but not the horses, as they were not considered in service until that time.

It is not known yet when we will leave here and enter the field of service, though it is not my opinion that we will leave here for several weeks yet, so if you will write me immediately on the receipt of this direct to this place, if not write to me at Guinea Station in Care of Capt. Brown Col. Richarson's Battallion.

I was down in town to day and saw Col. Spitler, who told me that Gen Jones was ordered to fall back to Harrisonburg, and that he intended to start to Page on next monday though the legislature will not adjourn until Tuesday. He expects that if Jones falls back that that country will soon be overrun by that Yankees again, and wishes to get to Page before they come. He said he would hear from them again this evening, and would then determine whether he would start a Monday or not. I gave him seventy ($70) dollars to give to you, which you will take and credit me with it, if it makes no difference to you.

I got my clothing that I left in Richmond last Spring, that is my jacket & sham, my pants he let a black boy ware them out that lived with him last year. I told him it was all right, as they were of small force.

We have had a great deal of wet cold, and windy weather this month. It has been snowing for the last 36 hours until to day, it has been raining nearly all the time. We have no shelter for our horses, and sometimes it seems as if they almost freeze. If we were in some woods we could soon build shelters for them, but we ar here in the fair ground and at some distance from any woods. We get plenty of grain for them though hardly enough of long feed.

Our rations are yet very short. We sometimes eat all at one meal that we draw for all day, and then feast [he means fast] the balance of the day or buy something.

Our trip down here cost me $15. all the money that I started with. Lt. Lionberger thinks he can draw it for us yet.

If the Yankees get in Page before we get an opportunity to send our saddles & bridles home we will box them up and send them to Gordonsville or some other place where they can be got. If you write here direct to Camp Lee near Richmond Va. Care of Capt. Brown Col. Richarson's Battallion. Nothing more at present but remain

your affectionate son Isaac

Cousin Ella Buswell writes to John with more news of marriages, romances, and yet another sighting of Sue Coffman. John T. Johnston, wounded at Antietam in September, 1862, does not return to duty until early 1864. Philip McInturff is later to succeed Ambrose Booten as minister of the Mill Creek church. "Old" Malinda Higgs, wife of Thomas, is 58 years old. Martin Rothgeb was discharged from the militia in February, 1862, and he has no further service record. His bride, Matilda, is to die the following September. The Yankees still hold Winchester, and the transfer of Lee's Body Guard to Imboden's command remains just a rumor.

Leaksville Virginia
March 29th/63

Cousin John

You must not think I have forgotten <u>Little Jonnie</u> any one but him. I wrote to you about three weeks ago and gave it to Jack Johnston he said he was going in a few days to his Co. but the last I heared of him he was still at home; I expect will wear it out before he gets there; I think it goes very hard with him to start.

Mary & myself were up to Reuben Aleshire to day did not have quite so nice a time as when you & George went with us. Reuben is not quite so lively as he used to be. There were Preaching at the Seminary last Sunday, <u>Mr McInturf,</u> little Sue was there the first time for two [weeks?,months?] I have seen her; she looks as well as ever is staying at Mr Long now.

It is almost Easter & I hope we will have a better time than we had last Easter; the Yankees guarding our house & searching ever place they could get in & the rain a pouring down. untill another Easter I hope you will all be at home and we will have peace; We have had so much bad weather this winter; I hope it will be better after this month; but then I expect <u>Old Jack</u> will have you a travilling & you will have a hard time again this Spring & Summer; but if you *only keep your health you can make out better. I am afraid the Pneu-monia will be very bad this Spring; there are some about now Old Mrs. Higs is very sick with the Pneumonia.*

You had better be a looking out or you will be left in the back-grounds; Martin Rothgeb and Matilda Huffman tied the knot last week after a long talk about it; I reckon he thinks he will be exemp now he has a Dunkard; I would not be much surprised to hear of A. Huffman tieing a knot while he is here; though I think he had a[s] well wait for a while; I guess Perry Kite would not care if the Yankees would leave Winchester so he could go down that way.

Pappa is going to start to Richmond in the morning and will go out to see you I guess; I will send this by him and see if you will get it;

We are all well except Mother she is nearly well though she does not go out of the house yet,

I heared the Dixie boys that joined Lee's body Guard have been transfered to Imboden instead of Lee; about what they might expected;

I will stop for this time; hopping to hear from you soon I remain as ever your affectionate Cousin

S. Ella Buswell

John writes home with news of Co. H soldiers and a request for some supplies. Alexander H. Keyser and George T. Wilson both recover their illnesses in time to be wounded at Gettysburg. Samuel Rothgeb remains sick and then on hospital duty, eventually at Lynchburg, through January 1865. William T. Young, Capt. of Co. K, 10th Va. Inf., was discharged in April, 1862. David Coffman and Frank Yowell, both of Co. D, 7th Va. Cav. were captured on December 11, 1862, and have been exchanged at City Point on April 4, 1863. Joseph F. Stover, wounded at Kernstown in March 1862, has returned to duty just this January and was discharged and sent home on February 19.

Sunday Morning   Camp Winder
Apr. 12th 1863

Dear Parents:

as an opportunity affords itself of sending you a letter by hand, thought I would send you a few lines; though I have nothing of much importance to write. I have not rec^d a letter from any of you for some time. We are still at our old camp, didn't think when we first came here that we would remain here one month, & now we have been here nearly four, can't think it possible that we will remain here long any more, this beautiful weather. It is the opinion of a great many that we *will make the advance & not fighting Joe. Hooker; as we might have expected of him. He sends up some of his Aeronauts nearly every day, guess they think that there are too many troops around here for them to cross. I heard from good authority that there are 95.000 effective men in this department of the army; 13.000 of unarmed men, a large number. There has been a good many guns brought in during the winter, yet the supply is inadequate.*

A. H. Keyser George T. Wilson starts home in the morning on sick furloughs for twenty days, don't think Wilson ever will be able to stand service has been complaining all winter. Saml. Rothgeb was sent to the Hospital about a week since, went to Staunton I think. Mother, I would be glad if you would send David & I a few pieces of soap as we don't draw but very little, that smells like carn; (some say it is made of mule[s] when they die), also my cotton pocket handkerchief, & my two check shirts as these are nearly worn out; the handkerchief I think you will find the outside room up stairs in the chests. Send these by the first opportunity. We are looking for Capt. Young down here every [day], think he will have a box for David & I. Squire Shuler expects to come down before long. I guess that David Coffman & Frank Yaowell are at home now, I heard they were on the way several days ago; a man of the Regt. was with them at Chicoga Ill. told us that they were on their way home. Father, I have never heard whether you got the money I sent you about two months ago, or not. I sent it by Joseph F. Stover, it was $415.00. I close expect to hear from you soon.

From your affectionate Son John.

P. S. The chaplains of the Brigade have had a protracted meeting for the last month, have had a good many mourners hope they are sincere; they administer the ordanance of baptism frequently. I hear them singing at the Chapel now.

The Page Greys have decamped on April 29 from Camp Winder near Guinea Station, and now Isaac Hite writes with news of the Battle of Chancellorsville on May 1-4. Here, Stonewall Jackson receives his mortal wound, and Gen. A. P. Hill is also wounded. Total losses for May 1-4: Union– 1512 killed, 9518 wounded, 5000 missing; Confederate– 1581 killed, 8700 wounded, 2000 missing.

Brig. Gen. Frank Paxton, in command of the 1st Virginia Brigade, is killed after sharing his premonitions with an aide. During the seven months of his command, Paxton personally has been converted from a profane agnostic to a quiet and humble Christian, no doubt partly through the influence of Jackson who regularly attended services with the men at their V-shaped chapel constructed at Camp Winder.

May 4/63
Guinia Station

Dear Father:-

As I have a moment to stop here I will drop you a few lines. We came here last night (Capt. Browns Company) with some six hundred and fifty Yankee prisoners taken yestarday in the fight on the plank road above Fredericksburg.

There arrived, also this morning some two hundred more. I can tell you as yet but little of the fight. We arrived here: that is at Lee's head quarters: from Richmond on Thursday 30th, and from that time until we had orders to bring those prisoners to this place, we were engaged in guarding roads coming from the field of action, taking up all our men that felt disposed to straggle from the army. Yestarday while the fight was going on we were back in the rear guarding Yanke prisoners and also taking up starglers. The other company of this battallion have been acting as couriers since we have been here as they were better acquainted the roads. The fight of yestar[day] was a very bloody one.

I have heard that Gen. Jackson had one of his arms shot off, and that A. P. Hill was also wounded. As for the Companie's from Page I have heard nothing from though it reasonable to suppose that the casualties [to] them must to have been Considerable. This leaves us all well and hope will find you all the same.

We have got to leave so I must close. We are going toward Lees head quarters.

Yours as ever
Isaac.

The "Companie's from Page" and indeed all of the Stonewall Brigade have been heavily engaged at Chancellorsville. Losses to the Brigade total 54 killed, 430 wounded, and 9 missing, including 10 killed and 50 wounded in the 33rd Regiment. From the Hites we have no first-hand account, but in a letter to his brother dated May 8, George Buswell gives battle details and then summarizes Company H casualties:

> *I sum up the casualties in our company as follows: Simeon Lucas, killed on the field. Benj. F. Miller, mortally wounded by shell in leg, had his leg amputated, has since died. James E. Miller, a brother of Ben's, through leg by ball, leg amputated above the knee. Return Nichols, severly through face. [Both James Miller and Return Nichols are to die of their wounds within a month.] [Benjamin F.] Beahm, severely in arm near shoulder, had part of bone taken out, would have been amputated at shoulder joint, but for his begging. Dr. Baldwin, who attended to him, thinks he is doing very well. Early Cubbage, flesh wound through arm at elbow. George Koontz, in face near the eye. Philip Somers, in arm. Franklin Rothgeb, flesh wound in arm. John W. McCoy, finger off, James Menifie (O. Sergt.), on shoulder, has come up. Bushrod Oden, slightly on side, has come up. I believe Robert Aleshire was slightly wounded on arm, came up next day. James Henry Cubbage was accidentally wounded on Tuesday, his gun went off whilst he was trying to draw the load, he was badly bruised. I understand Jacob F. Knight, who was complaining & had a pass to fall to the rear, was wounded in leg.*
>
> *... One or two of the boys in our company got behind & did not get in the fight. Those that were in did very well. Ambrose Hite did very well, was in a fine glee in time of the fight, did not appear to mind the balls at all. Capt. Shuler acted well. I do not think I ever at any time in the army, or out of the army, saw him more cool. ...*

After suffering the amputation of his mangled arm, Gen. Thomas J. Jackson dies on May 10. His death is a tragedy to the Confederate cause and a source of great grief to the First Virginia Brigade. Though refused by the exigencies of war from escorting the remains to the Richmond funeral and Lexington burial, the men receive some solace on May 30 when, by act of the War Department, they are designated as the Stonewall Brigade, the only Confederate unit to have such a sanctioned nickname.

Marking the beginning of the Gettysburg campaign, Lee moves two of his three Army of Northern Virginia corps northwestward from Fredericksburg to Culpeper Court House. J.E.B. Stuart's 8000 man cavalry corps stages two grand reviews, one on June 6 at nearby Brandy Station and the next in Culpeper Court House. Isaac writes a brief note to accompany his package to Mann Spitler's store. Edward Trenton Brumback is reported serving in the 43rd Va. Cav.

WINTER AND SPRING 1863

C. C. House, June 7/63

Dear father:-

We arrived here this evening. Nearly all the forces have left Fredericksburg, and come to this place. On last Friday evening there was an artillery duel below Fredericksburg. The result I did not learn. I have no time to write at present. I send you by Trenton Brumback, 1 pr. drawers 1 comfort and 1 round about which he will take to Luray by stage and leave them at uncle Mann's Store. I have more clothes than I can carry to do my horse justice. Martin Gander will have some clothes in the same sack

My eyes are about as they were when I left. I have not seen David nor John since I arrived in camp though I suppose they are now encamped in this vicinity somewhere.

Yours as ever
Isaac M. Hite

We have no other report on the condition of Isaac's eyes. Ewell's corps including David and John's Stonewall Brigade is indeed in the vicinity, but two days later moves into the lower Shenandoah Valley and is soon to fight the Second Battle of Winchester.

CHAPTER 9

Gettysburg

*"Is it so?
Yes, tis so, John is dead."*

Under its new brigadier, James A. Walker, the Stonewall Brigade participates in the Second Battle of Winchester on June 13 to 15, 1863, liberating that city from Federal occupation and capturing more than 4000 Union troops with only minor Confederate losses. The 33rd Regiment plays only a supporting role. Then after crossing the Potomac and bivouacking several days on the old Sharpsburg battleground, the brigade joins Lee's army in the Pennsylvania invasion, reaching Carlisle on June 27.

From this deepest northern penetration the brigade marches south again as the Gettysburg campaign gets underway on July 1. Ordered to the extreme left of the Confederate line, they spend July 2 astride the Hanover Road, waiting for orders to attack. Meanwhile the enemy is consolidating positions from Culp's Hill on his right, west and south through Cemetery Ridge, to Little Round Top on his left. Late that afternoon there is a desultory and ineffective attack on the Union right, too tentative and too late both for the impatient men and for General Lee.

Finally in the early dawn of July 3, the Stonewall Brigade and the rest of Ewell's corps begin a concerted attack on the now-reinforced Union position on Culp's Hill. Perhaps as a harbinger of the drama and defeat of Pickett's celebrated charge later that day, three desperate attacks are driven back with heavy losses, and Ewell's part is played out.

To the Hite family in Page County, the first personal news of the battle probably comes in this letter from Michael Shuler, Captain of Co. H. Sparing the immediate family from an impersonal notification, he writes Uncle Stage with this account of the grim results.

Gettysburg

July 12th 1863

Mr. A. S. Modesitt
Dear Sir,

    I take this Method of informing you of the severe wound that John P Hite received in the Battle of Gettysburg on Friday the 3rd Inst. and his condition when I last saw him:- in order that you may inform his father and family correctly. He was wounded early in the day. The ball entered his right shoulder and ranged down towards his left side where I thought it still remained. In the evening he appeared much more relieved. Our line on the left was changed and the Hospitals of Ewells Corps were removed to the right some 5 or 6 miles leaving the old ones with all the wounded that were unable to be moved liable to fall in the hands of the enemy.

    Five were left from My Company viz. Jno P. Hite, David Wood[,] Weakly, & W$\underline{m}$ A. Keyser, & W$\underline{m}$ Purdam. David Hite & A. H. Keyser were left with them for nurses. I suppose the Yankees took possession on Saturday. To be candid I believe John is mortally wounded — though there are some hopes still that he is not. David remained with him and will give him all the help and attention the Yankees will allow.

    I was slightly wounded in the head on Friday Evening. Have not been with the Company since. Will, however if I Continue to improve so fast, be with it in a few days. Don't think there has been any general engagements since the 3rd I am staying at private Quarters about 8 miles from Winchester. My respects to your Family &c.

Very Truly Yours &c
M. Shuler

In margin: *The loss in my Company was I regret to say very heavy as far as I know – 4 killed and 15 wounded. 3 missing supposed to be wounded.*

Of those left in hospital John Hite dies next day, July 4; David Wood, who, on a technicality, was once spared being shot for desertion, dies July 17; Wyatt B. Weakly is paroled from a Union hospital on August 24 and remains on sick leave through December, 1863; William Keyser is exchanged at City Point in November, 1863, admitted to Chimborazo Hospital at Richmond, and furloughed in November, 1864; William Purdam is absent wounded through December, 1863. Of those left as nurses, David Hite is imprisoned at Point Lookout and exchanged in March 1864, Alexander H. Keyser is exchanged and admitted to Chimborazo Hospital

144 THE PAINFUL NEWS I HAVE TO WRITE

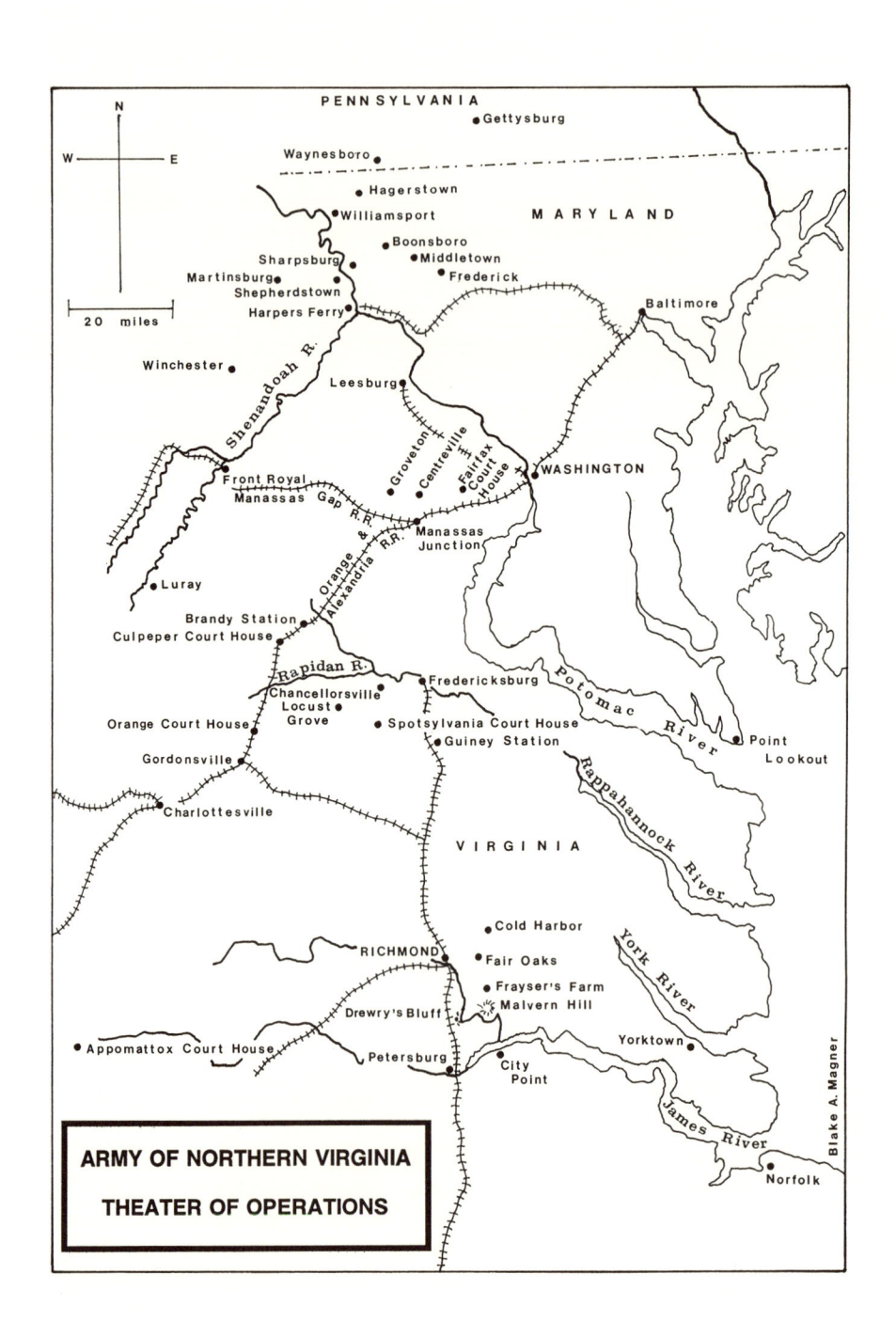

ARMY OF NORTHERN VIRGINIA
THEATER OF OPERATIONS

Gettysburg

in November, 1863, returned to duty, captured again in May, 1864, and finally paroled in January, 1865.

Isaac Hite's personal experience of the battle must be much like that of Martin Gander, his fellow in Lee's bodyguard, who left this note on the 50th anniversary of the battle:

> *Gettysburg, Pa.*
> *July 2, 1913*
> *I placed 4 guards around the old stone house on the hill, the personal headquarters of Gen. Lee the evening of July 1, 1863 about 5:30 P.M. at the command of Adj. Gen. Taylor, who was in the field headquarters across the street in a tent with Col. Douglas. I delivered messages from Gen. Lee at the house to Gen. Ewell and Gen. Johnston all during the 2 days battle.*
> *Sgt. M. V. Gander*
> *39 Bat Gen. R. E. Lee*
> *Courier & Scout*
> *Luray, Va.*

Isaac's letter to the family is dated just one day after Michael Shuler's. It lists Co. H casualties John Rosenberger and Ordnance Sergeant James W. Menifie killed on the field, plus William Purdam who survived, though badly wounded. Until shortly before this time, the practice on both sides has been to return prisoners to their lines soon after capture, on parole until certified as exchanged on a one-for-one basis. But because of questions on the Confederate treatment of captured Negro troops and the fear that Confederate parolees would too soon be returned to service, the agreement has broken down. David is not released until exchanged in March, 1864.

> *HeadQuarters A. N. Va.*
> *Camped near Hagerstown Md.*
> *July 13, 1863*
>
> *Dear Parents Sisters & Brothers,*
> *This morning I write to you, and the painful news I have to write I thought David had written before this. Is it so? yes, tis so, John is dead. He fell mortally wounded on the 3rd day of July early in the morning, and those who saw him last of the Company, thought he was dying that same evening when the army fell back. By his earnest*

request, and David's desire he was left with him to wait on him in the last, and to have him as neatly buried as he could in the enemy's Country.

He was shot—the ball entered the right side just below the armpit, passed through near the heart to the left side, ranging down and to the front, and stopped just before Coming through. Shortly after his left side turned black which shows that the ball lodged just under the skin. He fell, and from the wound it would seem that he could not have lived an half an hour, yet he was still alive late that evening. He was conscious of his situation, and prayed for death that he might be relieved of his suffering. While they were carrying him from the fiel[d], he told them if they were in any danger to lay him down, and save themselves, as for himself he would soon die. This he told them several times, but they succeeded in getting him to the hospital without danger.

But alass he is gone! He was the second son and brother to be called from this world of trouble to eternity. We hope he has met William around God's eternal throne sin[g]ing songs of praise to His Holy name. I am sorrow [sic] that I did not write sooner since I have heard that David was left with him. I thought that he had left with the army, and had written the particulars to you long ago. I could not hear until yestarday I suceeded in getting to the Company, when I first heard where David was, and more fully about John. I was told on the evening of the 4th by Joseph Huffman that John was mortally wounded, and supposed to be dead before that time, but the army had done fallen back so that the hospital which John was taken to was, before that time in the hands of the enemy. I thought it useless to attempt to go back then any more, knowing that David and the rest of the Company had done all they could for him.

I was glad to hear that David had stay'd with him to mark his grave if he could do nothing more. I suppose he will be parolled in a short time, and sent home until exchanged.

It is hardly necessary for me to say anything of the battle of Gettysburg at this late date as you no doubt have heard through other channels before this of its magnitude, and the great slaughter of human lives. Thousands again fell on both sides, and on the 3rd day the earth around seemed almost to tremble from the mighty thundering of heavy artillery. Genl. Picket's division charged the enemies hights at one time with between four and five thousand men, and returned with only about eight hundred. Genl. Pettig[r]ew who was to support Picket—his men failing to do their [duty], and like sheep before woolves fled in confusion. The Yankees seeing this turned on Picket and mowed his men by thousands. What a sacrafice of life—the souls that are hurried off to eternity. Genl. Lee seeing this sent word to Genl. Johnson who was at the other end of the line that the right wing of our army had been unsuccessful, when a retreat was at once determined upon.

I received father's letter a few days ago dated July 5th stating that mother was then sick. I hope she has gotten well again, yess before this sad news shall reach her. I have now written the particulars so far as I could get them from the Company. David will know more when he returns. May his funeral [wait] until some future day, when if it be His will the family may all have met together. John W. Rosenberger, William Pirdham, and the Ord. Sergeant of the Comp. were killed dead on the field.

Our army now has been drawn up in line of battle for the past two days, the right and left extending near the Potomac in the shape of a half moon. The center is some four miles from the river. I have been nearly the whole length, and all the way strong entrenchments have been made. The river is now fordable on horse back. Pontoon bridges will be laid across in a day or two more. This leave[s] me well.

From your affectionate
son & Brother I. M. Hite

And on the same sheet of paper, Isaac writes to his sister, Ella.

July 13th 1863

Dear Sister Ella:

I received a letter yestardy directed to David. I took the privilege to open it when I found a letter from Diana to David, and one from you to John. I will keep them until I have and opportunity to send them to you. Little did you think when you were writing yours that he who you were writing to would so soon be gone. But alass he is no more! It was written in the spirit and affection of a sister, but was too late to revive him any more. While his body lies beneath the enemies soil at Gettysburg, we hope his spirit has passed to a better world where no enemy can again hurt him. They have done all they can do; they have killed his body but his soul forever liveth, and my prayer to Almighty God that it be in the mansions of eternal bliss. After being wounded he expressed his desire to die–he wished to be relieved of his suffering. Oh may it be that he then had communion with the Father of mercy, and promise of a crown of glory.

From your
Affectionate Brother I. M. Hite

July 13, 1863
Bountiful hand of Providence

148   THE PAINFUL NEWS I HAVE TO WRITE

Isaac next writes to his sister Mary Ann and her husband John Burner. "Campbelle from Luray" is probably George W. Campbell of Co. H. Isaac's opinion that the "trip" was a total failure is echoed in the memoirs of John N. Opie, a 5th Va. cavalryman, that "the whole campaign was a blunder."

July 18th 1863
Camp at Bunker's Hill

Dear Brother & Sister:-
I wrote to them at home on the 13th, but did not get to send it until a few days ago, of the death of John. It is possible that the letter may not have reached them, though I suppose you have heard of his death before this. In that letter I wrote all the particulars so far as I could get them from the Co[m]pany. He was mortally wounded on the 3rd, early in the morning by a ball entering his right side just below his arm, and pasing through near his heart to the left. The ball did not Come entirely through but very near as the skin turned black shortly after he was wounded. He was conscious of his situation and wished to die that he might be relieved of his suffering. He told Lt. Buswell as soon as he was shot that he was killed, and said it seemed as if their were a dozen balls in his body. Campbelle from Luray saw him late in the evening and said he could scarcely talk above a whisper any more, and he did not think he would hardly live until the next morning. He was shot in the morning before firing his gun.
David was sent back to the hospital with him, and stayed with him after the army fell back from Gettiesburg. He is now in the hands of the Yankees, but I suppose will be sent across the lines again as soon as he can be spared from the hospital. It is likely he will be kept to wait on other wounded for awhile.
The whole army recrossed the river on the 13th & 14th. A majority crossed on pontoon bridges, though many had to waid. The Yankees pressed our rear hard, thought they got no prisners except some straglers.
Gen Lee was evidently driven out of Maryland, and on the whole I consider the trip a total failure, for he certainly expected to go farther than he did, and not come back as soon as he did. The few cattle and horses that were captured will not begin to pay for our losses, besides the army at this time is in very low sp[i]rits. The ranks of the regt's have been thined tremenduous since we passed along here about four weeks ago.
Now upon the whole I begin to think sometimes that our cause is getting very gloomy. This army has been driven out of Maryland, and

GETTYSBURG

Vicksburg has fallen, besides every thing appears to work badly. This leaves me well and hope may find you the same. Write to me soon. Direct to H.Q.A.N.Va. care of Capt Brown, Richarsons Battallion.

Your's & Isaac M. Hite

A personal description of the experience of Co. H in the Gettysburg campaign is provided by further excerpts from the diary of George D. Buswell.

Wed. [July] 1st. Reveille at 5 am. Marched at 7. Crossed the Blue Ridge, formed line of battle about 2 miles beyond Gettysburg. Marched about 28 miles. Our advance troops had a considerable fight at Gettysburg today; drove the Yankee's back.

Thurs. 2nd. Were aroused about sunrise. Some skirmishing in our front. We advanced a short distance & lay in line. A little skirmishing & cannonading all day. Heavy cannonading commenced on our right at 4 pm. Continued until sunset. Also infantry fighting. The 2nd, 3rd, & 4th Brigades were engaged. The Yankees have an excellent position on the top of a mountain Southeast of town. Our Brig. was placed in line of Battle on the mountain side about midnight. Capt. [George C.] Eastham Co. "I" was killed by a ball from the skirmishers.

Fri. 3rd. Slept a little this morning before light. The 33rd Regt. opened the fight at this point before daylight & sunrise, (3:30). When we had fired all our ammunition, we were relieved by the 4th Regt. We had hard fighting here nearly all day, in which our Brigade suffered severely, Our Company lost 4 killed, 17 wounded, 3 mortally. The killed are — 1st Sergt. Menifie, 2nd Sergt. Rosenberger, Privts. Wm. Jenkins & Haley Morris. Mortally wounded, John P. Hite, Wm. Purdam & David Wood. Wounded Capt. Shuler, Corporal David Stombock, Privates Wm. A. Keyser, John P. Beaver, George T. Wilson, Benjamin F. Price, James T. Purdam, Reuben T. Coffman, Wyatt B. Weely [Weakly], John W. Phillips, Joseph W. Bailey, Corporal E. J. Rothgeb, Prvts. Wm. McAlister & G. W. Campbell. We failed to carry the works in front of us. We fell back after midnight, were not followed by the Yankees. Our Company went into the fight with 36 men, had 21 killed & wounded, 4 of them slightly, returned to the Company for duty in a day or two.

Buswell's list matches that of Capt. Michael Shuler, though the official lists of wounded omit a few of those named here. His diary continues with an account of the army's retreat across the Potomac.

Sat. 4th. Lay in line on the hill west of town until midnight. A little skirmishing near town. Hard rain in the evening, Brought us 3 days rations.

Sun. 5th. Moved out of line about 2 am. The 4th, 33rd, & 10th Regts. were thrown out on the left flank as skirmishers. Were very near being fired on by Gen. Longstreet. Were drawn in about 12 oclk. Moved slowly until after night. The Yankees follow us up.

Mon. 6th. Moved on after sunrise. Killed some hogs for meat rations. Crossed the Ridge & bivouacked before night near Waynesboro.

Tues. 7th. Marched to within 3 miles of Hagerstown. The 33rd Regt. marched in rear of the army. The Yanks followed, but were not troublesome.

Wed. 8th. Very rainy. Our Brigade was moved out on the road about 1 1/2 miles towards Leitersburg to attend to some yanks, but they kept their distance & we came back to camp.

Thurs. 9th. The 4th & 33rd Regts. went on picket, relieved the 2nd Regt. The left of the 33rd was on out-post.

Fri. 10th. Some firing in our front today. We were relieved by the 42nd Regt. We marched to within a few hundred yards of camp, when we were about-faced & thrown out as skirmishers east of the road. Were withdrawn & marched 2 miles beyond Hagerstown on the Williamsport road.

Sat. 11th. Formed line of Battle about a mile from Hagerstown, threw-up fortifications, remained here all day.

Sun. 12th. Lay still all day. Some skirmishing in our front, more on our right & left. The Yanks are fortifying beyond town.

Mon. 13th. Moved to the left at 2 am. Formed first in one rank, then our line being strengthened by some of Gen. Jenkens dismounted Cavalry, we formed in two ranks. Remained here until about 9 pm. Then we moved out of line & towards Williamsport. Road muddy.

GETTYSBURG

Tues. 14th. Marched from town to the ferry from midnight until day light. We waded the Patomac, it was waist deep. We bivouacked for the night at old Camp Stevens, 3 or 4 miles below Martinsburg.

As the beaten and disspirited Army of Northern Virginia continues its retreat up the Shenandoah Valley, Cousin Bettie Strickler writes to Bettie Hite about the situation at New Market. Selina Strickler, 31, is listed as head of household in the 1860 Shenandoah County census, with her mother Mary, 64, Elizabeth (Bettie), 29, Mary, 27, Nancy, 22, and Milton, just 7. Brother James Strickler with his wife and seven children live next door.

New Market, Va   July 19th 63

Dear Cousin Bettie

With pleasure I seat myself this lonely Sabbath evening as I have been writing to Mary Gander I thought I would also drop you a line or two to let you know that I have not for gotten you although I believe you P[a]ge girls have forgotten me, you have something of more importance perhaps to study about, I should not wonder if you have in this war time but just come over and we will talk the matter over we will talk about the war and everything else.

Oh are these not troublesome times one battle after another is all we can hear and our friends being killed and wounded. oh, if you could see the wounded that have been going up the road since the last battle and it would make your heart ache. they have taken the Baptist Church in New Market for a Hospital to feed the wounded and dress their wounds and then they send them on to other hospitals. the citizens just do it themselves. they country people send in vegitables and the town Ladies cook it and keep a table set all the time just for the passing wounded. the men dress the wounds. I think it is better than the way they had to do at first. they just had to go about the country and get some thing to eat where ever they could get it and a great many of them suffered as much with hunger as they did with their wounds, they are nearly all walking

there seems to be just as many brave acting now as there was at the first

have you heard from your brothers since the fight or was they not in the fight. Well cousin I must stop writin and go and get supper. We have a Gentleman and Lady and servant boarding here they are what

I call high quality folks. they want a good deal of waiting on. they have been here since the first of June. they are from Baltimore. he is assistant quarter master and is to issue the rations for the soldiers that is passing who are in service

I must close by sending my love to all enquiring friends. Tell cousin Ann Mauck I intend looking for you all next Saturday and if you dont come I will pull your noses when I see you again come come come and dont put it off any longer

So no more at present give my love to Ella and your mother

Bettie Strickler to
Bettie Hite

Since she does not yet know of John Hite's death, Bettie's impertinent threat can be forgiven. As we shall see, the proposed visit is long delayed.

Two months later, when Isaac Hite writes his father again, the family still has not gotten a first-hand report of John's death. Lee has withdrawn from the Rappahannock, and is now headquartered just south of the Rapidan. Meade has occupied Culpeper County. Longstreet's Corps has been sent to Tennessee to support the Chickamauga campaign. The major battle anticipated in this letter never takes place. John P. Beaver of Co. H was wounded at Gettysburg, and for an unknown reason his father, Daniel, is apparently at army headquarters. Martin Biedler's farm is not far from the Hite homestead and on Isaac's route back across the Ridge.

HeadQuarters
Army Northern Virginia
Sat. September 19th 1863

Dear Father:-

You have been looking for a letter no doubt before this, as I promised to write shortly on my return, but as all were quiet when I got here, I neglected writing any so[o]ner. At present there is a good prospect for another fight shortly. You have already heard that the Yankees have ocupied Culpeper C. H. and driven our cavalry force back to near the Rappadan River some four or five days ago. They are yet just across the river in large force – I suppose Meade's whole army.

Today it was supposed a fight would commence, but as yet I hear no firing – at 10 O,clok A.M. The troops I think ma[r]ched out this morning by day-light, but to what point I do not know. Genl. Lee has not moved his head quarters yet, now I don't suppose he will if the

GETTYSBURG

153

fight comes off just below here on the Rappadan. Instead of Genl. Ewell's Corps leaving here as I told you when at home, it was Genl. Longstreet's. Genl. Longstreet moved his head quarters soon the next morning after I got here. One of his divisions was then at Richmond. It is reported here that his Corps or the larger portion of it has gone South. The Couriers from our battallion that were with him were sent back to their Companies.

Daniel Beaver got a letter from John Beaver a few days ago stating that he had gotten home. It is possible that he would know something of David and John if you were to see him. As yet I have heard nothing of them, though I have no opportunity, as all who get back from there from Page make that county their first place to visit.

I still have my horse yet, and I think his eyes are getting some better.

I saw Martin Biedler the morning I left, and he told me that he had several horses to sell, but as he was in a hurry and so was I, did not stop to look at them. I have been thinking since I have left that if you did not care, I would try to buy a horse in the army that is tolerably well broken down, and send him home, to run on pasture. Sometimes I can meet with good chances, which would pay me much better than to buy a high priced horse and bring him here, ware him out, and then sell him for little or nothing. Daniel & Braska could tend to him so that he,d cost nothing more than what grass he would eat.

There has been some very hard showers of rain here within past few days. Today it cl[o]udy and very cule for this season of the year. Nothing more. Write to me soon. From your

Affectionate son Isaac

To Daniel Hite

With John dead and David in a Federal prison camp, news of the armies comes only in letters from Isaac, and, for a time, we lose direct contact with the **Page Greys**.

Memoritechnica.

—:o:—

JOHN P. HITE departed this life July 4th, 1863. He fell mortally wounded on the 3rd, in the morning before sunrise and died the next morning about six o'clock. He was shot in making a charge up a steep mountain, and exposed to two fires, one in front and one from the right flank; it is supposed he was shot from the right flank; he was struck in the right shoulder, the ball ranged downward, passed through near the heart and lodged in the left flank just under the skin He was sensible of his situation and prayed for death, that he might be released from his suffering, about night he fell into a stupor and became unconscious and died the next morning. His age was 22 years 7 months and 20 days; he was a member of the 33rd Regiment Va. Volunteers, and belonged to the Stonewall Brigade. He fell in the memorable Battle fought at Gettysburg Pa., he was buried by his brother David, two miles north of Gettysburg. There he lies slumbering in his mother dust till Gabriel's trumpet shall bid it rise.

Memorial Notice From John Hite's Funeral Service September 10, 1865.

CHAPTER 10

Homefront and Headquarters (1863 & 1864)

*"If Diana has made my hat, I wish you would send it down.
I will soon be bareheaded and barefooted."*

Back in Page County, Mollie Gander invites Bettie Hite to join her for a trip to their Strickler cousins in New Market—a visit long postponed in deference to the death of John Hite.

River Dale Sept. 23rd 1863

Friend Bettie:
Ann and I have concluded to go over the mountain saturday evening and we want you to go with us. I ask Father for the horses to day and he said we could have them but he wanted them again Tuesday morning so we will come back monday evening if nothing happens. You must tell your father to be certain and let you have a horse for we are not going to stay long. Mary Strickler was over last sunday and she said we must be certain to come. they are to be preaching at their house on monday now you must be certain and come try and get here till one o'clock

From your friend
Mollie

Later, Ella Buswell writes to Bettie Hite about her family's move, prompted by Col. Thomas Buswell's governmental duties, to Salem, Roanoke County. Lt. George Buswell reports in his diary that he has been at home from August 29 to September 10, and Capt. Shuler has been on furlough from September 24 to October 15. During this period, the Stonewall Brigade is camped with the rest of the army along the Rapidan, and there has been no significant military action. Mart is Martin Gander, Bettie's future husband.

The Painful News I Have to Write

Roanoke Co Virginia
Oct 16th 1863

Dearest Bettie

I guess I cannot better employ myself this rainy day than by writing to an old friend. We arrived at our new home Wednesday; had a very pleasant time untill Wednesday it commenced raining and it raining yet. I have not seen Roanoke yet scarcely. It has been to cloudy and rainy we can not get out anywhere. We have made the acquaintance of one family, our nearest neighbor, Mr. Parish; our wagons has not come yet; we went there and stayed all night; they seem very nice; the old woman reminds me very much of Mrs. Gander:

We stayed all night at Cousin Edmona's Friday night and had a nice time; wish you could have been there; I saw Harvie he is about the same he used to be; I expect I will hear of his going to see Bettie; he promised to come out to see us but his promises are like pie crust, easily broken; or a long time in fulfilling them; Tell cousin David Coffman Goodbye for me. I did not get to speak to him after I left you; You must take good care of Ambrose [Rothgeb] this winter; I expect you will go to school to him.

I have not heard from Brother George since Capt. Shuler cam home. I am getting anxious to hear from him; I fear they have had a fight it is so rainy; and it always rains after a fight; I wrote to Cousin John Rosenberger yesterday; we cannot do anything untill the wagons come; I think they will surely come today; we passed them Monday 15 miles below Lexington; if I had known it would have taken them so long we would have stayed a day or two longer in Rockingham; We came through Staunton, Lexington and Buckhannon [Buchanan] and several other small towns; we passed through some very prettie country and some very rough & hilly; Rockbridge is I believe the roughest county we came through. I do not know if it is all like it was along the road; We had our provision with us would stop side of the road feed the horses & eat; we were as you said, like <u>Gipseyes</u>. I have not eat at a table since I left Rock[ingham]. our table is in the wagon; we use the <u>mess chest</u> for a table; we live like soldiers; cook by the fire; we bought a cook Stove the other side of Buckhannon; but had to leave it for the wagon to bring.

The cars are just passing, they pass in about 300 yards of the house; they pass three or [four] times a day; We have to cross the RailRoad to get to our nearest neighbors. it is something to see for anyone who has never see them; I would like to have seen you and all the girls before I left but it was impossible to get around; I hope you have gotten the things we left at Mr. Sibert's for you;

I presume you all were at Millcreek last Sunday at preaching; I thought of you. I know I shall miss old Mill Creek more than any other church in Page; for I have had very nice times there; I would like to know how they get along with there Singing;

I believe I will stop for this is such bad papper; I doubt if you can read it; if not send it back and I will write it over; I do not believe I asked you to write to me; it was not because I did not want to write to you but because I did not think of it; I want you to write and give me all the news of Page; if it will not take to much of your time from writing <u>to Mart</u>.

We are all well all stood traveling very well. Mother was complaining some with the headaches; Please don't expose this poorly written letter; I will try and do better next time; Give my love to all inquiring friends & accept a good share for yourself: Hoping to hear from you soon. I remain

your sincere friend
S.E. Buswell

In November, Isaac Hite writes from Brandy Station, near Culpeper Court House. We do not know whether Daniel Hite ever made a trip to the army encampment either with or without Henry Gander, Isaac's future father-in-law. Martin and Isaac now are serving together in Lee's body guard. Diana is the wife of David Hite, now in a Yankee prison camp.

Camp Near Brandy St.
Tuesday Nov 3rd 1863

Dear Father:-

All has been quiet here for some time past, more than once in a while there is a little picket fighting along the line. The weather is now very fine, and a good time for putting up winter quarters, which some of the soldiers are doing, though I hardly think we will winter so low down as this. Forage can not be had here in sufficient quantities to do the army this winter. I have nothing of interest to write at present, but as I have been looking for a letter from some of you for some time, and [as] it seems that none is Coming I have concluded to write again and try to stir you up. Bettie or Ella has not written to me since I left home. Write some times whether you have any thing to write about or not.

Father as you have never visited the army since the war Commenced, I think you and Henry Gander could splice teams and come down this fall. Gander has one horse wagon which you could hitch to, and make the trip in about four days, or come horse back just as you choose. Do not forget to bring something along to eat, for rations are getting very scarce here. The beef that we get for some time is so rank that we can't eat, therefore we have nothing but dry bread. If Diana has made my hat I wish you would send it down by Martin Gander. I shall soon be bareheaded and barefooted. A requisition was again sent in this morning for shoes and clothes, but whether we can get them I do not know as we have been duped so often.

Nothing more at present. hoping this may find you all well, I remain your affectionate son

Isaac

We don't know if the proposed September visit actually took place, but now Bettie Strickler again urges Bettie Hite to pay a visit to New Market.

New Market Sh. Co. Va Dec 13th

Dear Cousin

I seat myself this morning for the purpose of droping you a few lines to let you know that we are all well at present. hopeing this may find you all enjoying the same great blessing.

I had not heared from you I have almost come to the conclusion you have forgotten me and so I thought I would write and remind you that there was still such a being as myself in creation, now tell me what you have ben & doing and why you have kept your self so quiet so long

Well Cousin this is a lonely Sabbath. I wish you was hear to cheer my drooping spirits a little. it has been raining all the morning but it looks now as if it was going to clear off and I am in hopes we will have a bright day, I understand there is to be Singing at Mr Zirkles School house to day but I do not think there will be many there. I should liked very much to have ben there as it is the first singing that has bin in the in the [sic] neighbour hood for about two years

Well Cousin Bettie dont you wish this war was over and we could enjoy ourselves as we once did. I think we would know better how to appreciate good times than we once did. it seems that we can hear of nothing but trouble and distress through out the land

Cousin [Benjamin] Frank[lin] Strickler [10th Va. Cav.] was wounded in the late fight at the Rapahannock. he is now in the Hospi-

tal at Richmond. he wrote for some of us to visit him and Sister Selina has gone. She thinks She will bring him home as soon as he gets able to be moved, that is if they will let him come.

Cousin I received a letter from your brother Isaac this morning. he is well. I wish you to write to me and tell me how to direct a letter to him. he wrote but it is on such bad paper that I cannot make it out. his Captains name is what I must to know. and let me know if Cousin David is still a prisoner

nothing more at presant but remaning your effectionat cousin
Bettie Strickler

Come over soon, my love to all the family

As a courier for the headquarters staff, Isaac has kept a horse throughout his enlistment, and here, from relatively quiet winter quarters, he writes another letter about horses. Daniel Beaver, father of John P., seems to be visiting headquarters again.

Head Quarters A.N.Va.
Camp near Orange C.H.
December 13,/1863

Dear Father,

As you wished to know in your letter a short time since, how my horse was getting, and as I wrote to Daniel about a week ago that he was doing very well, and thought then, perhaps he would stand it until near Spring, but since I have come to the conclusion that he would be entirely broken down by that time, and possibly injured in some way, and as I will have to have another, I shall therefore try for an leave of absence in a week or two. I write you this therefore to make some inquiries who has a horse to sell that would be likely to suit. Horses next Spring will, I am afraid be much higher than they are now, and as I will have to have another I think it would be best to b[u]y now. I will pay you what is right to keep this one until Spring. Mr. Beaver was wondering a few days ago whether you had that plow point that you promised him, and if you still have it he says "he wishes you would keep it until spring when he will want it." I have no news to write. I received a letter from Bettie a few days ago. This leaves us all well, and hope will find you all the Same.

Yours affectionately
I. M. Hite

THE PAINFUL NEWS I HAVE TO WRITE

Isaac Martin Hite 1835–1898

From daguerrotype circa 1858.
Newspaper clipping found in frame under picture:

What a pitiful set these old bachelors are!
Every person of taste must allow;
And to kiss one—believe me, I'd rather by far
Give a buss to my mammy's old cow.

HOMEFRONT AND HEADQUARTERS 1863 & 1864   161

As the new year begins, Isaac has apparently made the trip home to get the horse. He now writes to sister Ella and alludes to the major recruitment effort undertaken to replenish the ranks depleted since Gettysburg.

Head Quarters A.N.Va.
Camped near Orange C.H.
January 26/64

Dear Sister Ella,
I arrived in Camp safe on the second evening after leaving home. I got as far as Criglersville the first nigh[t], and staid with a man by the name of Story. I was down to the 33rd Regt. a few days ago. Tell Father that I saw Capt. Shuler and he said that he had written to him a few days before concerning John's back pay, and in what manner to proceed to get it. He would have written sooner, but their was some dispute concerning the clothing money which he did not assertain until quite recently.

Since I Came to Camp their has been a strong talk of sending a portion to the Bat. back to some place to recruit the horses, but as the old Maj is always contrary to reason and justice, I suppose therefore that it will not be done.

Yestarday there was some clothing issued to the company again, but as mine happened to be tolerably good I could not get any. In order to get any clothing from the government any more, one must lay round in camp most naked for a month or two. We had one fellow that had been waring nothing but drawers for some time.

The weather is very warm and fine now. It really looks more like spring than the middle of winter. Tell all who may ask concerning our Comp. that it is nearly full, and that if they wish to join it, they had better hasten here immediately. We are only allowed a few more. Recruits are coming in every day. This leaves me well.
From your affectionate brother Isaac

Meanwhile, life in Page County continues. Bettie Hite has indeed become a pupil of cousin Ambrose B. Rothgeb who, after losing his hand with the Dixie Artillery at Malvern Hill in July, 1862, has resumed the job of schoolmaster. He now sends the tuition bill.

The Painful News I Have to Write

Bethlehem Feb 10/64

Cousin Daniel
   Sir, The session of my school being half out, one half of the subscription money, according to my terms is now due. You can send me the money if you have it to spare & I will send you a receipt.

Very respectfully
AB Rothgeb

½ Subscription	$12.50
1 Spel. & bot ink	
9 Shts. pap.	$3.50
Amt	$16.00

And on small piece of lined paper, triple-folded, comes a dinner invitation for the young ladies from Barbara Rothgeb, Ambrose's mother and a neighbor of the Gander family.

March 23rd 1864

Bettie & Ella Hite,
   You are respectfully invited to come and take dinner at my house on Friday next.

Very respectfully
Barbara Rothgeb

When he hears of David's exchange from a Yankee prison, Isaac writes home from his Battalion of Scouts, Guides, and Couriers. The price of horses reflects the great inflation in Confederate notes. John's funeral is to wait until the end of the War.

Battalion S.G.&C.
Aprl. 4th 1864

Dear Father,
   I received your letter a few days ago stating that David had gotten home. I would like very well to get there while he is at home, and think perhaps I will get there about the first of May.
   I have some idea of selling my horse to a member of the company who has none, which if I do, I can get another horse detail. He offers seven hundred dollars in new issue which I have concluded to take as soon as he gets the money if he does not back out.

Homefront and Headquarters 1863 & 1864

Whether I get there or not while David is there, you can have John's funeral preached if you wish, for if I cannot meet him there this time it is not likely that we both will get there any ways shortly.

If I do get off I will try to let you know a week or two beforehand.

It has commenced snowing again this morning. We have had mostly rough weather for some time. Day before yesterday it snowed and rained nearly all day. Every thing seems to be very quiet here now, which I suppose is on account of the roughness of the weather. Many here seem to be in good hopes that the war will end this summer, though I cannot hear of anyone having any good grounds for thus believing.

Your affectionate Son I.M. Hite

Not until July do we have any more communication from the army. We have no family letters on the great campaigns of the Wilderness, Spotsylvania, Cold Harbor, or Grant's assault on Petersburg which has forced the relocation of Lee's Headquarters to that vicinity. The fortifications at Drewry's Bluff on the James below Richmond have been unsuccessfully assaulted by Union Gen. Benjamin Franklin Butler on May 10, 1864. Thereafter, Butler's force is bottled up between Petersburg and Richmond and is effectively out of action until the end of the war. This situation continues as Isaac finally writes to Ella.

Camp Petersburg, July 24th, '64

Dear Sister,

I received Bettie's letter a few days ago, and was glad to hear from home again. There has not been much change taken place since I last wrote—for the past day or two there have been some troops sent from here; it is said, to Claffins Bluffs just below Druras [Drewry's] Bluffs on the James river. As preaching is about to commence in Camp I will stop until it is over.

Well Ella I have just returned from preaching and though the sermon was not as good as I have heard him preach on several former occasions yet it was a good one for camp. He has been with the army since the commencement [of the] war; for some time previous to the war he was pastor of the church at Bethel where the yankees at the commencement of the war were so badly whipped and routed.

The position of the two armies round Petersburg is yet the same. Picket firing is yet kept up nearly constantly, though shelling has nearly ceased. There has been no shells thrown into the city for several days. Mortar firing has been f[ar] more frequent than any other

164 **THE PAINFUL NEWS I HAVE TO WRITE**

for some time, more especially at night. They are very beautiful to look at. They are shot high in the air, making the arc of a circle, so that they will drop just behind the fortif[i]cations and explode.

It was reported here yestarday evening that Genl. [John Bell] Hood (who is now in command of Johnson's army) had whipped Sherman but as to day is Sunday we will get no further news until tomorrow.

On last Tuesday 19th we had a fine rain here which settled the deep dust, and made every thing look green again, though I do not think that most of corn fields here will make over a half crop. It is getting dry again. Tell Mother I drew a pair of pants a few days ago by hard work, as my old ones still look tolerably well since I patched them. When you write again let me know whether the orchard has much fruit in [it] and how the grapes and watermelons &c are doing.

A few furloughs are being given again, and if they are kept up until fall I think it will come my time about September.

This leaves me well and hope may find you all the same.

From your
Affectionate brother Isaac

Write soon.

Leaving Isaac and the "scouts, guides, and couriers" at Lee's headquarters, we return to the Page Greys of the Stonewall Brigade, now without any of the Hite brothers in the ranks.

CHAPTER 11

David: Declining Fortunes & a Third Fatal Blow

*"He has followed William and John
where wars are no more."*

We have no letters from David Hite. The only one of the brothers married before the war, his letters have been kept by his wife, Dianna (Cline), who is later to live with the Hite family until her 1879 remarriage to Rappahannock County widower E. S. Brown. And any letters in her possession are now lost to the family.

After his capture at Gettysburg, David has been transferred on July 28, 1863, to the U.S.A. General Hospital, Baltimore, and then on August 20 to the Federal Prison Camp at Point Lookout, Maryland. He is finally exchanged on March 17, 1864, at City Point, Virginia, and remains at home when cousin Ambrose Hite writes this letter to Bettie. Ulysses S. Grant, whose fighting reputation is known both North and South, has recently been named General-in-Chief of the Army of the United States.

Camp Stone-wall Brigade
Orange Co. Va April 15th [1864]

Dear Cousin;
I avail myself of the pleasure, this morning to drop you a few lines, to let you know that I am still in the land of the living. I am well at present and, hope these few lines may find you enjoying your self. I will now try & give you a little news about the army. Our army has recruited up right smart during this last winter. Our brigade numbers about eleven hundred. Some few of the men are deserting, & going to the yankys. Their are some six or seven out of our company, that intends to desert, they intended to go last night, but the Capt. found them out, & placed a guard out to catch them. So they found out that the Capt. had a guard out & never went.
I expect that they will attempt it again to night. I was up till eleven o'clock last night watching them.
We have a large force here on the Rapidann river. The yankys have a much larger force than what we have. Jen. Grant is in command of the yanky troops north of the Rapidann river. Jen. Grant

**David Christian Hite 1832–1864
Dianah (Cline) Hite 1834–Circa 1901?**

From daguerrotype, perhaps wedding photo, circa 1855.

DAVID: DECLINING FORTUNES & A THIRD FATAL BLOW

says he is going to Richmond this spring, but I think he will miss it. I thought some time ago that the yankys would prove too hard for us, as they had so many more men than what we had.

The yanks say that Jen Grant is the best Jen. that they have ever had in command of the Potomic. I heard good newes last night, which I hope may be true. I heard that Jen. Longstreet's corpse [that is, of course, corps] had arrived at Charletsvill Va. A Lieut. from the 2nd Regt. returned from furlough yesterday evening & said that he saw Longstreet at Charletsvill, which is thought to be a reliable tale. It is also reported that Jen. J.H. Morgan is on his way here to Join Jen. Lee. Jen. Morgan has command of about eighteen hundred cavelry-men.

I hope that these reports may be true. I hope that we may succeed in whiping the yanks this spring. Our summer campaign will soon commence, as the weather is getting so pretty. We have two drills a day, one before dinner, & the other one after dinner. I heard the other day, that David had reached home again. I suppose that report is true. I would like to see David very much, as it has been some time since I have seen him. I suppose he has lots of things to talk about.

I hope that he may have a long furlough. We have six in our mess now. I should have liked very much to been there at that in-for that occured sometime ago. I thought that you would have been one of the waitors, you and Mr. _____ some body els.

I heard that some of the girls of Page were very sorry, that those cavelry-men left the county. I do not mean <u>you</u> or <u>Ella</u>.

I must now bring my nonsense to a close, for I wreckon you are getting tired reading so uninteresting a letter as <u>this</u>. My love to <u>you</u> and Ella. Excuse bad writing & composition. Plese write as soon as this come to hand & give me all the newes.

I remain your sincere cousin A.M. Hite

There are no confirmed reports of desertions from Company H at this time, but the summer campaign does indeed soon commence—with disastrous results for the Stonewall Brigade. The first battle is that of the Wilderness, reported thus by George Buswell:

Thurs. 5th [May, 1864]. Ewel's corps is maneuvering in the <u>Wilderness</u> between Locust Grove & Wilderness Tavern. Became engaged about noon. Were engaged 3 or 4 hours in which our company lost heavily. The noble [Capt. Michael] Shuler was killed instantly. Others killed and mortally wounded, viz. Wm. R. Young, Philip M.

Somers, Joseph L. Cullars¹ & Willis Cubbage. Wounded; Sergt. E[dmund] J. Rothgeb, A[mbrose] C. Huffman, David Burns, E[dward] C. Mauck, Reuben Judy & Wm. S. Yates. We formed our lines after the firing ceased & fortified.

In just a few days, the armies have moved about ten miles southeast to Spotsylvania, and Buswell reports of the next engagements:

Tues. 10th. Am on rear guard. Right smart skirmish & artillery firing along our lines all day. About 7 pm the Yankees advanced in several lines on [Maj. Gen. Robert E.] Rode[s]'s & the left of [Maj. Gen. Edward] Johnson's Div. [George] Dole[s]'s Brig, Ga.'s, gave way to let them get about 200 yards in rear of our breastworks, but were finally repulsed by desperate fighting. In this fight Lieut. [Perry] Kite, Alfred M. Kite & myself were wounded. We reached the field hospital about midnight & had our wounds dressed. Lieut. Col. [George] Huston, commanding our Regt., also wounded.

Wed. 11th. My leg pains me some. No fighting of any consequence today. Wrote home.

Thurs. 12th. Slept but little last night. A most desperate engagement commenced at dawn this morning in which Maj. Gen. Johnson, Brig. Gen. [George H. Steuart] Stewart & a great part of Johnson's Div. were made prisoners. Lieut. [Charles T.] Chadduck & the greater part of Co. "H" were captured. J's Div. stood the blunt of this engagement & the heavy loss of prisoners was occasioned by the cowardice of the 2nd Brigade. My wound pained me a good deal last night but feels pretty easy today. Jessie W. Riley was slightly wounded on the heel. Eml Rothgeb reported killed or wounded. Lieut. [O.H.P.] Kite, Alfred Kite & [Jessie W.] Riley were sent to corps hospital. Captured today; Lieut. Chadduck, Sergt. [Charles A.] Young, Corpls. [B.F.] Coffman & [Daniel B.] Abbott, [James J.] Comer, [Ambrose] Hite, [John T.] Johnston, Ben Kite, J. H. Cubbage, [Bushrod] Oden, J. Ensign, A. H. Keyser. Seven of the Co. escaped.

The much briefer diary of Lt. Oliver Hazard "Perry" Kite gives these reports for the days of the Wilderness and Spotsylvania battles:

DAVID: DECLINING FORTUNES & A THIRD FATAL BLOW   169

Thur. May 5 - Left Camp pretty early, skirmishing commenced on our line about 11 oc A.M. Capt. Shuler was killed dead about 3 oclock P.M. Co H. had 8 wounded & 4 killed.

Tue. May 10 - Skirmishing commenced in our front. Early this morn, heavy cannonading on our lef Yankees made a charge on our left, in front of Doles Georgia Brigade, Georgia brigade gave way, Buswell, A. Kite & myself wounded.

Wed. May 11 - Things pretty quiet this morning. Skirmishing along the line of our Division, our troops in fine spirits, we still hold our breast works, no particular news.

Thur. May 12 - Heavy fighting cannonading this morning on our right. Yankees taken our works but we retaken them again, most desperate fight of the war, last 10 oclock P.M.

In these few days' battles, casualties to the Stonewall Brigade have reduced it to just 249 effectives and with no commanding officer. Total losses to Lee's army in the Wilderness are reported at 2000 killed, 6000 wounded, and 3400 missing. At Spotsylvania they are 1000 killed, 5000 wounded, and 3000 missing. Union losses are nearly twice that number, but Lee has no reserves to fill his depleted ranks.

No officers remain on duty in Co. H. Reports of the killed and wounded depend on diaries such as these, and, for the captured, on Union records. There are no official service records for the wound of Jessie Riley, the fate of Emanuel Rothgeb, or the capture of of Bushrod Oden. No record of any sort has been found for a William R. Young wounded on May 5 or for a J. Ensign captured on May 12. Though Buswell reports him mortally wounded on May 5, Willis Cubbage is listed as present on June 9. Of those reported captured, only John T. Johnston is exchanged in time to rejoin before war's end. George Buswell's wound becomes infected and heals very slowly. Multiple furlough extensions put him out of further action, though just at the end he makes an attempt to rejoin the company.

On May 14, the remnants of the Stonewall Brigade are combined with others, marking the end of this renowned fighting unit. The 33rd Virginia and fragments of thirteen other regiments become known as Terry's Brigade.

By mid-June this new brigade returns to the Shenandoah Valley with the rest of Early's corps. After driving the Federals from the upper valley they march north down the valley, and on July 5 invade Maryland once more. David Hite has rejoined Co. H some time before this date. Though they approach the defenses of Washington and badly frighten that city, Union reinforcements and their own diminished ranks force a retreat beginning on July 12.

Recovered from his wound, Perry Kite has returned to duty by late August and makes the following report in his diary:

Wed. Aug. 31 - Cool morning, no news of importance, washed pair of drawers, worte a letter to A. E. J., nice day, weather pleasant, health improving, 18 of Co. H in Camp, 16 Privates, 1 non-commissioned officer, & a Commissioned Officer Virg. Lt O.H.P. Kite, Sert't E.J. Rothgeb, Privates D.C. Hite, Peter S. Miller, A.C. Huffman, Jim Printz, Geo A. Rothgeb, Wm S. Yates, David Burns, Henry Aleshire, Early Cubbage, Robt Cubbage, Harrison W. Koontz, Geo W. Campbell, Joel Knight, Jessie W. Riley, M.S.S. Mims, Hiram Printz & E.C. Mauck No of members with Co H, 33 Reg't.

Meanwhile Sheridan's Union troops have moved into Winchester and are systematically plundering and burning the lower Shenandoah Valley. Finally in a strategic position on September 19, Early's troops move on Sheridan, meeting at Opequon Creek about three miles northeast of Winchester. Results are disastrous for the Confederates who, before the action ends three days later, lose 250 killed including Maj. Gen. Rodes, 1777 wounded, and 2813 captured. Sheridan loses 749 killed, 4440 wounded, and 357 missing, but drives Early from Winchester and the lower Valley. Perry Kite's diary reports simply:

Mon Sept 19 - Left Bunker Hill about 4 A.M. got to line of battle, fought the Yanks nearly all day. <u>I was wounded about 3 oclock P.M. wounded on Breast Got off field.</u>

DAVID: DECLINING FORTUNES & A THIRD FATAL BLOW 171

At home in Page County on September 22 and 23, two doctors probe unsuccessfully for the bullet in his chest, and, though later diary entries report signs of healing, his is to die on May 5, 1866, likely as a final result of this wound.

The last fatal blow to the Hite family is described in Isaac's letters of October 11 and 20.

Petersburg Va. October 11th 1864

Dear Father,
Your short letter dated the 22nd of Sept. just reached me this morning. It was the first I heard of the death of my dear brother. And it is true that he too has passed through the dark "valley of the shadow of death" to enter the world beyond the grave. He has followed William and John where wars are no more, and where the awful booming of cannon shall not be heard again.

If they rest quietly in Abraham's bosom as did Lazarus, they are much better off than here. Like those before him, he died in defence of his country, and no mortal man I believe, can ever say ought against them. He fell on the same day I suppose, that the brave general Rodes did, which shows that the great as well as the small are taken to fill the chasm to bridge the way for the triumphal car of liberty to pass. And yet thousands more may be taken to bridge the way, but surely that great Being who is too wise to err has not suffered this great sacrafice of human life in vain. And will those who survive this war, and are transplanted on the shores of liberty look back in a few thoughts to behold the bones of those who lie at the bottom of their security, or think for a moment they are the ones who died to reclaim them from phanatical thraldom. Many may not think; who pass safely through this war without scarcely loosing any kindred blood, of the many thousands that have died, but with the poor widows and the families whose members are being constantly taken, shall long cast a sigh over the tombs that soon will cover every hill top. May this people soon all turn to God that He will look down with a pitying eye, and stop this struggle. He and He only can stop it. The wisdom and the sagacity of the generals on one side seems to balance that of the generals of the oppo[site] side, and thus with varying success for nearly four years does this war still continue.

I hope you will write me the particulars about David so soon as you have an opportunity to do so. His remains I suppose were abandoned and left in the hands of the enemy unburied; if so they will never be found. It would be a great satisfaction to have his and John's remains brought home and interred there, but I fear it can never be done.

I suppose there is no mail to Page yet, though I have heard the yankees have fallen back down the valley. I fear to hear from there, for if Grant's order has been carried out, the valley has been stripped of everything, and the people left in a starving condition. I have heard from the lower part of the valley, and there it is said there is nothing left. Those once opulent and know not what poverty was are now beggars. And such is this war, to bring the proud and haughty to be beggars and to teach them that affluence and wealth may not always surround them.

We had a small fight on the north side of James river last Thursday in which we captured about six hundred prisners, and drove the yankees out of one line of breastworks. Lt. Lionbergers servant will will take this to Luray, and if you get it before he starts back I wish you would try and send me a pair of socks by him. I have gotten well of the chills somtime ago, and am well at present. I hope you all the same.

Your affectionate son Isaac

In the battles of Darbytown Road on October 7 and 13, including the "fight on the north side of the James" mentioned here, Union losses are reported at 105 killed, 502 wounded, and 206 missing. As the War continues to sap Confederate strength, Isaac's letters voice more and more of the frustration, vain hopes, and rumors which he shares with the rest of Lee's army.

Camp near Petersburg Va. Oct 20, 64

Dear Father,

But a few months ago the prospect for an early peace seemed quite favorable; indeed it so fasten'd on the minds of many, that they could not think otherwise. Then came the fall of Atlanta with some other reverses to our arms which soon settle the dark cloud on our side, and again the despondency of the people were more general perhaps, than at any previous date of the war. But now again I am glad to say this cloud is fast passing from above us, and casting its shadow once more on the yankee nation. Grant here and north of the James river has made several feeble attemps recently to storm our fortifications, but every time he has been so easily repulsed with heavy loss, that by the time the northern election is over he may abandon this route and pronounce it altogether impracticable. His efforts every time are growing more feeble, and unless he is heavily reinforced between this and their presidential election, I am of opinion there will be no further effort made to take Richmond this campaign. However they may rise and come with double energy between this and that time, but I believe that we have a sufficient force to meet any number that they can bring agains us.

Sheridan has been forced and compelled to retreat down the valley and thus made to abandon the idea of taken Lynchburg or Richmond from the back side. Hood has flanked Sherman in Georgia, and is now playing havock with his long line of communication in his rear.

Little positive reliable information is now furnished from the two contending armies in Georgia, yet, but little doubt is entertained but that Sherman and his army are in a very critical condition. These facts with others have revived the spirits of our army very much for the past week or two.

Our armies have also been rapidly filled up by calling in the reserves, and by an order of the secretary of war revoking all detales [special assignments?] made by that power. Our armies will be as strong this fall as they were last spring, but should they want another recruiting, I cannot see for my life where the men are to come from. If our independence is not gained within the next six months I fear we are a ruined people. The men that we had to recruit our armies next spring have been needed this fall. We now have all the men in the field, we have have no mor[e] to fall back on, and unless our independence is made secure before our present armies dwindle down we must and will be driven to our last and only hopes; that of coming under a monarchal government. We will have to do away with slavery—renounce self government and call on England or France to aid us to establish a limited mona[r]chy. I cannot see any other hopes in case we fail. The Richmond papers are speaking of Southern field negroes for soldiers, by promising freedom to all who will enlist as such. But this I do not believe would do us any good. If northern negroes will not fight who have been enlightened and permitted to enjoy many privileges, It is not reasonable to suppose that a Southern field negro will, who are kept in total ignorance of everything pertain[ing] to real happiness or freedom. Besides if this is a white man's government let white men sustain it or let it fall.

I received your letter yestarday dated 13th. I also received the one you wrote shortly after you heard of David's death. I answered that one the next day after getting it, and sent it by Lt Lionberger's boy who was going to Luray. In your last you stated that David was not dead when he was abandoned and left to the mercy of the yankees. I suppose you have no hopes of his recovery. There can be but little *hopes of his recovery if both legs were cut off above his knees, though more extraordinary ones have been known since the war. I wish when you write you would write more particular about him, and let me know what was the opinion of those who saw him last, that is if you have heard any of them express it.*

Your last letter almost sickens me to think how mien the cowardly yankees have done. I would seem like enough to provoke the Heavens to wrathful vengeance, and change every sprig of grass to venimous adders to sting the villians to destruction. This destruction of property was done by an order of Grants, for says he "if this war is to continue another year longer let the valley be a desert waste." Sheridan in one of his reports to Grant says "all day Saturday and Sunday the work of destruction continued." Your loss is much less than I expected it would be. I was most sure the barn would be in ashes with perhaps nearly all the grain and hay.

Mr. [Reuben] Dadisman's loss must to have been heavier than any one elses for far around. He has been very unfortunate and with many others must be very low in spirits. I imagine there must have been a deep gloom of sadness and despair pervading all classes when this work of destruction was going on. The Heavens were lit from the heard earned labor of thousands, while they could only stand spectators and see the food of life melting into ashes.

When you write again, write me all the particulars. Your last was looked for much sooner than it came, and gave me much relief to know that things were no worse than what they are. This leaves me well and hope may find you all the same.

Yours farewell I.M. Hite

David's body is never found. His funeral with that of brother John is celebrated the following September. And just one more letter from Isaac is to mark the closing months of the war.

Memoritechnica.

—:o:—

DAVID C. HITE departed this life September 19th 1864. He fell mortally wounded in the memorable battle at Winchester, about two hours before sundown. He was struck by a cannon ball, taking both legs nearly off between the body and the knees. Some of the company being close by, went to his aid, but found his situation such that he could not be moved and the enemy pressing very close. They told him his situation was such that he could not be moved and he told them to lay him down and do the best they could for themselves; they did so and placed his knapsack under his head and left him; that is the last we have ever heard of him. It is supposed that he bled to death in a very short time. He belonged to the 33rd Regiment Va. Volunteers, and the Stonewall Brigade. His body is now numbered among the dead, while his soul ever liveth and we hope forever at rest. He was wounded twice before, one time in the arm slightly and the next time in the neck badly. His age was 31 years 11 month and 3 days.

**Memorial Notice From David Hite's Funeral Service
September 10, 1865.**

CHAPTER 12

War's End and Epilogue

*"It is awful! Can a just God behold
such iniquity much longer?"*

Isaac, the last of Daniel Hite's soldier sons, writes the last of these wartime letters from Lee's Headquarters near Petersburg. Rumors of military movements, speculations about horses, and anguish for the Confederate plight precede his personal request for winter gloves.

Camp Near Petersburg Dec. 10, 64

Dear Father,
    For the past few days there has been a considerable stir among the troops. [Maj. Gen. G.K.] Warrens sixth Corps of the Yankee army started a few days ago for North Carolina—supposed he is making his way to the relief of Sherman. It is said that Warren taken with him a large quantity of supplies. Genl. A. P. Hill's Corps with two divisions of [Lt. Gen. Wade] Hampton's Cavalry, and I have heard also that [Lt. Gen. John B.] Gordon's division, have gone in pursuit. Gordons division passed through Petersburg a few days ago, but whether it has gone with Hill I have not positively learned.
    Nothing as yet has been heard from them. Sherman is said to be making his way towards the Atlantic coast, with [Lt. Gen. W.J.] Harde[e]s corps in his front opposing him, by blocading his roads, burning brid[g]es, and fighting him when he comes up. It was generally believed that a bloody fight would soon come of[f] here, but last night it sleeted and rained which will put off all hostile demonstrations for awhile, and perhaps for the winter, if the weather should continue rough for awhile.
    In my letter to Bettie a short time ago I said that I thought that the battallion would be disbanded for the winter. It is very uncertain now whether it will, though it is all the talk in camp. If it is disbanded I am one already detailed for to stay, so you need not look for me at all this winter.
    We are still drawing no corn and have not drawn more than a feed or two for past two weeks. All we get for our horses is a little hay and straw. They will all die before spring with this. In your letter you said that you had more horses than you could well winter, and that

War's End and Epilogue 177

you did not know what to do about selling one just now. My opinion is, that you had better sell this winter, for next spring horses will all be pressed into service close, and of course they will take them at government prices. Whether there will be any change made in the currency this winter is hard to tell, but if there is, the price that you could get of a private individual above the price that the government pays would perhaps more than make up for depreciation of the now present currency. Again you may keep them til spring, and still sell them for a great deal more than you can now by doing this before the government agents come round gathering up horses. I think from present appearances that there will be a great many horses wanted by spring.

Many of our soldiers here getting very mien. They club up in squads of six to a dozen and go through the country and do just as they please. The citizens fear them worse than high way robers. They shoot down stock, break into their meet houses, and take any thing that they want in present of the owner. They frequently shoot where the owners make any show of defence for their property. Not long since a child was shot and killed by one of this band who aimed to shoot the lady of the house who had reproached them for taken some of her property.

It is awful! Can a just God behold such iniquity much longer. I think it is alarming to see how fast this goverment is going to ruin. I fear we will never be a free people again.

If you have any chance I wish you would tell Mother to have me a pair of yarn gloves knit, and send to me. Eugene Flinn is now in Luray, and he may be there yet when you get this as he has a thirty day furlough.

I have been very unwell for the past four or five days with something like the chills. Nothing more at present but remain your affectionate

Son Isaac

The winter passes with a standstill in the siege of Petersburg and with no personal news from the front. An entry in George Buswell's diary confirms that Isaac has reached home at least once more before war's end:

Sun. *19th [February 1865]. Went with Sis to the preaching at Leaksville. Cousin Ella & Isaac Hite came home with us.*

Though he is not fully recovered from his leg wound, George Buswell describes his own failed attempt to return to the Page Greys in the spring and mentions the plans of Perry Kite and Charles Chadduck, also never realized. Martin Gander is reported at home in Buswell's entries of March 1, 12, and 29. He is not present to be paroled at Appomattox, nor is Charles E. Biedler, another one-time member of Lee's Bodyguard. Eugene Flinn, named in Isaac's letter above, does remain to the end. Ambrose C. Booten, the beloved pastor of Mill Creek Church, dies on March 29, 1865. Entries from the Buswell diary:

> *Wed. 15th [March]. Rainy. I went to Luray & made arrangements to start to camp on the 22nd inst.*
>
> *Tues. 21st. Went to Cousin A. Hite's with Mary & then to Luray & back. Got wet. Decided upon going to camp next Wednesday.*
>
> *Wed. 29th. Uncle Booten died this morning about 8 oclock. I started to the army. Took dinner at Mr. Noah Kite's, where Lt. Kite met me. We stayed all night at Dr. Jennings. Had a nice time, of course.*
>
> *Thurs. 30th. Started about 8 am, stopped a few minutes at Mrs. Kite's. We crossed the Ridge at Swift Run Gap, fed at Stanardsville & went to Liberty Mills. Rained nearly all day. Rapidan past fording.*
>
> *Fri. 31st. I went to Gordonsville & back. Learned that the R.R. would not be in running order to Richmond before the 10th or 12th of April. We, Lt. Kite & myself, went to Mr. Noah Henkel's for the night.*
>
> *Sat. 1st [April]. According to the conclusions of the previous evening, we started for home, fed & I took dinner at Criglersville. Fell in with Charlie Biedler & M. Crabill.*
>
> *Mon. 10th. Rainy. Lieut. Chadduck came up & told me that he and Lieut. Kite expected to start to the army next Wednesday on foot, so I could not go with them. I went out to see Lieut. Kite. Stopped awile at Mr. B's.*
>
> *Fri. 14th. Went to Honeyville & attended the funeral of R. Conner at Mt. Zion. Went to Leaksville, heard of the surrender of Gen Lee's army.*

War's End and Epilogue

We have no personal account of the sad last days of the war—the evacuation of Richmond and Lee's fighting retreat from Petersburg. Official records report that at Appomattox Court House, on April 9, 1865, I. M. Hite. Pvt., Co. C, 39 Batt'n Virginia Cavalry, is paroled with 1 Horse and equipments. Of Company H, the Page Greys of the 33rd Regiment, only Samuel Jobe, a teamster, is present to be paroled there.

Through the summer of 1865, the Page County country begins its slow return to normal. In September George Buswell attends the services for John and David Hite preached by Baptist ministers William C. Lauck and by Philip McInturff, the sucessor to Ambrose Booten at the Mill Creek church:

Sun. 10th. Went to preaching at Hamburg. Revs. Misters Lauck & McInturff preached J. P. & D. C. Hite's funerals. Went to night meeting at Leaksville with Miss Mollie G. & home.

In 1867 the remains of John P. Hite, with hundreds of others, are removed from their burial place near Gettysburg and buried in a common grave in Hollywood Cemetery, Richmond, Virginia.

Martin Gander marries Bettie Hite on December 21, 1865. They move onto the farm of Martin's bachelor granduncle, Isaac Maggart, supporting him until he dies on June 6, 1872. Martin and Bettie live until March 29, 1926, and September 15, 1927. Their Gander grandchildren, great grandchildren and great, great grandchildren live on the Maggart farm to this day.

Details of Isaac Hite's courtship of Mary Ann Gander are lost to us, but on February 6, 1868, he marries this Miss Mollie who once had a crow pick with John Hite. George Buswell's diary gives this report of the wedding and three days of celebration capped by the baptism of Mrs. Mary A. Ruffner, age about 43, "a very large lady":

Jan. 31st [1868]. I stayed all night with Isaac Hite. His time is drawing near, says he is getting <u>scared.</u>

Feb. 1st. Went home this morning. Thermometer at Cousin Daniel Hite's stood at 4° below 0.

Feb. 6th. Attended Isaac Hite's wedding at Mr. Gander's. Had a very pleasant time. The attendants were: Miss Ella Hite & myself; Miss Sallie Gander & Jos. Brubaker; Miss Annie Rothgeb & Jos. Brumback; Miss Ella Cline & Jno. Grove; Miss Cassie Brubaker & Amb. Hite; & Miss Ella Buswell & J.B. Compton. Officiating clergyman, Rev. Wm. C. Lauck.

Feb. 7th. Left Mr. Gander's at 11 A.M., went by White House & Hamburg & arrived at Cousin Daniel Hite's at 11:45. Only a few neighbors there besides the attendants. Of course had a nice dinnter & spent the evening quite pleasantly & tolerably merrily.

Feb. 8th. Party went to church at Mill Creek & to the river to witness the baptisim of Mrs. Joshua Ruffner, a very large lady. At the river our wedding party, after spending a very pleasant time, broke up; each gentleman taking his lady home. Jno. Grove & I took supper at Cousin D.H.'s & came home together.

An 1868 letter from the Jones family of Front Royal shows a continuation of the friendship begun during William Hite's convalescence, relapse, and death.

Miss E. Ella Hite Luray Page Co Virginia
Front Royal Sept 20

My Dear Friends Mr and Mrs Hite
Though some time has elapsed since we had the pleasure of hearing from you, yet it requires no effort to arouse all the the kindly feelings of former days, with me they are but as yesterday. but with so much to engroce our time we are too apt to neglect giving expression by keeping up on interchange of views and feelings by which we might more frequently be reminded of the flight of time and how rappidly we are passing away. the time is not far distant at farthest when I trust we shall all meet where there shall be no more parting of friends and if permitted to know each other there, Oh what a joyful meeting, and then to see our Saviour too, but then I am ready to ask can it be one so unworthy as I should enjoy such a blessing. we are having an evidence of the Christian Religion in the last hours of one who is now about to depart. Miss Mattie Reynolds who you no doubt remember (niece of Mrs Clouds). She took leave of the family this afternoon and is anxious to depart. She has been a very consistent Christian. her

health has been delicate for some time. her mother (Mrs Clouds sister) died last Spring. She too became much afflicted, we have had several very sudden deaths in our community recently. Major Brown son of Dr. Brown died & left a wife and 3 little girls a Mrs Bigs died suddenly left 2 children, several others in the neighbourhood.

Jane and Eva have gone to make Mrs Cloud a visit. She is living in Upperville Loudin Cy. enclosed I send you the Photograph of Mrs Caffroths family having made her a visit last Spring. I delivered your mesage. She with great pleasure complyed accomp[any]ing them with much love. I should have sent them early but waited until I could accompany them with a few lines.

her health has been very dellicate. She has spent the two last seasons at the Springs, Ella her oldest daughter spent her vacation with us, she is quite grown in Size, all unite in love to your family with a large share for your selfs and believe us as ever your friends

EA Jones

Sept. 28th 1868
Dear friend not having closed my letter I will tell you of the death of an other one out of our midst. Miss Lidey Jacobs daughter of Col. Jacobs one of the twins. She died this morning of Typhoyd fever.
your friend

Ea Jones
Mr and Mrs Hite

Gideon Jones adds a pencilled note.

Dear Friends
We hope soon to hear from you. I will then write to you with assurance of my kindest regards for yourselves & family Yrs affectionately,

G.W. Jones

Daniel Hite, the father of the four soldiers, died on November 18, 1876. Young Daniel S. Hite married and raised a family on the Hite farm where he died on May 4, 1934. His descendants still own this property southwest of Luray. His sister Eliza Ellen (Ella) who never married, lived most of her life on the same farm, died on May 19, 1935, and is buried on the pasture knoll with her parents and brother William. Also buried there are Bettie and Martin Gander and his parents Henry and Mary (Coffman) Gander.

Nebraska Douglas Hite (Braskie) married and lived in Oakton, Virginia, until his death on April 19, 1936. His wife gave birth to sixteen children, including four sets of twins. Only one of the eight twins lived to maturity.

Isaac and Mary Ann moved with their five children to Cooper County, Missouri, in 1885. On October 24, 1886, he wrote to his mother, the only letter we have which is written just to her. On November 4, 1897 he wrote, perhaps a last letter, to his spinster sister Ella:

> *Your letter of the 2nd inst received a few hours ago... containing the sad news of Mothers illness... Of course I would like extremely well to be there if I thought I could get there to see her alive and in her right mind, but thinking this doubtful, and know she is in the best of hands and that all will be done for her that can be done, I forego to make the attempt to get there in time.... But the chief reason for my not coming by myself is, that I have heart trouble for several years and I do not know whether it would be prudent for me to venture so far from home alone... but if it is not the will of Him who rules and does all things well to meet her here again may I be prepared to meet her above where there will be no more parting. Give her my love and tell her I think often of her.*

Rebecca (Grove) Hite died on November 6, probably before this letter was delivered. Isaac died less than a year later on September 22, 1898. His widow, Mary Ann, the author's (great) Grandma Hite, survived him nearly 45 years and died on June 23, 1943, at age 101, the last of the generation to whom the painful news had come.

APPENDIX A

Bibliography

Sources for the primary text are described in the Preface. Major reference sources include:

Bowman, John S., ed. *The Civil War Almanac.* New York: World Almanac Publications, 1983.

Catton, Bruce. *Picture History of the Civil War.* New York: American Heritage, 1960.

Commager, Henry Steele, ed. *The Blue and the Gray.* New York: Fairfax Press, 1991.

Grabill, John H., "Diary of a Soldier of the Stonewall Brigade," from *Shenandoah Herald*, Woodstock, VA, January, 1909. Charles Affleck Collection, Winchester-Frederick Co. Historical Society, Winchester, VA.

Hewett, Janet B., ed. *The Roster of Confederate Soldiers.* Wilmington, NC: Broadfoot Publishing Co., 1995-6 (16 vols.).

Kite, O. H. P. *Perpetual Diary, Jan. 1 - Dec. 31, 1864.* Penciled transcription. Marjorie Copenhaver Collection, Winchester-Frederick Co. Historical Society, Winchester, VA.

Miller, Francis T., ed. *The Photographic History of the Civil War.* New York: The Review of Reviews Co., 1911, 10 vols.

Moore, Robert H., II. *The Danville, Eighth Star New Market and Dixie Artillery.* Lynchburg: H.E. Howard, Inc., 1989.

Owens, Debby J., compiler. *Page County, Virginia, Federal Census, 1860.* Luray, VA: Genealogical Society of Page County, 1992.

Reidenbaugh. Lowell. *33rd Virginia Infantry.* Lynchburg: H.E. Howard, Inc., 1987.

Robertson, James I., Jr. *The Stonewall Brigade.* Baton Rouge: LSU Press, 1963.

Shuler, Michael. *Diary, 11 June to 12 December 1862.* Manuscript, Library of Congress (2 booklets) [#859 in *Civil War Manuscripts*, Library of Congress, Washington, 1986].

APPENDIX A: BIBLIOGRAPHY

Smith, Robert L. & Betsy G. *The Family of Daniel Hite and Rebecca Grove*. Privately printed, 1994 [Page County Library].

Spratt, Thomas M., compiler. *Page County, Virginia, Men in Gray*. Athens, GA: Iberian Publishing Co., 1994.

Sutton, Jean Buswell. *Diary of George Daniel Buswell*. Privately published, 1992 [Page County Library].

Wallace, Lee A., Jr. *A Guide to Virginia Military Organizations*. Richmond: Virginia Civil War Commission, 1964.

APPENDIX B

Hite Family Group Information

Daniel Hite, was b. in Shenandoah County, VA, on Feb. 12, 1808, the first of six children to David and Susannah (Spitler) Hite. On June 18, 1829 he m. Rebecca Grove who was b. Oct. 11, 1806, fourth of ten children to Christian (Jr.) and Mary (Gochenour) Grove. Daniel Hite d. in Page County on Nov. 18, 1876, and Rebecca d. there on Nov. 6, 1897. Both are buried in the family plot on a knoll in the pasture behind the farmhouse near Luray. Children, all b. in Page County (Shenandoah Co. before 1835):

i. Susannah, b. Oct. 11, 1830, d. Sept. 6, 1831.
ii. David Christian, b. Oct 6, 1832, d. Sept. 19, 1864, m. Diana Cline Dec. 7, 1854. No children.
iii. Mary Ann, twin to David, d. Oct. 12, 1904, m. John Ambrose Burner May 6, 1852. Ten children.
iv. Isaac Martin, b. Oct. 15, 1835, d. Sept. 22, 1898, m. Mary Ann Gander Feb. 6, 1868. Five children.
v. William Francis, b. March 18, 1838, d. Nov. 17, 1861.
vi. John Pendleton, b. Nov. 14, 1840, d. July 4, 1863.
vii. Sarah Elizabeth (Bettie), b. June 14, 1843, d. Sept. 15, 1927, m. Martin Van Buren Gander Dec. 21, 1865. Seven children.
viii. Eliza Ellen (Ella), b. Dec. 18, 1845, d. May 19, 1935, unmarried.
ix. Daniel Simeon June 3, 1849, d. May 4, 1934, m. Barbara Elizabeth Shirley Dec. 5, 1872. Four children.
x. Nebraska Douglas (Braskie), b. Dec. 8, 1853, d. Apr. 19, 1936, m. Bettie Washington Huffman Dec. 17, 1874. Four sets of twins among their sixteen children, only eight living to maturity.

APPENDIX C

Chronology of Vital Events and Military Service

Materials in this book are presented in fairly strict chronological order except for Chapters 2 and 3 where the very different experiences of John and William Hite require separate story lines. These dates from the Hite vital and military service records provide the framework into which the human story is woven:

1 Jun 1861	William Francis Hite as 1st Lt. and John Pendleton Hite as private enlist in Co. H. (the Page Grays), 33rd Virginia Infantry, William D. Rippetoe, Captain.
5 Jul 1861	David Christian Hite is posted to Winchester as private in Co. E, 97th Virginia Militia, David M. Dovel, Captain.
21 Jul 1861	William is wounded in chest, 1st Battle of Manassas (Bull Run).
22 Jul 1861	Isaac Martin Hite enlists as private, Co. I, 97th Virginia Militia, also called 2nd Regt., 7th Brigade, John D. Aleshire, Capt. Posted to Winchester.
22 Aug 1861	John is hospitalized near Manassas with "camp or bone" fever.
9 Sep 1861	Isaac is discharged from militia service.
13 Sep 1861	John is returned to duty.
5 Oct 1861	William is returned to duty at camp near Fairfax C.H.
30 Oct 1861	William returns ill to Jones house in Front Royal.
4 Nov 1861	Isaac is called again to duty with Co. I. Serves as corporal until discharged after 31 Dec 1861.

APPENDIX C: CHRONOLOGY OF VITAL EVENTS

17 Nov 1861	William dies in Front Royal, Virginia, of typhoid fever and complications from his earlier wound.
19 Nov 1861	William is buried at the Hite family plot, Mill Creek near Luray.
22 Apr 1862	David is enlisted in Co. H, 33rd Virginia Infantry at Elk Run, Page County, by Capt. Michael Shuler.
1 Jul 1862	Isaac is named corporal, Capt. W. H. Chapman's Co. (Dixie Artillery), Virginia Light Artillery.
1 Jul 1862	David is wounded in the wrist at Malvern Hill.
28 Aug 1862	David is wounded in the neck at 2nd Battle of Manassas (Bull Run). Absent (wounded) through remainder of 1862.
4 Oct 1862	Dixie Artillery is disbanded. Isaac reassigned to Cayce's Company.
1 Nov 1862	John returns to duty as 1st Sergt. until 31 Dec 1862. Listed as private for May/June 1863.
9 Jan 1863	Isaac is transferred as private to Co. C. (Lee's Bodyguard), 39th Batt'n, Virginia Cavalry (Richardson's Batt'n of Scouts, Guides and Couriers).
3 Jul 1863	John is mortally wounded in attack on Culp's Hill, Gettysburg.
4 Jul 1863	John dies of chest wound. Buried near Gettysburg by brother David who is captured when left to nurse John and other Confederate wounded.
28 Jul 1863	David is admitted as prisoner to U.S.A. General Hospital, Baltimore.
20 Aug 1863	David is transferred to Federal POW camp at Point Lookout, Maryland.
17 Mar 1864	David is exchanged at City Point, Virginia.
19 Sep 1864	David is killed at Battle of the Opequon (3rd Battle of Winchester). Body not recovered.

APPENDIX C: CHRONOLOGY OF VITAL EVENTS

9 Apr 1865	Isaac is paroled with 1 horse and equipments at Appomattox Court House.
1866	John is reburied at Hollywood Cemetery, Richmond, Virginia.
6 Feb 1868	Isaac marries Mary Ann Gander, daughter of Henry and Mary (Coffman) Gander and sister of Martin Van Buren Gander.
20 Nov 1879	After living with the Hite family since David's death, his widow, Dianna, marries widower E. S. Brown, farmer, of Rappahannock County.
April 1885	Isaac moves with wife and four living children to Cooper Co., MO.
22 Sep 1898	Isaac dies, Cooper Co., MO.
23 Jun 1943	Isaac's widow, Mary Ann (Gander) Hite dies, Sedalia, MO.

INDEX TO NAMES

This is an index to every name except those of the immediate Daniel Hite family who wrote and received these letters. Names are indexed only on the first page of each letter or short episode in which they are repeated.

Abbott, Daniel B.   103, 168
Aleshire, Henry   84, 86, 89, 170
Aleshire, John D.   20, 41, 74, 82
Aleshire, Reuben   136
Aleshire, Robert   113, 140
Alger, James N.   106
Almond, Joseph   60
Almond, Mr. & Mrs. Mann   51
Ashbey, Col. Turner   93

Bailey, Francis M.   70
Bailey, Joseph W.   149
Baldwin, Dr.   140
Banks, Gen. Nathaniel P.   93, 112
Baylor, Col. William S. H.   106
Beahm, Benjamin F.   116, 123, 124, 140
Beauregard, Gen. P. G. T.   17, 33
Beaver, Daniel   152, 159
Beaver, John P.   25, 31, 44, 71, 85, 149, 152, 159
Berry, Joseph   53
Berry, Mark   52, 53
Biedler, Charles E.   178
Biedler, Martin   152
Biedler, Morgan   41, 69
Biggs, Mrs.   181
Blackford, Dr. Benjamin   57, 60
Blanham, Catharine   4
Booten, Rev. Ambrose C.   41, 61, 86, 87, 136, 178, 179
Booten, John Kaylor   104
Booten, Reuben S.   13
Bradley, Henry F.   12
Bragg, Gen. Braxton   122
Brittan, William A.   97
Broadus, Clarence L.   130
Brown, Maj.   181
Brown, E. S.   165
Brown, Samuel Bradford   130

INDEX TO NAMES

Brubaker, Mr.   52
Brubaker, Cassie   180
Brubaker, Daniel R.   107, 108
Brubaker, Joseph   180
Brubaker, Mary R.   110
Brubaker, Thompson   127
Brubaker, William A.   78, 123
Brumback, Edward Trenton   140
Brumback, Joseph   180
Burner, John A.   3, 21, 37, 64, 102, 128, 148
Burner, Mary Ann (Hite)   3, 20, 21, 148
Burner, Sue   129
Burns, David   168, 170
Burnside, Gen. Ambrose   83, 128
Buswell, Abram   4, 14, 81
Buswell, George Daniel   4, 12, 14, 38, 41, 96–98, 100, 101, 105–107, 112, 123–124, 133, 136, 139, 148, 149–151, 155, 167–168, 169, 177–180
Buswell, Mary (Mollie)   4, 14, 41, 81
Buswell, Rebecca (Spitler)   4, 157
Buswell, Sarah Ellen (Ella)   4, 6, 13, 25, 38, 81, 136, 155, 180
Buswell, Lt. Col. Thomas   4, 28, 64, 66, 89, 107, 108, 119, 123, 155
Buswell, Wesley   4, 14, 81
Buswell, William (Willie)   4, 42
Butler, Gen. Benjamin Franklin   163

Caffroth, Mr. & Mrs.   51, 181
Caffroth, Ella   181
Cameron, Mr. (John?)   46
Campbell, George W.   148, 149, 170
Carson, J. H.   50
Cave, Calvin H.   53
Chadduck, Charles T.   29, 45, 65, 98, 123, 124, 134, 168, 178
Chapman, Mr.   110
Chapman, Elizabeth   71
Chapman, William A.   71
Chapman, William Henry   104
Cline, Ella   180
Cloud, Mrs.   180
Coffman, Benjamin F.   106, 119, 124, 168
Coffman, Cumberland G.   29
Coffman, David   80
Coffman, Mrs. David C.   52
Coffman, David J.   25, 81, 84, 137, 156
Coffman, Emily   51, 80
Coffman, Martin   107

Index to Names

Coffman, Reuben Y.   29, 149
Coffman, Susan (Sue)   80, 81, 124, 126, 131, 136
Comer, James J.   168
Comer, Reuben   41, 113
Compton, J. B.   180
Connor, R.   178
Corbin, Nancy   20, 110
Crabill, M.   178
Cubbage, Early   140, 170
Cubbage, James Henry   140, 168
Cubbage, Robert   114, 170
Cubbage, Simpson   54
Cubbage, Willis   106, 124, 168, 169
Cullars, Joseph L.   113, 114, 168
Cummings, Col. Arthur Campbell   8, 11, 30, 98

Dadisman, Reuben   20, 174
Davis, Pres. Jefferson   28, 102
Davis, Mary Jane   13
Davis, Sarah   13
Decker, John   117
Decker, Joseph F.   114, 115
Doles, Brig. Gen. George   168
Doran, Mr.   131
Dorraugh, James H.   13
Dosh, Willie   49
Douglas, Col.   145
Dovel, David M.   12, 21, 41, 59, 66
Duncan, Rev. Mr.   54

Early, Gen. Jubal   170
Eastham, George C.   149
Echols, Col. John   97
Ensign, J.   168, 169
Ewell, Gen. Richard   99, 101, 113, 116, 142, 145, 153, 167

Flinn, Eugene   177
Frazier, Eli M.   97
Frémont, Gen. John C.   108

Gander, David Henry   4
Gander, Frances (Fannie)   4, 6, 25, 31, 64, 80, 82, 85, 107, 130
Gander, Henry   4, 64, 108, 157, 181
Gander, Isaac Franklin   4
Gander, Joseph Thomas   4

INDEX TO NAMES

Gander, Martha Ellen (Mat) 4
Gander, Martin Van Buren 4, 13, 28, 37, 38, 81, 84, 118, 130, 141, 145, 155, 157, 178, 179, 181
Gander, Mary (Coffman) 4, 156, 181
Gander, Mary Ann (Mollie) 4, 6, 25, 28, 38, 64, 80, 124, 130, 151, 155, 179, 182
Gander, Sarah Jane (Sally) 4, 82, 180
Garnett, Gen Richard C. 68, 73, 89, 95, 97
Gibbons, Col. Simon Beauford 100
Gibson, Brig. Gen. Randall L. 13
Gochenour, Mary 3
Good, John L. 114
Gordon, Gen. John B. 176
Grabill, John H. 18, 133
Grant, Gen. Ulysses S. 83, 87, 163, 165, 172
Grant, Rev. Mr. 14
Graves, Mr. 133
Graves, Trenton 68
Grayson, Benjamin F. 11
Griffith, George 116, 119
Griffith, Henry H. 53
Grimsley, Daniel A. 129
Grove, Christian 3
Grove, Christian, Jr. 3
Grove, John H. 131, 133, 180
Grove, Joseph 127
Grove, Mary F. 127
Grove, Rebecca 3

Hampton, Gen. Wade 176
Hardee, Gen. William J. 176
Harman, John A. 24
Henkel, Martin 110
Henkel, Noah 178
Herndon, Rev. Richard N. 51
Higgs, Malinda 136
Higgs, Thomas 136
Hill, Gen. A. P. 105, 113, 116, 124, 138, 176
Hite, Abraham 3, 64, 110, 133
Hite, Ambrose M. 6, 13, 14, 127, 132, 140, 165, 168, 180
Hite, Andrew 3
Hite, Daniel 3
Hite, Frances (Fannie) 14
Hite, John 3
Hite, Martin 21, 71
Hite, Susan Rebecca (Becca) 14, 64

INDEX TO NAMES

Hite, Susannah (Spitler)   71, 133
Hood, Gen. John Bell   164
Hooker, Gen. Joseph   129, 138
Hough, Dr.   55
Huffman, Ambrose C.   114, 122, 132, 137, 168, 170
Huffman, Ann   126
Huffman, Isaac   27, 28
Huffman, Joseph Benton   68, 84, 146
Huffman, Matilda   136
Huffman, Mr. Joseph   37, 38, 42, 71
Huston, Col. George   168

Imboden, Gen. J. D.   137

Jackson, Gen. Thomas J. (Stonewall)   7, 17, 19, 24, 33, 38, 43, 47, 69, 73, 83, 93, 95, 98, 99, 102, 115, 124, 136, 138, 140
Jacobs, Lidey   181
Jenkins, Gen. D. C., Jr.   96, 149
Jenkins, William   149
Jennings, Dr.   178
Jennings, Mr.   102
Jobe, Samuel   179
Johnson, Gen. Edward   147, 168
Johnston, David   40
Johnston, Jennie   80
Johnston, John T. (Jack)   34, 82, 98, 103, 119, 136, 168, 169
Johnston, Joseph   13, 51, 52
Johnston, Gen. Joseph E.   12, 13, 17, 33, 68, 96, 98, 104, 145
Jones, Earnest A. (Erna)   5, 48, 50
Jones, Elizabeth A.   5, 48, 49, 54, 57, 180
Jones, Evaline   5, 48, 181
Jones, Gideon E. (Edgar)   5, 48, 49, 50
Jones, Gideon W.   5, 22, 48, 49, 50, 51, 57–60, 181
Jones, Harrison B.   65, 71, 75, 98
Jones, Henrietta (Bettie)   5, 48, 50
Jones, Jane C. (Jennie)   5, 35, 58, 60, 181
Jones, Gen. John M.   33, 135
Jones, Lt. Col. (later Gen.) John R.   60, 124
Jones, Miriam   5, 48
Jordan, Francis H.   12, 13
Jordan, Gabriel   79
Judd, Daniel   12, 34, 81, 83
Judd, Emily C.   34, 83
Judd, Samuel N.   34, 83
Judy, Martin V. B.   54

INDEX TO NAMES

Judy, Reuben 168

Kagey, Millie 83
Keeler, Arthelia 81
Keller, Appolonia 3
Keys, Naomia G. 133
Keys, William Asbury 133
Keyser, Alexander (Sr.) 46
Keyser, Alexander H. (Hamp) 29, 45, 46, 119, 137, 143, 168
Keyser, John 107, 108
Keyser, William A. 143, 149
Kibler, David 110
Kite, Alfred 122, 168, 169
Kite, Andrew Jackson (Jack) 13, 38
Kite, Benjamin 168
Kite, George 114
Kite, John W. 30, 45
Kite, Martin Van Buren 53
Kite, Noah 178
Kite, Oliver Hazard Perry (Perry) 46, 53, 65, 84, 98, 113, 123, 127, 137, 168, 170, 178
Knight, Jacob F. 140
Knight, Joel 53, 170
Koontz, Alexander H. 122, 123
Koontz, George W. 98, 103, 140
Koontz, Harrison W. 170
Koontz, John N. 123
Koontz, Martin Van Buren 19, 28

Lampkins, Soloman 29
Lauck, Rev. William C. 179, 180
Lawrence, Woodford M. 29, 70
Lee, Col. Edwin G. (Ned) 112, 119
Lee, Brig. Gen. Fitzhugh 124
Lee, Gen. Robert E. 7, 104, 115, 119, 124, 140, 142, 145, 146, 148, 152, 163, 167, 178
Letcher, Gov. John 12, 28, 36, 57
Lincoln, Pres. Abraham 129
Lionberger, John (Sr.) 67, 110
Lionberger, John Henry 89, 130, 134, 172, 173
Lionberger, Virginia 67
Litman, Capt. 77
Long, Frances A. (Mrs. Peter) 133
Long, Gideon B. 13, 19, 80, 81, 98, 103, 119
Long, Isaac 36, 57

INDEX TO NAMES

Long, Peter 69
Long, Susan 80
Longstreet, Gen. James 105, 114, 117, 150, 152, 167
Loring, Gen. William W. 83
Lowe, Prof. Thaddeus S. C. 55
Lucas, Simeon 139

Maggart, Isaac 107, 110, 179
Marr, Capt. John Q. 7
Martin, Albion 121, 123
Marye, Lucy 133
Mauck, Ann 152
Mauck, Edward C. 114, 168, 170
McAlister, William 149
McClellan, Gen. George B. 95, 108
McCoy, John W. 140
McDonald, Col. Angus W., Sr. 40
McDowell, Gen. Irvin 17, 105
McInturff, Rev. Philip 136, 179
Meade, Gen. George G. 152
Meem, Gen. Gilbert S. 12, 28, 89
Menifie, James W. 58, 71, 98, 103, 114, 140, 145, 149
Mercer, Maj. G. D. 94
Middleton, John J. 53
Miller, Benjamin F. 139
Miller, James E. 140
Miller, Paul 19
Miller, Peter S. 170
Miller, Samuel 66
Mims, M. S. S. 170
Modesitt, Andrew 4
Modesitt, Augustus Staige 1, 4, 12, 28, 37, 48, 50, 56, 58, 60, 64, 142
Modesitt, Elizabeth (Bettie) 4, 79
Modesitt, James R. 13
Modesitt, John W. 41, 114
Modesitt, Lucy Virginia (Jennie) 4, 71, 79, 133
Modesitt, Martha 4
Modesitt, Mary (Hite) 4, 12
Modesitt, Mary Ellen 4, 6, 13, 67, 71, 79
Modesitt, Rebecca 4
Modesitt, Willie 72
Morgan, Gen. J. H. 167
Morris, Haley 149
Morris, John 84
Morris, Simpson 84

Index to Names

Murphy, Col. George W.   8

Napolean, Louis   24
Neff, Col. John Francis   29, 98, 105, 112, 114
Nichols, Return   53, 97, 113, 140
Nicholson, Dr.   29

O'Ferrall, Charles T.   129
Oden, Bushrod   140, 168, 169
Offenbacker, Thomas M.   12,
Opie, John N.   148

Page, Capt.   117
Parish, Mr.   156
Paxton, Brig. Gen. Frank   122, 138
Pender, Gen. W. Dorsey   124
Pendleton, Col. William Nelson   18, 46
Perry, Joseph   106
Pettigrew, Albert H.   130
Pettigrew, Gen. J. J.   146
Petty, Mr.   59
Phillips, John W.   149
Pickett, Gen. George E.   146
Pope, Gen. John   114, 115
Porter, Gen. Fitz-John   114
Price, Benjamin F.   149
Price, Gen. Sterling   83, 91.94
Printz, Hiram   170
Printz, Irenus P.   53, 114
Printz, Isabias A.   116
Printz, James F. (Jim)   170
Purdam, William   143, 145, 149

Reader, Michael   3
Reid, Peter C.   129
Reynolds, Miss Mattie   180
Reynolds, Col. Samuel H.   113
Rhodes, Caroline   129
Rhodes, Emily   129
Rhodes, John H.   129
Rhodes, Lafayette   129
Rhodes, Nancy   129
Rhodes, Sarah   129
Riley, Jesse W. (Jessie)   106, 168, 169, 170
Rinica, Andrew   71

INDEX TO NAMES

Rippetoe, Mary (Mollie) 55
Rippetoe, William D. 5, 7, 11, 16, 19, 33, 36, 45, 54, 55, 57, 60, 65
Robertson, Newton J. 103
Rodes, Gen. Robert E. 168, 170, 171
Rogers, Arthur L. 117
Rosenberger, John 156
Rosenberger, John W. 124, 145, 149
Rothgeb, Alexander (Elic) 13, 25, 37, 40, 42
Rothgeb, Alexandria 109
Rothgeb, Ambrose B. 37, 40, 107, 108, 130, 156, 161
Rothgeb, Annie 180
Rothgeb, Mrs. Barbara 162
Rothgeb, Barbara Ann 13, 25, 31, 37, 40, 82, 86
Rothgeb, Catherine 20
Rothgeb, Daniel 109
Rothgeb, Edmund J. 81, 84, 124, 149, 168, 170
Rothgeb, Emmanuel (Man) 77, 85, 109, 168, 169
Rothgeb, Franklin 77, 81, 85, 122, 123, 140
Rothgeb, George A. 170
Rothgeb, Isaac 13, 37, 98
Rothgeb, Martin 77, 85, 89, 136
Rothgeb, Mary J. 84
Rothgeb, Reuben 64, 77, 89, 109, 122
Rothgeb, Samuel 137
Ruffner, Mark 123
Ruffner, Martha R. 81
Ruffner, Martin 31, 40
Ruffner, Mary A. 179
Rust, William O. 48, 51, 55

Shaffer, Isaac 64, 89
Shaffer, Israel 116
Shaw, Col. H. M. 83
Shenk, Ambrose Booten 5, 7, 45–48, 53, 56, 61, 65, 80, 91, 94, 96, 97, 98
Shenk, Mary Ann 97
Sheridan, Gen. Philip H. 170, 173
Sherman, Gen. William Tecumseh 164, 173, 176
Shields, Gen. James 94, 95, 108
Shirley, Martin 109
Shuler, Squire John 46, 83, 113, 123, 138
Shuler, Michael 5, 7, 16, 46, 53, 56, 98, 112–118, 119, 123, 134, 140, 142, 145, 149, 150, 155, 161, 167, 169
Sibert, Mr. 156
Slave (Burner), Charles 128
Slave (Jones), Bet 50

Index to Names

Slave (Jones), Kitty 50
Smith, Daniel 19
Smith, Gen. G. W. 33
Smith, John J. 97
Smith, William H. 42, 43
Smoot, Dr. Henry J. 13, 71
Somers, Philip M. 140, 168
Somers, Silas A. 19, 114
Sowers, Peter 19, 51, 55
Spitler, Abraham 3, 110
Spitler, Joseph 82
Spitler, Col. Mann 8, 12, 13, 28, 59, 134, 140
Spitler, Susannah 3
Spitler, Tom 27
Steuart, Brig. Gen. George H. 168
Stombaugh, David 114, 149
Stonebarger, Andrew J. 116
Story, Mr. 161
Stover, Abraham 13
Stover, Joseph F. 78, 97
Strickler, Abram 64
Strickler, Benjamin Franklin 158
Strickler, Cate 37, 40
Strickler, Elizabeth (Bettie) 151, 158
Strickler, Emmanuel 47
Strickler, James 151
Strickler, Mary 151, 155
Strickler, Milton 151
Strickler, Nancy 151
Strickler, Selina 151, 159
Strole, Hiram P. 103, 114
Stuart, Gen. J. E. B. 105, 124, 134, 140
Summers, Mr. 60
Switzer, Samuel 106

Taylor, Adj. Gen. Walter H. 145
Tobin, Mr. (Albert?) 109
Trinty, Hiram 35
Turner, Dr. James 57
Tyler, Susan M. 51

Van Dorn, Gen. Earl 94

Walker, Brig. Gen. James A. 142
Walter, James William 89

INDEX TO NAMES

Walton, David K.   119
Warren, Gen. G. K.   176
Weakly, Wyatt B.   143, 149
Webster, Charles William   29, 46, 68, 114
Webster, Samuel B.   46
Whitestone, Albert W.   100
Whittier, John Greenleaf   115
Wierman, Benjamin B.   123
Wilson, George T.   124, 137, 149
Wilson, John J.   113, 114
Winder, Gen. Charles Sidney   97, 106, 112
Wise, Gen. Henry A.   83
Wood, David   143, 149

Yager, Mr.   54
Yates, William S.   168, 170
Young, Charles A.   114, 168
Young, Mr. (Daniel T.?)   110
Young, Emma   37
Young, William R.   167, 169
Young, William Townsend   79, 84, 137
Yowell, Barbara (Grove)   37
Yowell, Cate   37, 40
Yowell, Ella   14, 37, 40, 42
Yowell, Francis W. (Frank)   13, 25, 26, 31, 37, 38, 137

Zirkle, Mr.   158
Zollicoffer, Gen. F. K.   78

GENERAL INDEX

Albemarle County, Va. 99
Alexandria, Va. 25
ambrotype 65, 68
Aquia Creek 65, 122

Ball's Bluff, battle of 35
balloons 138
Baltimore, Md. 152, 165
Bank of Richmond 48
Bath (Berkeley Springs), W.Va. 73, 74
Blooming Furnace 75
Bolivar Heights 116, 117
Brandy Station, Va. 140, 157
Buchanan, Va. 156
Bunker's Hill, Va. 93, 170

C & O Canal 69
camp and soldier life 8, 30, 46–48, 65, 66, 68, 69, 75, 79, 80, 88, 91, 95, 99, 123, 161, 163, 167
Camp Flowing Springs 66
Camp Harman 24, 30, 36, 45, 46, 48, 52, 57
Camp Jackson 21, 22
Camp Lee 130, 135, 136
Camp Maggot 21
Camp Petersburg 163
Camp Stephenson 70
Camp Stone-wall Brigade 165
Camp Winder 121, 123, 134, 137, 138
Carlisle, Penna. 142
Cedar Mountain, battle of 112, 113, 121, 122
Cemetery Ridge 142
Centerville, Va. 34–36, 46, 52
Chancellorsville, battle of 138–140
chaplains 138
Charleston Harbor 7
Charlestown, Va. 66, 116
Charlottesville, Va. 167
Chickahominy River 106
Chickamauga Campaign 152
Chimborazo Hospital 143
City Point, Va. 165

GENERAL INDEX 201

court martial 52, 65, 91, 121–123
C.S.S. Virginia 94
Culp's Hill 142, 149
Culpeper Court House, Va. 113, 140, 141, 152

Darbytown Road, battle of 172
desertion 22, 32, 33, 40, 52, 53, 71, 81, 86, 95, 98, 121, 122, 129–133, 165, 177
discipline 43, 112, 120
disease and sickness 10, 21, 24, 28–30, 37, 40–42, 45, 49, 50, 52, 55–57, 59, 60, 82, 97, 102, 122, 128, 137
Dixie Artillery 104, 107, 114, 115, 118–120, 134, 161
Doles's Georgia Brigade 168, 169
draft 14
Dranesville, battle of 70
Drewry's Bluff 163
drill 10–12, 16, 33, 44, 47

England 72, 87, 173

Fair Oaks, battle of 104, 105
Fairfax Court House, Va. 30, 31, 36, 45, 52, 68
Fairfax Station 52–54
food 8, 10, 13, 18, 30, 37, 42, 43, 50, 52, 68, 69, 70, 73, 102, 115, 123, 124, 130, 135, 150
Fort Donelson, Tenn. 87
France 43, 173
Frayser's Farm, battle of 107
Frederick, Md. 115, 116
Fredericksburg, Va. 120, 140, 141
Fredericksburg, battle of 120, 128, 129
free blacks 128
Front Royal, Va. 19–21, 27, 36, 44, 45, 48–51, 56–59, 102, 180

Gettysburg, battle of 97, 137, 143, 145–149, 161
Gordonsville, Va. 136
Greenwood Station 100
Groveton, battle of 114
Guinea Station 120, 123, 135, 138

Hagarstown, Md. 150
Hampton Roads, Va. 94
Hancock, Md. 73
Hanging Rock, Va. 82
Harper's Ferry, battle of 116, 117, 119
Harpers Ferry 17, 66, 68, 116

Harrisonburg, Va. 101, 102, 135
Hollin Ferry 115

Irish 43

James River 163

Kelly's Ford, battle of 133, 134
Kernstown, Va. 43, 95
Kernstown, battle of 96, 97, 137

Leaksville, Va. 81, 178
Lee's Body Guard 130, 136, 145
Lee's Headquarters, Gettysburg 145
Leesburg, Va. 35, 36, 41
Lexington, Va. 140, 156
Liberty, Va. 101
liquor 10, 33, 35, 43, 71, 91
Luray, Va. 7, 51, 58, 64, 66, 67, 79, 133, 141, 178
Lynchburg, Va. 79, 137

Malvern Hill, battle of 106, 107, 120, 161
Manassas, Va. 95
Manassas, First Battle of 18–20, 51
Manassas, Second Battle of 113, 114, 120
Manassas Gap Railroad 17
Manassas Junction 65
Martinsburg, Va. 14, 16, 69, 73, 75, 79, 116, 119, 120
Maryland Heights 66
Mason and Slidell Affair 72
Massanutten Creek 110
McDowell, battle of 100–102
militia 77, 79, 81, 82, 86–89, 91, 104, 134
Mill Creek 110, 133, 136, 157
Mill Springs, battle of 78
Monocacy Junction 115
morale 8, 11, 22, 24, 56
Moss Neck, Va. 120, 121, 123
Mt. Jackson 95, 96
mulattoes 128
Murfreesboro, battle of 122

Nashville, Tenn. 87
New Centreville, Va. 65
New Market, Va. 133, 151, 155, 158

General Index

Newtown, Va. 95, 96
Norfolk, Va. 95

Opequon Creek 170
Orange and Alexandria Railroad 17
Orange Court House, Va. 113, 159, 161

Page Artillery 47
Page County, Va. 1, 3, 53, 98, 100, 108, 109
parole 118
pay 42
Pea Ridge, battle of 94
Pendleton, Va. 101
Petersburg, Va. 171, 172, 176
Petersburg, siege of 163, 164, 172
Pickett's Charge 146
Point Lookout, Md. 165
Port Republic, Va. 99
Potomac River 69, 70, 74, 75, 115, 117, 142, 150
prisoners 41, 76, 139

Rapidan River 152, 153, 155, 165, 178
Rappahannock River 123, 134, 152
religion 163
Republican Party 88
Richmond, Va. 56, 94, 104, 105, 107, 136, 140, 159, 167
Roanoke Island, battle of 83
Romney, Va. 41, 73, 75, 76, 83

Savage Station 106
Seven Days Battles 105–108
Seven Pines, battle of 104, 105
Sharpsburg, battle of 118, 119
Shenandoah River 3, 17
Shenandoah Valley 1, 7, 17, 170
Shepardstown, Md. 117
slaves 128
Spotsylvania, battle of 168, 169
Stanton, Va. 130
Staunton, Va. 100, 107, 138, 156
Stonewall Brigade 91, 98, 99, 112, 115, 120–122, 139–142, 155
straglers 139
Strasburg, Va. 43, 95, 96-

U.S. Monitor 94

Virginia troops
- 2nd Virginia Infantry 150
- 4th Virginia Infantry 150
- 5th Virginia Infantry 97, 106
- 6th Virginia Cavalry 129
- 7th Virginia Cavalry 40, 69, 89, 93, 97, 107, 129, 137
- 10th Virginia Cavalry 84, 158
- 10th Virginia Infantry 79, 100, 137
- 17th Virginia Infantry 48
- 27th Virginia Infantry 70
- 35th Virginia Cavalry 133
- 37th Virginia Infantry 96
- 39th Battalion, Virginia Cavalry 130, 145, 179
- 43rd Virginia Cavalry 140
- 97th Virginia Militia 59, 66, 74, 133

Washington, D.C. 22, 170
Waynesboro, Penna. 150
Wilderness, battle of 167–169
Williamsport, Md. 116, 150
Winchester, Va. 12, 14, 17, 20, 26, 41, 43, 44, 55, 59, 64, 65, 68, 70, 71, 74–76, 78, 79, 81, 83, 91, 93, 95, 96, 101, 102, 136, 170
Winchester, Second Battle of 142
Wise Legion 83
wounds 18, 20, 24